Trotsky and the Origins of Trotskyism

Alfred Rosmer

Boris Souvarine, Emile Fabrol and

Antoine Clavez

Trotsky and the Origins of Trotskyism

with an introduction

by Al Richardson

Francis
Boutle
Publishers

First published in English by Francis Boutle Publishers
23 Arlington Way
London EC1R 1UY
Tel/Fax: (020) 7278 4497
Email: trotsky@francisboutle.demon.co.uk
www.francisboutle.demon.co.uk

ISBN 1 903427 07 X

Printed in Great Britain by Bookcraft

Contents

7 **List of illustrations**

11 **Introduction**

19 **Part One**
'Bolshevisation' and 'Trotskyism' in France
20 Emile Fabrol – The Prelude to Stalinism
35 Antoine Clavez – The Bureaucratisation and Destruction of the Party
49 Emile Fabrol – The French Communist Party and Trotsky

67 **Part Two**
Boris Souvarine and Alfred Rosmer, 'Bolshevisation'
68 Boris Souvarine – How I Came to be Regarded as a 'Trotskyist'
79 Victor Delagarde, Pierre Monatte and Alfred Rosmer – Second Letter to the Members of the Communist Party: The Reply of the Three Expelled
94 Alfred Rosmer – About the 'Final Warning' Given to Trotsky: The Myth of 'Trotskyism'
115 Alfred Rosmer – A Ridiculous Gesture: The Central Committee of the French Communist Party Addresses a Demand to Trotsky

120 The Nucleus – Reply to Trotsky's Two Requests

139 **Part Three**
On the Planet Without a Visa – Alfred Rosmer
141 Chapter One, In Turkey
154 Chapter Two, In France
166 Chapter Three, In Norway
187 Chapter Four, In Mexico (Part One)
214 Chapter Five, In Mexico (Part Two)

243 **Index**

List of illustrations

10 Trotsky and Alfred Rosmer at the Second Congress of the Comintern, 1920
114 Alfred Rosmer (1877–1964)
140 Trotsky in hunting outfit at Samanli, Turkey, November 1931
186 Marguerite and Alfred Rosmer with trotsky, Natalia Sedova and Sieva in Mexico

Acknowledgements

Our thanks go to the excellent French magazine *Prométhée* for permission to translate the first and most of the second section of this book. The whole of the third section we owe to the Centre d'Etudes et de Recherches sur les Mouvements Trotskyste et Révolutionnaires Internationaux (CERMTRI) website, and to Ted Crawford, who wrested the French text from it. To Ian Birchall and George Paizis and the magazine *Revolutionary History* go our thanks for allowing us to reprint the third item in our second section. Meticulous correction of the English by Richard Kirkwood and Harry Ratner has prevented the translator from making too much of an ass of himself, and without Paul Flewers our presentation would be even more confusing than it has turned out to be. We would also like to thank David King for permission to reproduce the photographs of Alfred Rosmer, Trotsky and Rosmer at the Second Congress of the Comintern and the Rosmers, Trotsky, Natalia Sedova and Sieva in Mexico.

This book was compiled by his friends to celebrate Clarence Chrysostom's eightieth year, and his sixty-second as a revolutionary. We would like therefore to thank Lizzy Ali, Glynn Beagley, Barry Buitekant, Ted Crawford, Ian Donovan, Paul Flewers, Mildred Gordon, Chris Gray, Brian Green, Mike Jones, Gloria Lazenby, Esther Leslie, George Leslie, Sheila Leslie, Ron Lynn, Philip Marchant, Gustav Mowitz, Pat Nightingale, Bob Pitt, Richard Price, Al Richardson, Jim Ring, Alejandra Rios, Bruce Robinson, V Skanthakumar, John Sullivan and José Villa.

David King Collection

Trotsky and Rosmer (to his right) at the Second Congress of the Comintern (1920)

Introduction

The subject of this book needs no introduction, to socialists or communists, to scholars of modern Russian history, nor, indeed, to anyone interested in world politics during the last century. Not only was Leon Trotsky one of history's major architects, but, as Isaac Deutscher reminds us, he was one of its prophets as well. The development of the Soviet Union from a sole mafia monopolising state power to a myriad of smaller ones competing for it was one of his more melancholy predictions. In more ways than one, as the famous secularist Frank Ridley once said, Trotsky 'belongs to the ages'.

As a revolutionary, Trotsky did not believe either that history was the work of great men, or that the rest of us have to be the playthings of anonymous social forces. Likewise the author of the pieces collected and translated here was no less of an individual in his own right, a revolutionary trade unionist, a courageous opponent of modern warfare, a revolutionary thinker, a historian, and a literary critic. Alfred Griot (1877–1964), who took his pseudonym of Rosmer from Ibsen, was already involved in revolutionary journalism well before the First World War. He first met Trotsky when they struggled against the war in 1915, and continued his acquaintance until the Old Man's death 35 years later. He was Trotsky's closest ally in creating the French Communist Party and in regulating the trade union activity of the Comintern. He was among the first to alert the world to the power struggle going on in Russia after the death of Lenin, to reconstruct a European network of anti-Stalinist revolutionaries, and to help Trotsky clear his name in the face of the Moscow trials. He is thus the ideal person for tracing the development of Trotsky's thought, for describing his personal fortunes, and for assessing his significance in the broad sweep of history.[1]

Of particular interest is the final section of this book, the five additional chapters written by Rosmer for Trotsky's *My Life*. The original autobiography ends in 1929, but when Rosmer was preparing a new French edition in 1953 these chapters were added to complete the picture. They take the form of an intricate mosaic, extracted where possible from Trotsky's works and carefully selected with two aims in view. The first was to use Trotsky's own words when describing what happened to him, so preserving the expressions and texture of the original book. The second was to provide excerpts from his major writings expressing the essence of his thought, or the range of his foresight. Since Rosmer only rarely indicates the sources of his quotations, an effort has been made to identify and footnote them, with some success. The text here has been amended to agree with the standard English translations, even where this has given rise to awkward expressions when we take into account the surrounding French. Nonetheless, we are sure that English readers will appreciate having this major historical work in their hands, for as a first hand source it ranks alongside those of Victor Serge and Natalia Sedova, Jean Van Heijenoort and Pierre Naville, as well as serving as a useful supplement to the standard works of Deutscher and Pierre Broué. The extracts taken from *The Revolution Betrayed* and *In Defence of Marxism* rejecting 'state capitalist' and 'new class' theories have taken on an added interest since the collapse of the Soviet Union, which has inevitably reopened the debate as to what it really was and why it fell so easily. Our admiration for Rosmer's conscientiousness and fidelity to his subject can only increase when we realise that at the time he was selecting them he no longer shared Trotsky's views.

For good or ill, Trotsky's place in the history of the twentieth century is no longer in dispute among serious commentators, but the same cannot be said of the movement he founded. Trotskyism signally failed to establish itself as a revolutionary alternative to Stalinism. Most of its adherents are content to explain this by the massive repression to which it was subjected, or by unfavourable objective circumstances. The more farsighted point to the failure of its perspectives in the aftermath of the Second World War. Yet, paradoxically, one of the deepest reasons was its growing similarity to the movement it came into being to oppose.

Trotskyism has always disputed Stalinism's claim to be the

continuation of Leninism. And it is true that the historical and political analyses that make up the first two parts of this book are damning indictments of the fake 'Leninism' and 'Bolshevism' specially constructed to condemn Trotsky by Zinoviev, Bukharin, Kamenev and their associates,[2] including the cult of 'the Party', the self-proclamation of its leadership, the military concept of 'democratic centralism', the attempt to substitute party for class, which involved rejecting the united front with the mass organisations, and the leftist verbiage intended to justify these things.

Denying that any of these policies have any links with Lenin's thought and practice, Trotskyists claim to be the only true Leninists. This is all the more surprising because the ideology and practices of 'Leninism' and 'Bolshevism' were specifically constructed to exclude them. For 'Leninism', a most un-Marxist orthodoxy, and 'Trotskyism', a heresy, were invented at the same time, during Lenin's last illness, and for the same purpose, to discredit Trotsky in the succession struggle. Yet the ways of dealing with dissidents in their groupings, the personality cults of their leaders, their internal regimes, the absurdity of their pretensions, and even their pronounced mendacity about their own pasts show that all too many Trotskyist organisations bear more than a passing resemblance to Stalinism. So here we have a major historical mystery, that Trotskyism asserts its fidelity to a 'Leninism' that was created to oppose it, whilst inheriting a real legacy from the Stalinism whose antithesis it claims to be.

This is why, if anything, the first two parts of our collection are more instructive for our present understanding than the more attractive narrative that follows them, for they go right to the heart of the mystery of the origins of Trotskyism. The unbroken continuity of the Trotskyist movement is largely a myth. There have been, in fact, two distinct waves of 'Trotskyism' outside the USSR. The first, the generation of AE Reade in Britain, Ludwig Lore and Max Eastman in the USA, Souvarine, Monatte and Rosmer in France, some German comrades and the majority leadership of the Belgian Communist Party, left few traces.[3] The modern international Trotskyist movement, almost without exception, goes back to a second wave originating in the Joint Opposition in the USSR. The majority of its personnel were Zinovievists rather than Trotskyists. It is all the more ironic that prominent in this second wave were Treint, Cannon, Fischer and Maslow, Zinovievists who were largely instrumental in excluding the first wave of Trotskyists in their own countries. Against this background today's leftist rhetoric, manipulative attitude to the mass movement, operation through 'front' organisations, exaggerated pretensions to Leninism and Bolshevism, and unpleasant internal regimes are all too easily explained. For example, Cannon's admiration for Zinoviev continued to be openly expressed long after he had formally assumed the mantle of Trotskyism.[4]

The first wave of Trotskyism was far smaller, more diffuse and less coherent than the second, and was far less self-consciously 'Bolshevik'. It is not at all surprising that it failed to last. It probably had as much in common with the outlook of Rosa Luxemburg, whose name was bracketed with his at the time, as it did with Trotsky's. This first wave can be loosely divided into two categories – literary figures such as Eastman, Souvarine, and Reade and Millicent Shooter in Britain, and a more working-class based opposition such as Rosmer, Monatte, the majority leadership of the Belgian Communist Party and the Greek ArcheioMarxists.[5] So saying that it failed to last is a statement that requires further qualification, because the two components failed to last in different ways. Apart from the assistance that Eastman later provided in translations and royalties, the literary figures who supported Trotsky – Reade, Souvarine, Shooter – soon faded completely from the scene, and even Eastman in any case never joined the movement. The working-class based opposition survived longer, but in another form, because in each case it already had a cohesion and ideology of its own before it became associated with the Comintern, and in a sense had never been completely assimilated into it. Thus *Révolution prolétarienne* survived as an anarcho-syndicalist tendency, the ArcheioMarxists, after flirting with Trotskyism in the early 1930s, reverted to a rather petrified and dogmatic existence, and the Belgian group all but disappeared. Rosmer alone supplied a link between the two waves, and even he did not remain in the second wave for very long. Antoine Clavez makes the telling point that Rosmer never joined the Fourth International.[6] And although its founding conference was held in his own house, it is equally significant that whilst his account of Trotsky's last exile often talks about the idea of a Fourth International, he does not even describe its actual foundation.

The second wave originating in the Joint Opposition in the USSR was centrally directed, ideologically coherent, considerably more numerous and more fitted to survive politically, and this is the more recognisable face of Trotskyism as we see it today. It should nonetheless be noted that there are considerable differences in character and politics between the two waves, not the least being that Trotsky specifically repudiated the first. The first wave in fact denied that it was 'Trotskyist' at all, as did Trotsky himself at the time. So here, as with the Tories, a name came to be accepted by a movement that was first used as an insult by its enemies. But the main point to remember is that this opposition was still undifferentiated, part of a general European movement of protest against the methods of 'Bolshevising' the Comintern that also included Paul Levi, Brandler and Thalheimer in Germany, Serrati and Angelica Balabanoff in Italy, and others elsewhere.[7] The specific identity of 'Trotskyism' outside the USSR is a later construction.[8]

This book cannot deal with the whole debate, since it has to limit itself to the part Rosmer played in it. But those who have the patience and time should also read *The First Open Letter of Rosmer, Monatte and Delagarde* and 'The Letter of the 280' (Helmut Gruber, *Soviet Russia Masters the Comintern*, New York, 1974, pp. 61–72), Max Eastman's *Since Lenin Died* (London, 1925), and Trotsky's various statements (*The Challenge of the Left Opposition, 1923–1925*, New York, 1975, pp310–8), which are freely available elsewhere.

Readers who wish to reconstruct the points and order of the controversy will be able to link to these other sources by paying careful attention to the footnotes. Only a few extra details are necessary. Eastman informs us that it was Trotsky himself who entrusted him with the 'carefully guarded secret' of Lenin's *Testament*, and that further information, 'accessible only to insiders', was provided by Rosmer and Souvarine, both then members of the Executive Committee of the Comintern.[9] Souvarine was the first to learn of the clashes between Trotsky and the rest of the leadership. On his way back from Moscow, he had a conversation in Berlin with Radek, who 'revealed his disquiet as regards the conflict that had already arrayed the Moscow Politbureau against

Trotsky'.[10] Souvarine later met Trotsky in Moscow on 9 May 1924, and his impression then was that 'Trotsky is on the whole confident. It has been a defeat, but day-to-day experience shows that he was right, so he confided to Rosmer, and his popularity has become enormous, and even disquieting. It is now a matter of knowing how to wait, and to hold firmly on to his positions.'[11] The actual text of Lenin's *Testament*, reproduced from Krupskaya's own copy, was sent by a trusted messenger to Souvarine in Paris.[12] He himself considered that publishing *Since Lenin Died* would embarrass the Opposition, but Rosmer took the opposite view.[13] Finally, if we might add a little local colour, it was the most cynical Stalinist these islands ever produced, Palme Dutt, the writer of the most unpleasant of the attacks on Eastman, who also wrote privately to him saying that the Politbureau of the CPGB 'might decide' to publish Eastman's reply to his detractors.[14] Clearly, Dutt still wanted to keep his options open, as is suggested by other evidence from this time.[15]

Al Richardson

Notes

1. For more on Rosmer, see *Revolutionary History*, Volume 7, no 4, 2000. His full-length books include *Le Mouvement ouvrier pendant la première guerre mondiale* (Paris, 1936) and (in English translation) *Lenin's Moscow* (London, 1971).
2. Zinoviev later admitted as much (LD Trotsky, *The Stalin School of Falsification*, London, 1974, pp71–9). The first actual user of the term 'Leninism' appears to have been Kamenev, in a polemic with Ossinsky (*Pravda*, 24 March 1923). Bukharin seems to have been the main promoter of the idea of a barracks discipline within the party. The phrase 'iron cohort' mocked by Rosmer (below, p39) was one of his favourites, first appearing as the title of one of his articles in 1922.
3. For AE Reade, see Sam Bornstein and Al Richardson, *Against the Stream*, London, 1986, pp1ff; Harry Wicks, *Keeping My Head*, London, 1992, pp38, 42–5, 175; John McIlroy, 'New Light on Arthur Reade: Tracking Down Britain's First Trotskyist', *Revolutionary History*, Volume 8, no 1, 2001. For Ludwig Lore, see Theodore Draper, *American Communism and Soviet Russia*, New York, 1960, pp106–9. For Souvarine, see Pierre Broué, *Histoire de l'internationale communiste, 1919–1943*, Paris, 1997, p380. On the Belgian Communist Party, see *Revolutionary History*, Volume 7, no 1, 1998. Eastman's relations with Trotsky are traced by Ernie Stubbins, 'Max Eastman —From Fellow-Traveller to Witch-Hunter', *Socialist Press*, 1 October 1980. The others are sufficiently dealt with in the text below.
4. For example, James P Cannon, *The First Ten Years of American Communism*, New York, 1973, pp186–7. For Cannon's Zinovievism, see also *Revolutionary History*, Volume 4, no 3, Summer 1992, pp110–3; Volume 5, no 1, Autumn 1993, pp106–7; Walter Kendall, *Journal of Trotsky Studies*, no 2, 1994, pp225–31. The truth of Cannon's evolution towards Trotskyism is clearly set out by Phil Valenti, 'Towards a Myth-Free History of "American Trotskyism": The Myth of the Origins', *The Campaigner*, Volume 6, no 2, Spring 1973, pp32–44. For Cannon's attitudes to Lore, Trotsky and 'Bolshevisation', see Irving Howe and Lewis Coser, *The American Communist Party: A Critical History (1919–1957)*, Boston, 1957, pp152–4.
5. Like all generalisations, this one obviously has its limitations. Monatte and Rosmer were also great lovers of literature. It is no accident that Rosmer took his pseudonym from a character in Ibsen, a writer whom Trotsky also admired. See 'Autour d'Alfred Rosmer: Entretien avec Collette Chambelland', *Prométhée*, no 5, May–July 1990, p13.
6. Below, p43.
7. To begin with Giacinto Serrati (1874–1926), the leader of the Maximalist wing of the Italian Socialist Party, opposed joining the Comintern on the basis of the 'Twenty-One Conditions'; Angelica Balabanova (1877–1963) disapproved of the slanders against the Italian Socialist Party, and rejoined it after her expulsion from the Communist Party in 1924. The forms 'Bolshevisation' took in Britain are touched upon by Wicks, op cit, pp. 41, 46.
8. It was only after Trotsky's exile outside the Soviet Union that he began to lay down criteria for clear lines of demarcation between the various oppositional groupings. See LD Trotsky, 'Groupings in the Communist Opposition', 31 March 1929, *Writings of Leon Trotsky, 1929*, New York, 1975, pp80–5.
9. Max Eastman, *Love and Revolution*, New York, 1964, p. 428.
10. Boris Souvarine, in *Le Contrat social*, Volume 9, no 6, 1965.
11. Boris Souvarine, Letter, 12 May 1924.
12. Eastman, op cit, p. 452.

13. Op cit, p. 443.
14. Op cit, p. 451.
15. See Bornstein and Richardson, op cit, pp16–7.

Part One

'Bolshevisation' and 'Trotskyism' in France

The Prelude to Stalinism

Emile Fabrol

From *Prométhée,* no 3, November 1989–January 1990, pp3–9

The decay of Communism was already obvious when Lenin died on 21 January 1924. After his death, it proceeded at increased speed. In his last speech, at the Fourth Congress of the Communist International, Lenin had warned the communists of all countries against a mechanical and slavish imitation of Russian methods. Zinoviev made such imitation into a compulsory rule. Moreover, under the pretext of 'Bolshevising' the parties, he introduced totalitarianism into the whole life of the Communist International. By means of the emissaries he sent into the sections, he suppressed all opposition just before the Congress. Wherever resistance appeared, the most varied means were used to crush it. It was a war of attrition where the workers were doomed to lose to the functionaries, who, having all the time they needed, imposed endless discussions. Tired of the struggle, all those who had indulged in criticism and were overwhelmed by the weight and authority of the International gave way provisionally, or left.

At the Fifth Congress of the Communist International, in July 1924, Zinoviev, beaming, proclaimed:

> 'We have achieved one hundred per cent "Bolshevisation".' He thought his rule was assured. At the peak of his personal triumph, he could not imagine that the most obscure of the triumvirs would rise above him within two years, and 10 years later would have him felled with a bullet in the cellars of the Lubyanka prison. From now on it was Moscow without Lenin. (Alfred Rosmer, Conclusion of *Lenin's Moscow*, published in 1953)

If it is true that the French section of the Communist International was created by the split that took place at the Eighteenth Congress of the SFIO [*Section Française de l'Internationale Ouvrière*], it is no less true that it was only politically the case after the Fourth Congress of the Communist International in November 1922. We might also add that the gestation of the Communist Party in France was no easy matter. The militants who struggled against the SFIO, which had quietly taken part during the war of 1914–18 in the *Union Sacrée*, were not very numerous. Whether they were in the Socialist Party, like Souvarine or Loriot,[1] or whether they were revolutionary syndicalists, like Rosmer, Monatte, Monmousseau or Sémard,[2] the supporters of the Committee for the Resumption of International Relations, which then became the Committee for Joining the Third International, had been able to resist the wave of chauvinism that led European Social Democracy to induce workers to fight other workers. They had very quickly grasped the importance of the October Revolution, but by 1926, with very few exceptions, like Monmousseau or Sémard, most of them were no longer party members, either expelled or had left.

Lenin himself noted in February 1922 that 'the process of transforming the old type of European parliamentary party – which in fact is reformist and only slightly tinted with revolutionary colours – into a new type of party, into a genuinely revolutionary, genuinely communist party, is an extremely arduous one. This is demonstrated most clearly, perhaps, by the example of France.'[3] This was as true on the organisational level as it was on the political. His opinion was confirmed by the first two years of the existence of the French section of the Communist International. It is generally accepted that this period provides the classic proof of the necessity for banning factions and tendencies within the Communist Party. Very few historians of the workers' movement have gone into detail on this factional struggle and it is not our task to do so here. But to explain the effects of 'Bolshevisation', we must emphasise one very important point. From the Congress of Tours to the Fourth Congress of the Communist International it was the Centre that led the party. The Centre, in the language of the time, was that former faction of the SFIO which, even if it was not wholly won over by the October Revolution, had understood that it was no longer possible to defend an openly social democratic policy to the working class. The best-known representatives of this swamp were Cachin and Frossard.[4] They had only been observers at the Second Congress of the Communist International in 1920, whereas the non-members of the SFIO, like Rosmer, Lefebvre, Lepetit and Vergeat,[5] had been full delegates. The obsession of this Centre was, if not the elimination, at least the marginalisation of the Left originating from the Committee for Joining the Third International, which was living proof of their past as collaborators. To the extent that at the First Congress (in Marseille in 1921) the failure of Souvarine to be elected to the leading committee forced those on the Left who were to resign so as not to be used as a cover for the policies of Cachin and Frossard. Better, or more exactly, worse, the Second Congress in Paris in October 1922 totally eliminated the Left from the party's central leadership. Things came to such a pass that a month later the Communist International adopted desperate measures in the face of the obvious risk that the Congress of Tours would be to no avail. It reinstated the Left in the leadership, and nominated as joint General Secretaries, Frossard and Treint.[6] But the Communist International did not stop there, it adopted a programme. This programme, which still possesses an amazing freshness, allows us to envisage constructing a revolutionary party in what was one of the most important imperialist countries in Europe at the time. Let us judge it as a whole by recalling the main thrust of this 'programme of work and activity': organising resistance to the capitalist offensive, creating factory councils, carrying out the United Front, struggling against the tendencies to dissipate and fragment activity, struggling against French imperialism, struggling for the right of the colonial peoples to independence, etc.[7]

It was this statement that led Trotsky to write in the preface of his book *The Communist Movement in France* in March 1923, 'Naturally the greatest difficulties still lie ahead. But there is one thing we can say positively: in France a real communist party is living and breathing, fighting and growing.'[8]

A Process of Splitting

The work of constructing an authentic communist party was obviously only beginning. Without being naive, and knowing that no human creation is immune from degeneration, one could speak of promising beginnings.

In fact, being capable of leading a campaign against the occupation of the Ruhr by Poincaré's troops, a veritable act of war on the part of French imperialism,[9] and being capable of leading an anti-militarist struggle meant being capable of struggling against one's own imperialism. Knowing how to struggle, even against the current, against your own imperialism is no less than the touchstone for any revolutionary stance. The work begun by the intervention of the Fourth Congress of the Communist International had to be consolidated and deepened. The departure of Frossard and the arrival of Monatte, Barbusse[10] and Monmousseau showed that the French section of the Communist International was on the way to becoming the party that would allow the working class to embrace Communism, to become conscious of its rôle as the leading force, and to gain the ability to destroy the exploitative system.

But to progress towards this aim, the French section of the Communist International had to become solidly rooted in the working class, and particularly in the concentrations of workers that were the large factories. Getting established there meant being present there, being active, and being organised as a party. On this matter, replying to Treint who had accused him of seeking to remove the trade union commissions of the party from the control of the party itself, Monatte wrote, in the *Bulletin communiste* for 9 May 1922: 'I know very well that the presence and activity of the workers would invigorate the party, and would not only proletarianise it, but would also create within it a necessary counterweight to the spirit of parliamentarism, Blanquism and putschism.'[11]

However, this effort came up against the struggle, to begin with more or less secret, and then more open after the death of Lenin, that shook the leadership of the Russian section of the Communist International. What is conveniently called the triumvirate (Zinoviev, Kamenev and Stalin) was struggling with Trotsky and the Left Opposition. The French section could not remain outside this conflict, any more than the other sections of the Communist International. Moreover, Trotsky enjoyed an evident popularity in France. He had been present at the very first meeting of those who had opposed the imperialist war between 1914 and 1918, and who came together at the Zimmerwald Conference[12] with the others, including Lenin. He was the one who had 'followed' the French section on behalf of the Executive of the Communist International, and was one of the main architects, as chairman of the French Commission upon which Lenin also sat, of the decisions of the Fourth World Congress. For all these reasons at least, the leading committee (apart from Treint and Suzanne Girault)[13] condemned the attacks on him. We might add that in a letter to Zinoviev (who was then Chairman of the Comintern) on 10 September 1922, Humbert-Droz, who was the representative of the Comintern in Paris, proposed Rosmer as future General Secretary to save the French party threatened with strangulation by an emerging bureaucracy devoted to Treint.[14]

Thus it was that the French party was the first section to go in for witch-hunting 'Trotskyists'. Under this label were eliminated from the party all those who opposed the liquidatory line of the triumvirate, that is, essentially, the very first people to struggle to join the Third International. Souvarine was expelled by the Fifth Congress of the Comintern in June 1924, and Monatte and Rosmer in December 1924, before the Clichy Congress began. Loriot and Dunois[15] left the PCF after the so-called *Letter of the 280* in 1925 (a letter also signed by a sympathiser, Georges Cogniot).[16] If we can put it this way, we had to wait until 1927 before this sort of expulsion could be carried out in the Russian party.

The first thing that can be said is that under the label of 'Bolshevisation' it was in fact an extension into the Comintern of a conflict that was shaking the Russian party: the first steps in a method of leadership which, once it had definitively triumphed, was to result in terrible destruction.

We can summarise the argument as follows: 'You disagree with the party leadership, you are a "Trotskyist", you are a

Social Democrat, you are a traitor.' This implacable logic inevitably led to expulsion, and to political murder if the party leadership also wielded state power.

The roots of this policy, so alien to Communism, were to be found in the setback to the German revolution of 1923. This setback put an end for the time being to the perspective of the immediate progress of the revolution in Europe. It was the cradle of the theory of 'Socialism in One Country', and of the USSR as a besieged fortress. The Comintern leadership lost confidence in the revolutionary capacity of the working classes in the bourgeois states, and assigned to them as their main task, and indeed their only task, the defence of this fortress as it stood. The dialectic gave way to mechanical reasoning, and the belief that the defence of the USSR would take place by means of the world revolution, and by the breaking of other links in the chain of imperialism became literally unthinkable to those who presided over the destinies of the Comintern, even if it had been set up in 1919 as 'The

An Unsolicited Confession

The crisis inside the party has created a state of siege within it. The party had to be saved, and prevented from degenerating into a social democratic party; it must struggle against the right, and quickly reorganise itself. All this resulted in a decline of open criticism and free discussion within the party. It was enough to make a few critical remarks, not to be in complete agreement on one detail, to be regarded as being on the right, however distant you might be from Rosmer, Loriot, Souvarine and Monatte ... As a result of the crisis in the party the principles of democratic centralism were applied in an erroneous and mechanical manner, often using far too brutal methods towards party members.

Extracts from the article signed by Alfred Lepetit, the pseudonym of the Comintern representative Guralsky,[17] *which appeared in the* Cahiers du bolchévisme, *15 June 1925*

World Party of the Revolution'. Under these circumstances, those who were opposed to the policy being followed necessarily became class enemies.

What 'Bolshevisation' Was

Apart from the witch-hunting of the 'Trotskyists', in fact 'Bolshevisation' was to be the start of a process that would end in fully-fledged Stalinism, in other words, a break with communist principles. Perhaps such an assertion would have raised a howl a few months later. Today nothing justifies us doing anything in half-measures so as not to upset anybody, and run the risk of a new period of total imperialist domination. Even if it has to cause splits, these splits can only be welcome and clarifying.

'Bolshevisation' meant the birth of bureaucratic methods in the faction of the working-class movement that had come out of Social Democracy. It meant invective in the place of political debate, even if this was firm and unyielding. Under the pretext of seeking homogeneity among the different currents that went to make up the PCF, it meant imposing an authoritarian unity. The high point of this method was Treint's article 'Against the International Right'.

Little by little, the congresses of the party only ratified the composition of the central leadership. Thus Thorez,[18] elected as a candidate member to the Central Committee at the Third Congress (in Lyon in 1924) and then a full member at the Fourth (in Clichy in 1925) was co-opted onto the Political Bureau and appointed Organisational Secretary (a key post for the 'Bolshevisers') in July 1925 (Duclos, *Mémoires*, Volume 1, p243).[19] The Fifth Congress (in Lille in 1926) limited itself to confirming this decision of the apparatus. We might add that at the congress the membership of the Central Committee rose from 37 to 80, resulting in the arrival of a mass of completely new members totally ignorant of the political struggle within the party. Now a superficial democratisation (this congress condemned Treint's practices) concealed the strengthening of bureaucratisation. 'Bolshevisation' meant the formation of an extensive apparatus that made the decisions in the place of the militants. In the *Cahiers du bolchévisme* (no 25) we find this gem which achieved unanimity among all the general secretaries, but reduced the Central Committee to a rubber stamp and militants to people simply carrying out orders: 'The General Secretary has an essentially political rôle, having complete general control over all spheres of the party's activity ... The General Secretary examines all the questions presented to him. He solves current questions, and decides upon those that must be submitted to the Central Committee, the Political Bureau, or the Organisational Bureau.' Things could not be clearer! It comes as no surprise to learn that in 1924 articles devoted to organisational matters made up 65.1 per cent of *Bulletin communiste*, and 67.7 per cent of the *Cahiers du Bolchévisme* (figures quoted by Danielle Tartakowsky in *Les premiers communistes français*, 1980).

'Bolshevisation' meant breaking up the party structure. With the correct intention of organising the party in the workplace, the 'Bolshevisers' decided that there should only be factory cells, and threw themselves into forming them without taking account of concrete reality, and only allowing themselves 12 months to complete the project.

It goes without saying that there is many a slip between cup and lip. The non-organised members were attached to a factory cell. The consequence of this arbitrary procedure, apart from a rapid fall in membership, was a real atomisation of the party. This atomisation was a real gift to the leadership. It shut off the militants from each other, it allowed opponents to be isolated and expelled more rapidly, and it made the apparatus the complete master of the party. This structure is still in place.

Politically, 'Bolshevisation' meant the denial of the immediate past, that of 1923, as can be judged from several significant examples. In an article that appeared in the *Cahiers du bolchévisme* for 1 July 1925, referring to the struggle against the war with the Rif, André Marty[20] allowed himself to write: 'the war took us by surprise without our having any clear literature for the use of the soldiers and sailors'. This assertion is contradicted by the work undertaken in the struggle against the occupation of the Ruhr (*Prométhée*, no 2). Moreover, it shows the way of thinking – unchanged right up to today – which revolves around the following three-part schema: the party has a correct policy, it has made some mistakes, it has such and such tasks to accomplish. And we read the following complete lie in the *Cahiers du bolshévisme* (15 June 1925) under the pseudonym of Alfred Lepetit, the

Comintern representative Guralsky: 'There has never been in France an active and working communist party.' By 1929, Sémard was writing similar things.

Politically, 'Bolshevisation' represents a turning in of the organisation on itself, a surprising and revealing fact at one and the same time, noted by Danielle Tartakowsky (in *Les premiers communistes français*). In 1924 and 1925, the *Cahiers du bolshévisme* did not publish a single polemical article against the SFIO and the CGT. This turning in on itself led to taking up political positions as false as they were dangerous. In the *Cahiers du bolchévisme* for 28 November 1924, Treint wrote: 'Fascism, Social Democracy and Anarchism are essentially the close combination of anti-proletarian violence and social demagogy ... Because fascism was no longer enough, it was necessary to transform Social Democracy and Anarchism into fascist organisations.' In 1926 Sellier, of the ex-Centre[21] wrote: 'We are not on the road to fascism, we are there already.' (The Radical Party headed the government with the support of the SFIO.) Officially, the era of 'Social Fascism' had not yet been inaugurated, but with a similar outlook the defeat of 1933 in Germany is understandable.

Whatever the circumstances, a communist has no need of these fairy tales utterly devoid of any foundation in order to combat Social Democracy and Anarchism politically.

In Contradiction with the Theses of the Third World Congress

The organisational voluntarism that disfigured the Communist Party was in total contradiction to the organisational theses agreed at the Third Congress of the Communist International in 1921. We know that Lenin opposed Zinoviev at this congress. The latter tried to make the organisational weakness of the Comintern's sections the main cause of the failure of the revolution in Europe. Without neglecting this important question, Lenin considered that the situation was above all due to the fact that the majority of the working class had not yet been won over to the communist programme. This attitude contrasts with what was going to be the main keynote of Stalinism, that the party alone represents the entire class in itself, and consequently substitutes itself for it.

Now the theses agreed by the congress clearly stipulate that the party must be capable of 'being always in a position of leadership over the entire movement, a position which the party wins not by force but by the authority it derives from its great energy, ability, experience and flexibility'.[22]

These theses considered that 'Communist cells are the basic units for carrying out the day-to-day communist work of the party in the factories , trade unions, workers' cooperatives, military detachments, etc ...'[23]

These theses warn against a 'formal or mechanical centralisation [which] would mean the centralisation of "power" in the hands of the party bureaucracy, allowing it to dominate the other members of the party or the revolutionary proletarian masses which are outside the party'.[24] We might rightly say that this was a premonitory warning.

We can select the following points from these theses: firstly, 'serious tactical disagreements which surface during elections to the central body should not be ignored; on the contrary, they must be discussed by the central body, of which able representatives of the minority view must be members'.[25] Secondly, 'in order that every party decision is carried out fully by all party organisations and party members, the largest possible number of party members should be involved in discussing and deciding every issue'.[26] Can anyone give us an example of a single working-class organisation, Stalinist or otherwise, where these two points are scrupulously respected? In both cases we are at the opposite end of the spectrum from Article 42 of the statutes adopted by the PCF in 1926 (after the supposed elimination of authoritarianism as represented by Treint): 'Discussion of all questions that give rise to differences is completely free so long as a decision has not been taken.' When we take account of how these decisions were taken, discussion becomes superfluous, and violates the said statutes.

Finally, we might add that Lenin, ill during the Fourth Congress, only intervened to emphasise that these theses were 'too Russian'.[27] In this way, he wanted to say that the sections of the Comintern should not blindly follow the Russian model, and that these theses were not a list of recipes that would inevitably guarantee success. The theses could only really take shape in the real context of the class struggle. For this, Lenin advised studying the history of the Russian Revolution and the reality of revolutionary struggle.

The 'Bolshevisers' only retained the discipline, strong

leadership and centralisation. Let us ask a small question in passing, worth its weight in gold. Why did the expression 'democratic centralism' contained in the theses disappear from the vocabulary afterwards? The 'Bolshevisers' made a clean sweep of the theses of the Third Congress and the remarks of Lenin at the Fourth Congress. Concluding his final intervention, Lenin said: 'If they do that, I am sure the prospects of the world revolution will be not only good, but excellent.'[28] But it was not done!

The Consequences of 'Bolshevisation'

The results of 'Bolshevisation' were naturally of two types: organisational and political.

On the organisational side, we should note that despite the authoritarian and bureaucratic methods, or the circulars of the all-pervading apparatus, the French Communist Party did succeed over the years in gaining a real implantation in the working class. The creation of workplace cells came up against the repression of the bosses, and resulted in the sackings of numerous militants. But to this difficulty of an objective character one should add the disastrous effects of the destruction of the local organisations. The political methods brought in by 'Bolshevisation' caused a drop in membership, a 70 per cent turnover in the party (according to the report by Sémard to the Lille Congress in 1926) and the disappearance from the leadership of those who had struggled for adherence to the Third International. If formally the party had come out of the split at the Congress of Tours, politically it was a new party.

Another tangible result of this period was the formation of cadres who came from the working class. But this formation had a contradictory character.

Souvarine, with the delicacy typical of him, noted in the November 1925 issue of *Bulletin communiste* (after his expulsion, he again took up this title abandoned by the leadership of the French Communist Party in favour of the *Cahiers du bolchévisme*):

> The party lacks cadres? A good discovery, but a bit late. They get rid of seasoned militants by all sorts of means ... then we are informed we are short of cadres. Nothing could be easier ... It is enough to

> create cadres by conveyor belt methods. And we set up a second Leninist school for them. What is a Leninist school? It is a collection of pitiable types, selected for their docility and subjected to a regime of carefully prepared subjection. They are made to stumble through formulae, recite clichés, and imitate 'the higher ups'.

Let us look a little closer at the courses in the French Communist Party's schools of this period. The main teacher at the Bobigny school was Alfred Kurella (a German militant who ended his career on the Central Committee of the East German Communist Party).[29] In his pamphlet *Rôle et méthode de l'enseignement léniniste*, Kurella waged war against general education, which he said 'attracted the worker imbued with a real thirst for knowledge into the domain of bourgeois sciences, led him to abandon the struggle, in order to join the enemy ranks'. This same Kurella, writing as 'Bernard' in the *Cahiers du bolchévisme* for 16 October 1925, forcefully affirmed that 'the methodical deepening of experiences undergone, and the study of theory cannot come before the day-to-day defence of the working class and the defence of the revolution, but must follow it'.

We might add that, again according to Kurella, 'the study of any subject must allow the correctness of the rules of our method to be proved'. The 'teaching' of the Bolshevisers went hand in hand with their military concept of organisation and their aversion to any critical spirit, particularly in anyone who had only one defect: to have had real revolutionary experience.

As Danielle Tartakowsky has correctly pointed out in her book *Les premiers communistes français*: 'By considering theory too much as if it were a finished product, correct for all time through all the changes resulting in the Russian Revolution and new types of parties, one prevents oneself from thinking about the conditions in which theoretical elaboration takes place.' And we might add that thus all theoretical development is forbidden: Marxist Gospels are created according to Saint Marx and Saint Lenin, and then Saint Stalin, Saint Mao, etc. The jihad becomes a must for the faithful, and produces its greatest number of martyrs in the ranks of the working class.

One last point shows that the 'Bolshevisers' had initiated a

The leaders of the Left (Souvarine, Treint and others), and its followers who decided to struggle against Frossard and his friends were in no way capable of linking themselves with the French workers' movement and of leading it ...

At the Boulogne National Council (January 1923), we might have thought that, guided by a leadership in which elements of the Left predominated, the party had become a good communist party. A year has been enough to show that we are not there yet ...

On the occasion of the discussion of 1923 in the Russian Communist Party, Souvarine indulged in tendentious information in order to induce the leadership of the French Communist Party, and then the party itself, to come out in support of the Trotskyist platform ...

In December 1926, our party, with the help of the International, eliminated a left danger (mechanical discipline and bad trade union work, which led to a separation from the masses). It also forced out of its ranks the microscopically small Treint-Suzanne Girault Group, which had joined Trotskyism and carried on factional activity ...

The Communist International has a French section which, 10 years after it was set up, still has great weaknesses, particularly in its rank-and-file organisation, and which makes political mistakes, but which has sincerely and resolutely taken the road mapped out by Lenin.

Pierre Sémard, extracts from an article that appeared in the Comintern pamphlet Dix années de lutte pour la révolution mondiale, *in 1929*

caricature of Communism. In their schools, one course was devoted to dialectic, and only one to 'Marx and Engels', but they preferred 'Leninism' to Lenin, as represented by Stalin's pamphlet *The Foundations of Leninism*. And as for the first two courses, they disappeared from the curriculum from 1925 onwards.

On the political level, apart from the struggle against the Rif war, which after all was to be the last correct approach of the French Communist Party to the colonial question, we should note the first signs of reformism on two important questions.

In the preliminary discussion for the Lyon Congress, Maurice Chambelland, a supporter of the Left,[30] expressed himself in this way:

> For the Communist Party, 1924 must not be an electoral year (general elections were due to take place that year, the first in which the French Communist Party would take part), since in that case our party would not even deserve its name. The 'parliamentary struggle' must not fill its horizon. There are many other tasks falling to it, a thousand times more important. What worries me about this pre-congress discussion is that comrades who have taken part in it up till now don't seem to have thought much about these things. They only talk about the electoral tactic. (*L'Humanité*, 10 January 1924)

Finally, there is the matter of part of a speech of Thorez to the Lille Congress of 1926 reported in this way by Duclos in his *Mémoires*:

> It was in the course of this congress that Maurice Thorez, overcoming the currents of national nihilism that had developed in our party in reaction to the chauvinism that had poisoned the working-class movement during the First World War, came out against the payment of the debts to the United States and Great Britain, so opposing the national interests of our country to those of the big capitalists on the other side of the Atlantic and the other side of the Channel. (*Mémoires*, Volume 1, p257)[31]

The worm was already in the fruit!

Here we are putting our finger on an incontrovertible point: organisational questions and political questions are intimately connected. When such organisational questions are posed in a working-class party with such sharpness, this means, speechifying aside, that its programme is not – or is no longer – wholly revolutionary. There is absolute incompatibility between a bureaucratic internal regime and a communist programme.

And to think that the 'Bolshevisers' were pretending to be proceeding in the name of revolutionary purity, and in the name of 'Leninism'! In fact, they ushered in Stalinism. Some, like Treint, Sauvage,[32] and Suzanne Girault – at the instigation of Zinoviev and Kamenev – were hoist on their own petard. Others like Thorez and the inevitable Cachin, along with Duclos and Frachon,[33] were, after the end of the Barbé-Célor affair,[34] to become the homogeneous and monolithic leadership to which the 'Bolshevisers' aspired. And we all know the extent of this disaster!

The Bureaucratisation and Destruction of the Party

Antoine Clavez

From *Prométhée*, no 3, December 1989–January 1990, pp 11–16

The struggle for the succession to Lenin that was to end with the seizure of power by the bureaucracy and the expulsion of Trotsky did not fail to cause ripples in the International. On 6 January 1924, Souvarine wrote to Zinoviev, then Chairman of the Communist International, that 'to attack Trotsky's authority is to lessen the prestige of the Russian Revolution ... for the French workers Trotsky means Bolshevism, the revolution and the Communist International'.[1] Trotsky had a watching brief on the French section for the Comintern, and had been the main architect of its real foundation, beginning in January 1923 with the departure of Frossard and company, an old social democratic politician connected with the bourgeoisie through the channels of Freemasonry and the League for the Rights of Man, and the arrival of the revolutionary syndicalists Monatte and Delagarde.[2] Zinoviev, Kamenev, and the most obscure of the triumvirs, Stalin, could not allow a situation to develop which would have brought the Comintern onto the side of the Russian opposition. Zinoviev used all the means at his disposal to win over the world organisation to the theses of the triumvirs, and transform it into a docile instrument of their policy, in the interests of the new masters of Soviet Russia. At the beginning of January, the leading committee of the French Communist Party had removed Treint, who was nicknamed 'captain' on account of his military authoritarianism which disrupted the party, from the Political Bureau of the PCF. This removal of what it was convenient to call the Left as opposed to the old Tours Centre allowed Zinoviev to break the leadership of the party, and find a champion coming from the pro-Bolshevik Left of the party. The plan of the Chairman of the Comintern was to reinstate Treint in the leadership of the party; his temperament was ideally suited to the task in hand – to bring the section into line. To carry this out it was necessary to convince the most spineless elements in the leadership, Cachin and Sellier, of the correctness of the theses of the triumvirate by trapping them between the rank and file and the top.

Manuilsky and Lozovsky[3] were sent on the spot to help Treint and Suzanne Girault hold on to their positions at the head of the Seine Federation with the aid of secret funds that had not been used during the German October. On 17 February, the regional conference gave the majority to the Treintist faction; from then on it would not be difficult to overturn the majority on the leading committee. The Cachins, Selliers and company, representing the old Centre, who had been deeply involved in the *Union Sacrée* during the 1914–18 war (Cachin had been sent to Italy by the government to get Italy into the war on the right side), were anxious to show their loyalty to Moscow, all the more so because this manoeuvre would allow them to get their own back upon those militants who had conducted themselves in a courageous and exemplary way during the war. The hour of the Johnny-come-lately Leninists had arrived.

At the meeting of the leading committee on 18 March, a 14-strong Zinovievist faction proposed a ready-made motion which was accepted, minus the votes of Monatte and Rosmer, and of Souvarine, who was absent. The Zinovievist theses had won out. It is the task of the party apparatus, under the influence of the Bolshevik Old Guard, formed in the school of Lenin and in two revolutions (1905 and 1917) to oppose any deviation. The Old Guard makes up the historic group that alone is capable of assuring cohesion between the different elements in the party, and of maintaining the Bolshevik line of the party.[4]

We came to the Bolshevik Party, obviously not always in a state of grace, and the first thing we were told was that a strict discipline needed to be imposed upon us, and for eight years we have attempted to subject ourselves to this discipline, and to understand it ... We cannot perceive without great bitterness what can result from this conflict, when men of such authority, and women of such authority, with such a past, with all the passion that they can muster, in spite of everything, set themselves against the overwhelming majority of the Russian Communist Party; they are liable, because of their prestige, their personal authority, and their past, their great past, to upset morale. This is serious, and it is this that disturbs me about their present state of morale... Factional spirit at the moment is a most regrettable thing. I am obviously not afraid myself, as I have unlimited confidence in the power of these men, and even if there were at the present time an opposition against the majority of the Russian Communist Party, made up of men who have an admirable and irreproachable past as revolutionaries, and even if they were to set themselves against it, the Russian Revolution will still not be defeated for all that. Only for some time now there has been great rejoicing in public opinion, among our enemies, and a deep sadness among the proletariat of the International. It is against this that we wish to protest ...

Extracts from the intervention of Cachin on the Central Committee of the PCF on 1–3 September 1926, in the Cahiers d'histoire de l'Institut Maurice Thorez, *nos 25–26, 1978*

The Bonapartist theses of the Thermidoreans[5] were thus adopted by the French Communist Party. Following on from the analysis of the political situation in Russia, the leading committee extended the concept to the parties in the capitalist countries:

> The more deeply a communist party gets involved in the tactic of the United Front, the more ener-

> getically it must struggle within itself against the survival and rebirth of the reformist and social democratic spirit, and against all the dangers of deviation from the United Front. It is by such an internal struggle against a possible danger from the right in a party immersed in the bosom of the material and ideological corruption of capitalism that a communist party can show that every daily struggle can only be successful if it prepares the struggle that leads to the dictatorship of the proletariat.

In the *Cahiers du bolshévisme* no 2, Treint explained what we are to understand by 'reformist and social democratic survivals':

> These revisionist tendencies are particularly aimed at the French party, for they are holding back the formation of revolutionary cadres endowed with a solid ideology. Comrades must understand that only the theory, tactics and practice provided by Lenin and applied by his pupils are truly correct, and that any other methods developed, even by the best revolutionaries (like Trotsky and Rosa Luxemburg) are false, and are only survivals of the old methods and theories of the social democratic left, or an erroneous reaction against these errors.[6]

In the opinion of the Zinovievists, it was therefore a matter of ridding the party of all the elements who had accumulated any experience. The only authentic revolutionaries were the recent members, who had got their training within the party, and were incapable of questioning the correctness of the general line. Why did you need a programme, if you were drunk on action?

The Fifth Congress of the Comintern excluded Souvarine at the request of the French delegation, when actually nothing of the sort had been envisaged in Paris. Explaining to party opinion how this came about, you could read in *L'Humanité* on 19 July 1924: 'It is the extent to which all the petit bourgeois survivals of the individualist "self" are destroyed that the anonymous iron cohorts of the French

Bolsheviks will be formed.' In their letter to the members of the French Communist Party, Monatte and Rosmer were able to write on this subject, 'it has been said that the party must become an iron cohort. But in reality, anyone who has proved his mettle must be broken ... We must bow, not before ideas or the decisions taken by the organisation, but before men. By this method it is not cohorts that are being prepared, but a regiment of slugs.'

In the conception of the leading team, putting the militants' values of self-sacrifice at the forefront would see the selection of cadres of a new type: they had to have performers strictly conforming to the limits of an apparatus, a structure for the one-sided application of tactics decided by a small leading circle. In this conception, it was not the party that made policy, but 'technical' authorities; the problem was no longer the theoretical elaboration and analysis of the concrete situation, but applying it. The big thing became in the French Communist Party what it became convenient to describe as 'organisational problems'.

When questions of power predominate in a party over political questions, and all political life becomes a bureaucratic farce, struggles lacking in inspiration do not take place in an open way, and only appear in a coded fashion. The screen for the Zinovievist operation in the Comintern was the proletarianisation of the parties and their mere presence in places of class confrontation. And whatever led to this was legitimate and necessary.

In his report before the Organisational Commission of the Fifth Congress, Piatnitsky[7] explained: 'All the local organs will be maintained, but they will no longer be elected by a plenary assembly of members and professionals, but exclusively by the cells, which will send their delegates to the district, regional and city conferences.'

The basic thing was therefore not the implanting of the party in working-class circles, but the atomisation of its members into little units with no links between them, subject to a hierarchy largely external to them. The idea of the party line tended to become immanent and mystical. At the same meeting, Sauvage explained: 'Our task [of "Bolshevisation"] was made all the easier by the speed and extent to which cells were set up, and comrades belonging to the cells automatically left the local organisations to which they belonged.' Thus through this process, the legal structures of the party that would have been able to prevent it were annihilated.

The *Bulletin communiste* quoted a resolution of the Seine federal bureau, a beacon federation of the Treintist clique, where we are clearly told how a factory cell ought to function: 'At each cell meeting, apart from questions that particularly concern the factory, a short speech about the slogans that the party should launch in the factory should be made by a delegate from the federal commission to the cells or the secretary; it is important that every speech should be followed by an exchange of views, and that everyone should take part in it.' A little talk and an exchange of views, this is what political debate in the party had become under the inspiration of Zinoviev! It is true that the question was not posed in their minds in this way, since the guarantee of the revolutionary nature of the line was the leadership made up of the disciples and pupils of Lenin. The programme exists, and after all, why bother any further, since it is only a matter of applying it?

However, putting in place the new structures at the base of the party could not fail to pose a certain number of problems. France was not at the time a country of great industrial concentrations, and the majority of the workers were in small enterprises; this was particularly the case with the communist militants. This single fact made it unlikely that many militants would come together in the same factory, and if it did happen, the problem of the employer's repression was immediately posed. Factory cells had to be created from what existed, and elements from other factories had to be enrolled in them. These artificial cells killed off life in the old sections without putting anything in its place. The new organisations created in this piecemeal way were destined to be lifeless, and caused a haemorrhage of militants. The militants who were capable of being active in this setting had to change their jobs frequently, with no opportunity of creating real links between the party and the masses. The new structure, not as yet devoid of all revolutionary will, was by its nature led to develop putschist tendencies, as happened a few years later in the infamous Third Period. It is not without interest to note in passing that Béla Kun,[8] the promoter of the disastrous theory of 'the offensive' opposed by Lenin and Trotsky at the Third Congress, was put in charge of the ideology of the Comintern by Zinoviev.

Point 11 of the resolution of the Third Congress of the Communist International explained that 'each party member should belong to a smaller working group: a committee, commission, board, group, fraction or cell. This is the only way party work can be correctly allocated, carried out and supervised.' And the resolution also insisted that they must also 'attend the general meetings of their local organisations',[9] for only work in small groups could allow effective general meetings to be held to direct the whole of the work of the party. A political division of work, real militant activity of the members, and local party organisation were the norm for any communist organisation before the Soviet Thermidor and the militaristic transformation imposed by Zinoviev.

Nor is it unworthy of note that in the same resolution the Communist International insisted on the fact that leading bodies must not be inordinately increased, and that there should be as few obstacles as possible between the rank and file and the top.

The implications of the new organisational orientation of the party were not clear to the rank-and-file militants. A massive surge of pseudo-revolutionary if not anti-Marxist exhortation and empty dialectic poured over the working-class Left, who were transmuted into an international right, and the basic problem was disguised behind the urgent necessity for communists to root their tactics and strategy in the structure of the class struggle, and therefore to be present in the factories, where it went on.

In an article entitled 'The Myth of Trotskyism' and published in *La Révolution prolétarienne* some months after his expulsion, Alfred Rosmer explained:

> A few years ago, when these questions could be discussed in the International, when the respective rôles of the party, the unions and the soviets were considered, we generally came to the conclusion that the party seemed to be the most temporary organism, and that it was either the soviets or the unions which would take on the dominant rôle in the building of communist society.[10]

Speaking of Treint in a letter to the editorial board of *La Lutte de classes* in 1929, Trotsky explained that Zinovievism was a mixture of extreme leftism and centrism, and that finally 'the ease with which Treint changes his appraisals ... [testifies] that Treint intends to apply Zinovievist methods within the framework of the opposition'.[11] For what in the end is Zinovievism, if not a particular view of the party and a number of authoritarian practices, with a view to militarising it and reducing the ranks of the party into docile instruments? There is obviously a whole gamut of arguments from ultra-leftism to centrism that a bureaucracy can use in the context of a political confrontation within the party; in this particular case what is most important is not the correctness of the analysis, or its relevance, but the higher interests of the party that will carry out the revolution. The only intangible thing in Zinoviev's thinking was the party and its physical set-up. When he took up a position against the October insurrection, it was not because he was in favour of critical support for Kerensky, for Lenin's *April Theses* were history by then, but because the party did not seem to him to be ready for it, for were there not in Russia millions of unorganised and non-Bolshevik peasants?[12] The same argument applied, according to him in Germany, that the party was not ready.

For Zinoviev, there was a correlation between building the party and preparing for the revolution. He was obsessed with organisational preparations.

Although it was not expressed openly, the deep differences during the few months of struggle that brought Monatte and Rosmer into opposition with the Comintern revolved around the link that united the working class and its 'natural' organisations, the trade unions, the strike committees, the soviets and the party. Winning the confidence of the masses and winning their the political leadership is one thing, but making the party the sole factor in the seizure of power is quite another.

Zinovievism put the emphasis on the construction of an apparatus which would take complete charge of the programme, the party and the revolution. Even if it is true that, as opposed to the Stalinists, the Zinovievists were deeply attached to world revolution, it nonetheless remains true that they nurtured bureaucratisation, reformist degeneration and outbursts of putschist fever. It may appear strange today to talk about Zinovievism, for even though it has undoubtedly left its mark on the process of Stalinist degeneration among the communist parties, nobody in the spectrum of the far left now proclaims its contribution to the working-class movement. Its traces remain, nonetheless.

There were two waves of expulsions from the Third International connected with the Russian question and the Stalinisation of the world organisation, the first at the end of 1924, and the second in 1925–26. The first wave is the one we have dealt with here, and it affected those militants who from the very beginning had opposed the effects of the Soviet Thermidor; those who were expelled, branded with the infamous stamp of 'Trotskyism' by Zinoviev, were condemned for tactical reasons by Trotsky, who, for example, asked Monatte and Rosmer to appeal against their expulsion to the Communist International.[13] Apart from the *Révolution prolétarienne* group, all political trace of them was lost. The second wave of expulsions was that of the Zinovievist leaders after the break-up of the triumvirate and the emergence of the Leningrad Opposition within the USSR, Zinoviev's stronghold. The uniting of opponents in the USSR behind the name of Trotsky encouraged the creation of Trotskyist groups in the rest of the world out of the personnel of the Zinovievist faction; that is how the Treints came to Trotskyism, which they had previously fiercely fought against. It was the same in Germany with the Fischer-Maslow group.[14] It was therefore these that in the 1920s provided the larger units of the Joint Opposition. As Oskar Hippe naively remarks in his autobiography: 'There was already a small Trotsky faction in Berlin ... in the party this group was regarded as a right-wing deviation. It did not put in an appearance ... later, these comrades had largely disappeared from active party work.'[15] And we might well ask why Rosmer, who lent his house in Barbizon for the founding congress of the Fourth International, never joined it.

The Trotskyist group where Zinovievist influence is most striking is Cannon's American SWP:[16]

> For the proletarian revolutionist the party is the concentrated expression of his life purpose, and he is bound to it for life and death. He preaches and practices party patriotism, because he knows that his socialist ideal cannot be realised without the party. In his eyes the crime of crimes is disloyalty or irresponsibility towards the party. (*The Struggle for a Proletarian Party*)[17]

Here, as with Treint, we see that adherence to the organisation as such is more important than adherence to the programme, and adherence to an apparatus that will make the revolution is paramount. Disloyalty to the apparatus therefore becomes the crime of crimes. Thrice loyal adherence to

> This shows the extent to which the communist movement is rotten today; even the best that is in it has been infected with Stalinist poison, and is now incapable of getting rid of it, and perhaps does not even want to. The leaders have learned how to control – with very simple methods and squalid manoeuvres – and the troops fall into line with pure and simple obedience; it seems that they would rather follow the chief than study and discuss for themselves the great and numerous problems of the time: they like to have everything done for them.
>
> *This reflection of Rosmer's was taken from a letter dated 17 March 1947 to Sara Jacobs.*[18] *It applies to the.methods of the Cannon leadership in the American SWP. And Rosmer says of Cannon in the same letter that he 'embarrasses Trotskyism more than he helps it'.*

the organisation is the only quality that a bureaucratic leader asks of his rank and file, so the party lives, but as for the line ...

Similarly, the idea according to which it is the party and its mechanisms that will make the revolution, and not the working class, leading people to consider the organisation more important than the real links with the working class and its natural organisations, the trade unions and soviets, places Cannonism in the Zinovievist tradition that subsequently went over to Trotskyism. Cannon's political legacy makes the essence of this trend clear. At the time of the destruction of the Fourth International in favour of entrism in the official communist parties, Cannon could find nothing better to save the SWP than to form a bloc with the apparatus, led by Barnes;[19] from an all-powerful tool of the revolution, the apparatus became an independent political entity, as if by accident! Devised to save Trotskyist orthodoxy, the manoeuvre ended 10 years later in the fusion of the SWP with the Pabloites,[20] against whom it had been devised.

Cleaning the slag of history out of revolutionary thinking has become more necessary than ever due to world developments. Even if the Leninism of the Soviet Thermidoreans and their continuators, whatever name they give themselves, is an abomination, the vitality of revolutionary thought and of communism, as a mode of analysis and of action, has not been overturned. Disillusion and cynicism are bad politics, communism itself is not dead.

We publish below a few of the successive opinions of the leadership of the French Communist Party on the period of 'Bolshevisation':

1964: *Manuel d'histoire du PCF*, pages 175–6

> With the support of the government, the bosses systematically intensified repression against communist militants. Social Democracy distorted and denigrated the party's effort and mocked its militants, whom it called 'cellulards'.
>
> These pressures had their echo among party members by way of Social Democrat or Anarcho-reformist survivals. The introduction of factory cells ended by crystallising the opposition of militants who showed themselves incapable of assimilating the basic principles of Marxism-Leninism: Anarcho-Syndicalists like Rosmer or Monatte, and members of the old Committee for Joining the Third International like Souvarine. In spite of the diversity of traditions claimed by these men, they united on a common platform, quite close to Social Democracy.
>
> Counting on the inexperience of party members and the mistakes made during the attempt to reorganise, and basing themselves on the inevitable difficulties encountered by many of the new cells, they carried on a struggle against the party over the factory cells, and urged a return to the old organisational forms. Persisting in their errors, they went over to factional and disruptive

work. They ended up repeating the social democratic lies against the party, the international communist movement, and the Soviet Union. The party had to expel them in 1924.

The struggle against this trend was all the more necessary because something similar was present in the Communist International. After the death of Lenin on 21 January 1924 some elements grouped around Trotsky actually began an open attack upon the principles of Marxism-Leninism.

1968: *Mémoires de Jacques Duclos*, page 269

The question of whether the victory of socialism was possible in the Soviet Union was the basis of the differences between the party and the Trotskyists, who were joined by Zinoviev and Kamenev, who at the time of the October Revolution had adopted a cowardly attitude that was severely condemned by Lenin.

The Trotskyists and Zinovievists demanded the right to form factions inside the Bolshevik Party, and tried to promote a policy of factional struggle within the Communist International.

I was myself from the very beginning opposed to the Trotskyist tendencies which ended with the expulsion of Souvarine from the party ranks, and I was just as hostile to the theses defended by the Trotskyist-Zinovievist bloc, one of whose leading lights in France was none other than Albert Treint, the 'feather plucker' who was thrown out of the party in his turn.

The discussions about the policy of the Bolshevik Party and the Trotskyist-Zinovievist theses had the great advantage of allowing communist militants to grasp the complexity of the problems our Soviet comrades had to resolve. The great majority of the party rejected the adventurist theses of Trotsky and Zinoviev, which clearly showed their lack of confidence in the future of the first socialist state, and consequently their belief in the necessity to spread the revolutionary struggle without taking account of objective reality, as if it were possible to do no matter what, no matter where at no matter what time.

1981: Danielle Tartakowsky, Le PCF, *Étapes et problemes*, Éditions sociales, pages 49–50

In the situation of 1924, marked by the death of Lenin, and the crisis opened up by it in the Russian party and beyond in the Communist International, this objective ('Bolshevisation') nonetheless largely overlapped with a second objective, distinct to begin with, which consisted of purging from the parties those elements suspected of supporting Trotsky in the conflict which set him against Stalin, Zinoviev and Kamenev. In line with the decision to 'Bolshevise' the touchstone of support for the positions of the now triumphant Troika, and deciding all opposition or reluctance to organise on the basis of factory cells to be irrefutable proof of a 'Trotskyist' deviation, the Communist International made use of Bolshevisation to sort out, by means of purges, conflicts which until then had been latent in its principle sections.

These purges, whether of right or left, which took place in the name of an orthodoxy then defined by Stalin's *Foundations of Leninism*, and the more fundamental decision to carry on political activity from now on at the main point of exploitation, that of the factory, so breaking with both the social democratic and revolutionary syndicalist traditions, provoked opposition, expulsions, and withdrawals. Souvarine was expelled for his strong support for the positions of Trotsky; cadres who had come from revolutionary syndicalism, such as Monatte and Rosmer, socialist leaders from the very beginning, such as Loriot or Dunois, and intellectuals who had joined it left the party one by one through a total incomprehension of what was going on. They either went back to the SFIO, or the revolutionary syndicalist movements still working, in spite of setbacks, in the trade union movement, or in the 'Trotskyist' organisations with their small numbers.

But that was not the main reason for the loss of militants.

Let us note that 'those who returned' to the SFIO only did so around the 1930s, that *La Révolution prolétarienne* founded by Monatte and Rosmer did not call itself 'communist syndicalist' to start off with, and that we had to wait until 1927–28 to see a 'Trotskyist' group emerge.

The French Communist Party and Trotsky

Emile Fabrol

From *Prométhée*, no 1, Summer 1989, pp 3–9, 19

In February 1922, Lenin emphasised that 'the process of transforming the old type of European parliamentary party – which in fact is reformist and only slightly tinted with revolutionary colours – into a new type of party, is an extremely arduous one. This is demonstrated most clearly, perhaps, by the example of France.'[1] This opinion of Lenin sums up perfectly the crisis through which the French section of the Communist International was then passing. The Fourth Congress of the Communist International in 1922 by adopting a programme of work and action for the French Communist Party, and by sorting out the composition of its leadership had put an end to a crisis that could have finished it off completely.

On the death of Lenin, the struggle that brought Zinoviev-Kamenev and Stalin into opposition to Trotsky and the Left Opposition overtook the Communist International, and particularly its French section. The struggle against 'Trotskyism' became the rallying cry against all those who opposed the policy of Zinoviev at the head of the Comintern, and of Treint at the head of the French Communist Party.

This is not only a historical question, it is a political one.

Under the Banner of 'Anti-Trotskyism'

In December 1924, Monatte, Rosmer and Delagarde were expelled from the French Communist Party. The motion to expel them stated that 'the arms acquired by Monatte, Rosmer and Delagarde from the arsenal of Pioch and Frossard, have at the present time been taken up by the whole of the bourgeoisie and directed against the party and against the International. Thus Monatte, Rosmer and Delagarde have taken part in the anti-proletarian and anti-communist offensive led by the combined forces of demagogic fascism and the fascistic Left bloc.'[2] Even though the one who put together this condemnation is none other than Treint, himself expelled in 1926 for 'Trotskyism', it is purely Stalinist phraseology.

This drive against those militants who had come from revolutionary syndicalism, having participated in the preparation for the Zimmerwald Conference at a time when the Socialist Party had been enmeshed in the *Union Sacrée*, and who, like Rosmer, had been members of the Communist International before the Congress of Tours, was launched in an article by Treint in the *Bulletin communiste* for 18 April 1924 entitled 'Against the International Right'. The article is a masterpiece of obfuscation ('our present day right has come from the old left'), of following the leader, and of an absence of political analysis. The methods of 'Bolshevisation' were set in motion. Twisting the facts and lying were its major components. Thus, again in the same article, Treint accused Monatte of wanting to form 'a network of trade union commissions independent of party control'. In the *Bulletin communiste* on 9 May 1924, Monatte, after noting that Treint alone and Sémard only vaguely had any memory of this, that the delegate from the Red International of Labour Unions did not remember it at all, and that the meeting's minutes had disappeared, stated on the contrary that 'it was solely a question of giving real life to the trade union commissions. That would have been enough, because I know very well that the presence and activity of the workers would invigorate the party, and would not only proletarianise it, but would also create within it a counterweight to the spirit of parliamentarism and the Blanquist and putschist spirit.'[3] In his reply to Treint, Monatte was posing real problems, which the 'Bolshevisers' did not want to see raised. They preferred invective, because they could not eliminate the party's most revolutionary elements just like that. Treint had of necessity to move fast and present the Comintern with a fait accompli, in order to 'prove' the existence of a faction in France of the supposed international right headed by Trotsky. In fact, in a letter to Zinoviev dated 10 September 1923, Humbert-Droz, the Comintern representative with the French Communist Party, wrote: 'Rosmer seems to me to be the only one with the necessary authority and at the same time the indispensable skill to be the party General Secretary.'[4] But it was out of the question for Zinoviev, then in a struggle against Trotsky, to have in the leadership of the French Communist Party a man connected with Trotsky since the First World War.

Treint conducted a campaign against *L'Humanité*, which was 'making the party lose its clear communist identity'. Monatte, Rosmer, Charbit, Antonini, Godonnèche[5] and Chambelland, who had been in charge of several pages of the French Communist Party's daily paper, resigned some time in April 1924. On 23 May 1924, the *Bulletin communiste* published their letters of resignation in which they put their fingers on the nub of the affair:

> We do it in the knowledge that urgent work to reorganise the party is necessary ... At a time when the electoral campaign is in full swing in which the party is giving the impression that it is largely taking part with the intention of capturing seats, it is natural that those members of the party who have come from revolutionary syndicalism should be treated as nuisances, and even threatened with expulsion.

And even if the electoral campaign of 1924 was carried out in the form of a bloc of the workers and peasants against the National Bloc (the bourgeois right),[6] and the left bloc (the SFIO allied with the Radical Party), and even if the French Communist Party had not yet sunk into the electoralism and legalism it was to make its own after June 1934, those militants who had in the past a healthy aversion to the SFIO's parliamentarism obviously could not support the slightest concession to this type of thing.

This was basically a correct position, even if it was also

true that they had not broken completely with the basic anti-parliamentarism of their own past.

In July 1924, at the Fifth so-called 'Bolshevisation' Congress of the Comintern, Souvarine was expelled for 'inadmissible personal and political concepts and practices completely incompatible with the communist movement'.[7] And even if it was universally accepted that Souvarine did have authoritarian tendencies, the real reason for his expulsion was otherwise. Treint and Zinoviev could not tolerate the fact that Souvarine had published in the *Bulletin communiste*, which he edited, 'but skilfully, in a tendentious manner',[8] some extracts from the political positions of the Opposition in the Russian party, that he had carried a motion on the leading committee (with 22 votes to two, those of Treint and Suzanne Girault) condemning the attacks against Trotsky, without even declaring his solidarity with the Opposition,[9] that he alone had taken up Trotsky's defence before the Thirteenth Congress of the Russian party, and after raising a subscription had published Trotsky's *New Course* in French.

Béthune, 15 April 1924

Dear Comrade

You have made good use of my modest subscription for the publication of Trotsky's pamphlet. I take the opportunity once more to assure you of my complete solidarity as regards the situation in the French Communist Party, as well as what concerns the international 'crisis'.

Fraternally,

Thorez

PS: Could you please reply as to the correct position that my federation should take up.

Letter to Boris Souvarine from the future 'greatest Stalinist in France'

As you can imagine, the struggle against 'Trotskyism' very quickly took on some momentum in the French party, perhaps even a pitch of desperation. The reasons for this were many. It was undeniable that Trotsky enjoyed a certain amount of popularity in the French Communist Party. As Chairman of the French Commission of the Communist International, Trotsky had played a decisive rôle in the decisions of the Fourth Congress. A fact worth noting is that at the time of Lenin's death in January 1924, *L'Humanité* had associated Trotsky with Lenin. On the 23rd, under the headline of 'Lenin is Dead', there were two photographs, one of Lenin and the other a representation of Lenin along with Trotsky and Kamenev; on the 25th there was an editorial entitled 'Farewell Ilyich! Farewell Leader!', signed by Leon Trotsky; on the 27th there was a photograph with the caption underneath of 'Lenin talking to volunteers setting off for the Polish front in the Theatre Square in Moscow in 1920', with one Lev Davidovich Bronstein at the foot of the rostrum (in the Stalinist version of this photo put out a few years later he had disappeared).[10]

In addition, Rosmer had been a member of the Communist International before the Congress of Tours, had signed the manifesto adopted by the Second Congress in July 1920, and had also (along with Lenin, Trotsky and Zinoviev, among others) signed the telegram from the Executive of the Communist International to the Congress of Tours, which along with Clara Zetkin's intervention[11] had induced the majority of the Eighteenth Congress of the SFIO to join the Third International.

The Beginnings of Bolshevisation

The plenum of the Communist International in 1925 declared that 'Bolshevisation consists in knowing how to apply the general principles of Leninism to each concrete situation in every country', and that 'the Bolshevisation of the sections of the Communist International consists of studying and applying in action the experience gained by the Russian Communist Party'.[12] Make sense of this if you can!

One thing was for sure, that the Zinovievs, Treint and others like Ruth Fischer in Germany, were carrying out an identical practice: wiping out any form of opposition, creating ideological conformity, and achieving 'one hundred per cent

Leninism', as a certain Al (surely Guralsky, the Comintern's representative in the French Communist Party) wrote in the *Cahiers du bolchévisme*, which had been published to replace the *Bulletin communiste*, on 28 November 1924. There was only one way to achieve this aim: 'Comrades must understand that only the theory, tactics and practice provided by Lenin and applied by his pupils are truly correct, and that any other methods and theories developed even by the best revolutionaries (like Trotsky and Rosa Luxemburg) are false, and are only survivals of the old methods and theories of the social democratic left.'[13]

Things could hardly be clearer about the objectives of the 'Bolshevisers'. Lenin's body was embalmed, and his thought and his practice were now fixed for ever as well. Those who raised questions or criticisms were only vulgar left Social Democrats, and therefore rightist elements (what sublime logic, or rather perfect twisting of the dialectic). Just as in self-respecting schools, bad pupils were to be expelled.

Under the pretext of a necessary organisation of the working class at the points of capitalist exploitation itself – forming factory cells – under the pretext of finally breaking with the remains of parliamentarist conceptions, and under the pretext of the necessary proletarianisation of the sections of the Communist International, they introduced only regimentation, bureaucratisation and political castration.

In their *Letter to the Members of the PCF* dated 22 November 1924, which they made public after the leadership's refusal to publish it in the party press, and which announced the end of their membership of the French Communist party, Monatte, Rosmer and Delagarde condemned this process:

> There is a lot of talk about homogeneity, alignment, and discipline. From top to bottom in the party, there has been a cascade of orders, which we are supposed to obey without understanding and especially without murmuring anything other than the ritual: 'Captain, you are right.' A mess-hall mentality is created and the habits of non-coms take over. The problem is only to find the right kind of apparatus to run things and full-timers to appoint. Soon the party bureaucracy will

> be able to go one better than that of the French state.[14]

We take the opportunity to ask our readers, to whatever organisation of the working-class movement they belong, who have had doubts about the effectiveness of their party, to think seriously about this quotation.

The apparatus became the apple of the party's eye. In the *Theses on the Policy of the PCF and the Problems Posed for the Communist International*, adopted unanimously by the leading committee of the PCF minus two against (Monatte and Souvarine) and one abstention (Rosmer), we note, as regards the struggle in the Russian party, this universally valid sentence and political credo of all bureaucrats and would-be bureaucrats: 'It is the task of the party apparatus, inspired by the Bolshevik Old Guard, formed in the school of Lenin and in two revolutions (1905 and 1917) to oppose any deviation.'[15] This was affirmed in 1931 by Ferrat in his *History of the PCF*, when he emphasised that one of the essential tasks the Fifth Congress of the Comintern assigned to the PCF was 'the formation of a real apparatus in the party'. Far be it from us to deny the need for an apparatus for a revolutionary party. But it must be kept to its proper place. It is the party that decides policy at its congresses, and it is the leadership, elected by the congress, that carries it out. For this reason, with our experience of the working-class movement, we can only share the disquiet of Marguerite Rosmer in a letter to Humbert-Droz on 11 April 1924: 'We are badly muddled and worn down by functionaries who come at us from all sides, the majority of whom are incompetent and bereft of political sense, but who always line up on the strongest side so as not to lose their cushy jobs.'

The origins of this phase in the formation of the French Communist Party are to be found in the struggle that was then unfolding in the leadership of the Russian party. As Danielle Tartakowsky notes: 'Bolshevisation was a weapon in the struggle that the Triumvirate (Zinoviev-Kamenev-Stalin) was carrying on against Trotsky.'[16]

'Bolshevisation' was one of the main consequences of the setback to the German October of 1923. We are only being true to history when we say that Lenin regarded the Russian October of 1917 as the beginning of the world revolution. The last congress held while Lenin was alive declared, 'only the seizure of power by the proletariat and the world socialist revolution can save humanity from the permanent catastrophe provoked by the continuation of modern capitalism'.[17] Now the end of 1923 marked the setback to the Bulgarian revolution, and above all to the German revolution.[18]

The occupation of the Ruhr by the French army could not fail to produce revolutionary consequences, and the defeat of the passive resistance supported by the German government left the German bourgeoisie in a dead end, *unless* the German Communist Party failed to draw the conclusions the situation demanded. But that is what happened! The defeat of the German October was above all due to the leadership of the Communist International. Thus Stalin dared to write in a letter of 7 August 1923 to Zinoviev and Bukharin: 'In my opinion, the Germans must be curbed and not spurred on.'[19] At the Thirteenth Congress of the Russian party, Zinoviev went on: 'In the same position, we would have had to do the same thing.'[20] But *Pravda* on 25 May 1924 drew quite another conclusion: 'It is clear that the [German] Communist Party then had the majority of the population with it; it would have been able to join battle, with all the chances of success.' This corresponds more clearly to the objective situation in Germany in October 1923.

The main result of this setback is what we may call the 'end' of the immediate and real possibilities for the development of the world revolution, even if Ruth Fischer continued to come out with smug optimism. It is what caused the birth of the all-pervading dogma of 'socialism in one country'. Whoever says 'socialism in one country' also says that there is 'no need of a world party of the revolution'. This change in the Third International was brought about by 'Bolshevisation'. Zinoviev began the project, he was principally responsible, and Stalin finished the job, until the organisation, which for a long time no longer had any meaning, was dissolved in 1943 on the altar of peaceful coexistence.

The Construction of the Revolutionary Party is Impaired

If there is any word in the language of the militant workers' movement whose sense is particularly ambiguous it is very much the case with 'Bolshevisation'.

First of all, we should take the opportunity to recall what Lenin thought about the word 'Bolshevik': 'such a meaningless and ugly term' which 'expresses nothing whatever but the purely accidental fact that at the Brussels-London congress of 1903 we were in the majority'. Ironically, he added: 'Perhaps I would propose a "compromise" to my comrades, namely, to call ourselves the Communist Party, but to retain the word "Bolsheviks" in brackets.'[21] This bracketed word came into its own after the death of Lenin.

For the French section of the Communist International, 1923 was to be the true date of its real separation from social democratic reformism. Even if the Congress of Tours had ratified its organisational break with the Social Democrats, it had not for all that created an authentic communist party. The French section of the Communist International did not appear to be completely distinguishable from the SFIO, to the extent that militant workers like Monatte and Monmousseau preferred to remain outside.

Trotsky pointed out in his report to the Fourth Congress:

> The French Communist Party has passed through a grave crisis. And this crisis of the party curiously coincides with the crisis of the French bourgeoisie and its state ... The coincidence of these two crises allows me to say, and to conclude, that the French party has not yet gained for its organisation, its activity and its autonomy that absolute freedom as regards capitalist society that is necessary to be able to profit, freely and greatly from the crisis of the latter.[22]

This was very much the start of the matter. In order to attain the objective of absolute freedom as regards the bourgeoisie, its state and its ideology, the congress adopted a programme of work and activity. We do not have the space to publish this programme.[23] We strongly advise our readers to study it carefully. It should put an end to all the talk about the theory of the soviet model being imposed on all the sections of the Comintern and the supposed lack of correspondence between the policy of the French section of the Communist International and the practical situation in France. We merely note that it includes organising the resistance to the capitalist offensive, creating factory councils, carrying out the

United Front, struggling against the tendencies to spread activity too thinly, intransigent struggle against French imperialism, and for the right of independence for the colonial population. All these points clashed with the policy followed after 1924, and above all after June 1934.

The year of 1923 was to be a baptism of fire for the French section of the Communist International and the programme that had emerged from the Fourth Congress of the Comintern – the struggle against the occupation of the Ruhr. This struggle was carried on in a revolutionary way that brought down terrible repression upon the French section of the Comintern. The year of 1923 was also when Frossard and his friends left, and also when Monatte, Monmousseau and Barbusse joined. The year can be regarded without any exaggeration as the real birth of an authentic Communist Party in France. This was, moreover, the conclusion Trotsky drew: 'The greatest difficulties still lie ahead. But there is one thing we can say positively: in France a real Communist Party is living and breathing, fighting and growing.'[24]

This impetus was halted by the beginnings of 'Bolshevisation'. Along with the practices already described, we might add a real change in the composition of the party. It is a remarkable fact, as Ferrat notes in his history, that the turnover rate of the party members was 70 per cent at the time. The same happened on the leadership level. The weight of the 'founders' within it was to diminish. At the Clichy Congress in 1925, new members of the leading committee represented 57 per cent of the whole, and those who had joined before 1923 only 24 per cent. At the Lille Congress in 1926, new men made up 61 per cent of the leading committee, and established members 14 per cent.[25] By 1926, the leading committee did not include any members of the left of the party of 1922. On the other hand, Cachin, the social patriot of 1914, was ever present, and he survived all the stages of the evolution of the French Communist Party until his death in 1958.

Such was the organisational and ideological state of the French Communist Party once 'Bolshevisation' had had its unfortunate effects. The *Manuel d'histoire du PCF* published by the leadership in 1964 considered that this was the time when the PCF 'began to forge a truly working-class collective leadership and to rid itself of the factions that had been organised within its ranks'. This is on the whole true as far as the facts go. But at what cost?

The cost was no less than a break in the process of constructing a revolutionary party in France, as a direct consequence of the beginning of the bureaucratisation of the Russian party. The party that came out of this period abandoned the prospect of world revolution, and entered its phase of reformism of the Stalinist type. Even if it did not change its name, it was no longer the French Section of the Communist International hoped for by the militants of the Committee for Joining the Third International, such as Raymond Lefebvre, Jules Lepetit and Marcel Vergeat, who had been full delegates at the Second Congress of the Comintern in July 1920.

We gave our support to the Communist International: we are not acquainted with 'Leninism' or 'Trotskyism'. While Lenin was alive the International was big enough to embrace Trotsky and so-called Trotskyism, as well as the Russian Workers Opposition and numerous elements who had come from revolutionary syndicalism in the rest of the world.

Leninism without Lenin frightens us. It comes under the guise of a name we obviously look up to, all the more, and perhaps even more so, than those who claim to follow him but completely trample on his last recommendations, and labour to undo and dismantle the revolutionary international structure that Lenin was determined to build.

In all countries the symptoms of malaise and abstentionism are showing themselves. If we take no notice, we will, under the banner of Leninism, be on the road towards a retreat of the International, a weakening of its forces, and a stifling of its thought.

Delagarde, Monatte and Rosmer, La Révolution prolétarienne, *no 1, January 1925*[26]

Notes

The Prelude to Stalinism – Emile Fabrol

1. Boris Lifshitz, called Souvarine (1895–1984) was a journalist and a leader of the left in the Socialist Party before he became a communist. He was the first supporter of the Left Opposition in France, but broke with Trotsky in 1929. His famous life of Stalin was translated into English by CLR James and published in 1939. See Michael Banda, 'Boris Souvarine, 1893–1984', in *Labour Review*, Volume 8, no 5, December 1984, pp45–7. Fernand Loriot (1870–1932) was a trade unionist and socialist, and an opponent of the First World War. He was secretary of the Committee for Joining the Third International, and later international secretary of the French Communist Party. He went into opposition in 1925, and helped found *Contre le Courant*.
2. Pierre Monatte (1881–1960) was a proof-reader, a pioneer syndicalist and an opponent of the First World War; Gaston Monmousseau (1883–1960) was an anarcho-syndicalist railway worker who later joined the Communist Party, and remained a loyal Stalinist to his death; Pierre Sémard (1887–1942) was a leading railway trade unionist and later General Secretary of the Communist Party, until he was replaced by Thorez in 1929.
3. VI Lenin, 'Notes of a Publicist', February 1922, *Collected Works*, Volume 33, Moscow, 1966, p209.
4. Marcel Cachin (1869–1958) had been a member of Guesde's party, and later a right-wing socialist who supported the First World War, when he had been sent with money to contact Mussolini and help bring Italy into the war. He remained in the leadership of the French Communist Party from 1921 onwards. Louis-Oliver Frossard (1889–1946) was General Secretary of the French Socialist Party in October 1918. After leaving the Communist Party he rejoined the SFIO.
5. Raymond Lefebvre (1891–1920) had been wounded at Verdun, but had opposed the First World War; Louis Bertho, called Jules Lepetit (1889–1920) was an anarcho-syndicalist jailed for his opposition to the war; Marcel Vergeat (1891–1920) was a lathe operator and a syndicalist who supported the Zimmerwald Manifesto. All three perished at sea near Murmansk on their way back to France. See Frederick Strom, 'How Lefebvre, Lepetit and Vergeat were Drowned', *The Communist Review*, no 1, May 1921, pp19–20; Victor Serge, *Memoirs of a Revolutionary*, Oxford UP, 1963, p112.
6. Albert Treint (1889–1971) was General Secretary of the French Communist Party after Frossard, and a supporter of Zinoviev, for which he was expelled in 1927.
7. 'A Militant Programme of Action for the French Communist Party', 5 December 1922, *Theses, Documents and Manifestos of the First Four Congresses of the Third International*, London, 1980, pp422–7.
8. LD Trotsky, 'Preface to *The Communist Movement in France*', 25 March 1923, *The First Five Years of the Communist International*, Volume 2, London, 1974, p340.
9. Raymond Poincaré (1860–1934) was President of France. He was largely responsible for sending French troops to occupy the Ruhr when Germany defaulted on her reparations payments in 1923. His right-wing electoral alliance, the Bloc national or Horizon bleu, ruled France in 1926–29.
10. Henri Barbusse (1873–1935) was a prominent novelist and an opponent of the First World War who joined the Communist Party in 1923, and wrote a biography of Stalin. He continued to play an important part in the French Communist Party's influence over the intelligentsia well on into the 1930s.

11. Monatte's words here have been corrected in accordance with the note that appeared in the *Bulletin communiste* for 16 May 1924. The passage originally read 'terrified' (terrifié') instead of 'invigorated' (tonifié'). Blanquism takes its name from Louis Auguste Blanqui (1805–1881), who advocated the seizure of power on behalf of the working class by a conspiratorial elite by means of a coup d'état.
12. The Zimmerwald Conference was an international gathering in 1915 of socialists in Switzerland opposed to the First World War. Its manifesto was drafted by Trotsky. See LD Trotsky, *The War and the International*, Colombo, 1971, pp86–9.
13. Suzanne Girault (1882–1973) was a Swiss who lived in Russia before the 1917 Revolution. She served as Rosmer's interpreter and came to France in 1922, where she was co-opted onto the Political Bureau of the French Communist Party. She was also an alternate member of the Executive Committee of the Comintern, and as such an ally of Zinoviev and Treint.
14. Archives Humbert-Droz, La Chaux-de-Fonds. Jules Humbert-Droz (1891–1971) was a Swiss pastor and a pacifist opponent of the First World War. He afterwards served as a Comintern functionary in a number of capacities, until he broke with Stalin at the time of the Trial of the Twenty-One. His archives are a rich source of information about Soviet foreign policy during this period. See Siegfried Bahne, *Origines et débuts des partis communistes des pays latins*, Archives Humbert-Droz, Volume 1, Dordrecht, 1970 (reviewed by Tom Kemp, 'Early Years of the Comintern', *Workers Press*, 5 January 1971).
15. Amédée Catonné, called Dunois (1879–1944) was a journalist and an anarcho-syndicalist. He left the PCF in 1927, and later joined the SFIO. He died in Belsen during the Second World War.
16. Georges Auguste Alexandre Cogniot (1901–1978) joined the PCF in 1921. At this period he supported Trotsky, an act he later regretted as a loyal Stalinist, and went on to become a parliamentary deputy, and later editor of *L'Humanité*. For the *Letter of the 280 Militants* (published in the *Bulletin communiste*, no 14, 22 January 1926), see H Gruber (ed), *Soviet Russia Masters the Comintern*, New York, 1974, pp67–72.
17. August Guralsky was one of the pseudonyms of Abraham Heifetz (1890–1960), along with Lepetit, Kleine, etc. He was a member of the Bund who joined the Bolsheviks in 1919, when he became a confidant of Zinoviev. He represented the Comintern in France, and then in Latin America. He was imprisoned during the purges.
18. Maurice Thorez (1900–1964) had supported Trotsky in 1923, being one of the first to respond to Souvarine's appeal for funds to publish Trotsky's *The New Course* (Jean-Louis Panné, *Boris Souvarine: Le premier désenchanté du communisme*, Paris, 1993, p142. See below, pp52, 77). But after he went to Moscow in 1925 and met Stalin, his rise in the French Communist Party was meteoric, and he was its General Secretary from 1929 onwards.
19. Jacques Duclos (1896–1975), a cynical Stalinist, was a pastry cook who had joined the PCF shortly after it was set up. He became a member of the Political Bureau, where he served as Thorez' right-hand man, and was also a Comintern agent in various parts of Europe.
20. André Marty (1886–1956) was the leader of the French naval mutiny in the Black Sea, and later a Comintern agent, especially during the Spanish Civil War. The Rif rebellion was a joint campaign directed by France and Spain against the Moroccan rebel Abd el-Krim, whose defeat of the Spanish army at Anual in 1921 was having an unsettling effect in the nearby French colony.

21. Louis Sellier (1885–1978) was a postal worker and a member of the SFIO who joined the Communist Party and was elected to the Presidium of the Comintern in 1922. He was then General Secretary of the PCF until he was replaced by Sémard, and was later expelled. The Radical Bloc, called the Cartel des gauches, was an electoral alliance of the SFIO and the Radicals led by Edouard Herriot.
22. Third Congress of the Comintern, 'The Organisational Structure of the Communist Parties, the Methods and Content of Their Work: Theses', 12 July 1921, *Theses, Resolutions and Manifestos of the First Four Congresses of the Third International*, London, 1980, Thesis 9, p236.
23. Thesis 12, op cit, p237.
24. Thesis 6, op cit, p235.
25. Thesis 45, op cit, p256.
26. Thesis 49, op cit, p257.
27. VI Lenin, 'Five Years of the Russian Revolution and the Prospects of the World Revolution: Report to the Fourth Congress of the Communist International', 13 November 1922, *Collected Works*, Volume 33, Moscow, 1966, pp430–1.
28. Op cit, p432.
29. Alfred Kurella (1895–1975) was a founder of the German Communist Youth, who later worked in the Comintern apparatus in Moscow, and as secretary of the International Committee against War and Fascism during the period of the Popular Front.
30. Maurice Chambelland (1901–1966), a revolutionary syndicalist and secretary of the CGT typographers' union, was a close friend of Rosmer.
31. The Dawes Plan of 1924 regulated the payment of German reparations and Entente war debts. Under it the USA loaned money to Germany, which paid it in reparations to Britain and France, which then paid it in war debts to the USA.
32. François Nicolas Sauvage (1879–1946) was the companion of Suzanne Girault, and represented the Seine Federation on the Central Committee of the PCF. He was expelled as a Zinovievist in 1928.
33. Benoît Frachon (1893–1975), a miner and metalworker, was a member of the SFIO before joining the PCF. He was a leading Stalinist trade union bureaucrat, and served on the Comintern Executive.
34. Henri Barbé (1902–1966) and Pierre Célor (1902–1957) were former youth leaders scapegoated for the fall in the French Communist Party's membership at the height of the Third Period. They were accused of forming a group within the party and of being corrupt (and even, in Célor's case, of being in the pay of the police), and were expelled by Thorez in 1932. They later went over to the extreme right. See Louis Couturier, *Les 'Grandes affaires' du parti communiste français*, Paris, 1972, pp9–17; Tom Kemp, *Stalinism in France*, London, 1984, pp92–6.

The Bureaucratisation and Destruction of the Party – Antoine Clavez

1. Boris Souvarine, *Letter to Zinoviev*, 4 January 1924, quoted in Jean-Louis Panné, *Boris Souvarine, Le Premier désenchanté du communisme*, Paris, 1993, p136.
2. Victor Louis Achille Delagarde (1890–1954) was a machine tool operator and trade union militant expelled from the PCF at the same time as Rosmer and Monatte, but without having had the opportunity to discuss with them.
3. Dmitri Zakharovich Manuilsky (1883–1959) was a member of the Inter-

District organisation led by Trotsky that joined the Bolsheviks in 1917. He worked for the Comintern in France and the Ukraine, and was later prominent in its central apparatus during the 'Third Period'. Solomon Abramovich Dridzo, called Lozovsky (1878–1952) was leader of RILU and on the Praesidium of the Comintern. He perished in the anti-Jewish purge launched shortly before Stalin's death.

4. *Le Bulletin communiste*, 28 March 1924.
5. Bonapartism, which takes its name from Napoleon, but more particularly from Louis Bonaparte, is a term used for authoritarian bureaucratic rule, often based upon the army; Thermidor 1794 was when the Jacobins were overthrown, and the reaction against the French Revolution began. Both terms are used by Marxists for the period of the retreat of a revolution.
6. Al (Guralsky), *Cahiers du Bolchévisme*, 28 November 1924. Rosa Luxemburg (1870–1919) was the brilliant theorist of the left of German Social Democracy, and later of the Spartacus Group and the German Communist Party. She was murdered by Freikorps in 1919 at the behest of the Social Democratic government. The animus of the Russian bureaucracy against her memory became even more pronounced later. See LD Trotsky, 'Hands Off Rosa Luxemburg!', 28 June 1932, *Writings of Leon Trotsky, 1932*, New York, 1973, pp131–42.
7. Ossip Aaronovich Tarchis, called Piatnitsky (1882–1939) was secretary of the Moscow Bolshevik organisation in 1917, and later a functionary in the Comintern. He perished in the purges.
8. The theorists of the Comintern held that capitalism had gone through three phases since the First World War, a first of revolutionary upheaval (1917–23), a second of temporary stabilisation (1924–28), and a third, which coincided with the Wall Street Crash, of renewed upheaval and the final crisis of the capitalist order. Every other tendency apart from Stalinism was accused of being fascist, or preparing the way for it. This time of extreme left-wing rhetoric and mad sectarianism is generally now known as the 'Third Period'. Béla Kun (1885–1937), with his 'theory of the offensive', had been responsible for an earlier policy of ultra-leftism in Germany in 1921, which was strongly condemned by Lenin.
9. Thesis 11, Third Congress of the Comintern, 'The Organisational Structure of the Communist Parties, the Methods and Content of Their Work', 12 July 1921, *Theses, Resolutions and Manifestos of the First Four Congresses of the Communist International*, London, 1980, p237.
10. Alfred Rosmer, 'About the "Final Warning" Given to Trotsky: The Myth of Trotskyism' (below, p102).
11. LD Trotsky, 'A Letter to the Editorial Board of La Lutte de Classes', 11 August 1929, *Writings of Leon Trotsky, 1929*, New York, 1975, p244.
12. Zinoviev and Kamenev had opposed the Bolsheviks' seizure of power in 1917, and even alerted the authorities by publishing an article about it in the open press, which led Lenin to denounce them as strike-breakers, and to propose their expulsion from the party. See VI Lenin, 'Letter to Bolshevik Party Members', 18 October 1917, *Collected Works*, Volume 26, Moscow, 1966, pp216–9.
13. The Thirteenth Congress of the CPSU in May 1924 had closed the debate on *The New Course*, and Trotsky could not reopen the controversy without being accused of a breach of discipline, which would not have the support of the rest of the Left Opposition. Trotsky was therefore obliged to disavow the support of Rosmer and Monatte. See LD Trotsky, 'A Statement on Monatte and Rosmer', 8

September 1925, *The Challenge of the Left Opposition, 1923–25*, New York, 1975, pp316–8. At the same time, he had to repudiate Max Eastman's book *Since Lenin Died (The Challenge of the Left Opposition, 1923–25*, pp310–5, and S Bornstein and A Richardson, *Against the Stream*, London, 1986, pp7–10). The statement repudiating Eastman's book was dictated by the party apparatus, and the same may well have been the case with the statement on Monatte and Rosmer.

14. Ruth Fischer (1895–1961) was a founder of the Austrian Communist Party, and leader of the KPD [German Communist Party] in 1924 along with Isaak Efimovich Chemerinsky, known as Arkady Maslow (1891–1941). Noted for their ultra-leftism, they came over with Zinoviev to the Joint Opposition. They cooperated with Trotsky for some years, and some of their followers, such as Oskar Hippe, went over to the German Trotskyists. Fischer later published an unreliable account of these years, *Stalin and German Communism*, Harvard UP, 1948.
15. Oskar Hippe, *... And Red is the Colour of our Flag*, London, 1991, pp89–90.
16. James Patrick Cannon (1890–1974) was a supporter of Zinoviev in the American Communist Party who had previously voted for the expulsion of the Trotskyists. He went over to the Left Opposition after his Cannon-Foster faction failed to gain Moscow's support for the leadership of the American party. See *Revolutionary History*, Volume 5, no 1, Autumn 1993, pp105–7.
17. James P Cannon, *The Struggle for a Proletarian Party*, New York, 1972, p15.
18. Sara Jacobs (1900–76), the wife of Jack Weber, was born in Poland and then emigrated to the USA. She served as Trotsky's Russian-language secretary while in exile in Turkey and France.
19. Jack Barnes inherited the leadership of the American SWP from Farrell Dobbs in 1972. A notorious machine politician, he was responsible for expelling many veteran American Trotskyists from the party and converting it into an advertising agency of the Cuban state.
20. 'Pabloism' is pejorative term derived from Pablo, the pseudonym of Michael Raptis (1911–1996), the head of the International Secretariat of the Fourth International at the time of the split with the International Committee in 1953. He was noted for his unscrupulous organisational practices.

The French Communist Party and Trotsky – Emile Fabrol

1. VI Lenin, 'Notes of a Publicist', February 1922, *Collected Works*, Volume 33, Moscow, 1966, p209.
2. *La Révolution prolétarienne*, no 1, January 1925. See below, p84. Georges Pioch (1873–1953) was a poet and journalist who had passed through Anarchism and the Socialist Party to become Secretary of the Seine Federation of the PCF in 1920–22. He had been expelled in 1923.
3. See *Bulletin communiste*, 16 May 1924.
4. Archives Humbert-Droz, La Chaux-de-Fonds.
5. Fraim Charbit (1892–1985) was a revolutionary syndicalist book worker, and a friend of Monatte. Antonini was a post office employee, and a founder of the postal workers federation in Tunisia. Upon his return to France, he became a member of the Executive of the Communist Federation in 1920. He left the PCF along with Monatte. Victor Francis Godonèche (1886–1942) was a trade union militant who had been a delegate to the RILU (Red International of Labour Unions) congress in 1921.
6. See above, section 1, p60 n9.
7. André Ferrat, *Histoire du PCF*, 1931. André Morel, called Ferrat (1902–1988),

was the General Secretary of the French Communist Youth, and was imprisoned for anti-militarist activity. He later joined the PCF's Political Bureau, and represented the party in Moscow. He was expelled in 1936 and set up the *Que Faire?* group, some of whose positions overlapped with those of Trotskyism, but he rejoined the SFIO in 1938.

8. André Ferrat, *Histoire du PCF*, 1931.
9. The Central Committee of the Polish Communist Party had reacted in the same way in December 1923. And we know what became of that, it was decimated by Stalinism (author's note). See *Revolutionary History*, Volume 6, no 1, 1996, pp38–9.
10. This is the famous doctored photograph. See David King, *The Commissar Vanishes*, Edinburgh, 1997, pp66–9.
11. Clara Eisner Zetkin (1857–1933) was the prewar leader of the German Social Democratic women, and a supporter of Rosa Luxemburg and Paul Levy, but who later went over to Stalin. She served on the French Commission of the Comintern, and spoke at the Congress of Tours to persuade the French Socialist Party to join the Third International.
12. André Ferrat, *Histoire du PCF*, 1931.
13. Ibid.
14. A Rosmer, P Monatte and V Delagarde, 'Open Letter to Members of the PCF', 22 November 1924, *Cahiers du Bolshévisme*, no 4, 12 December 1924, in Helmut Gruber (ed), *Soviet Russia Masters the Comintern*, New York, 1974, p65.
15. Archives Humbert-Droz, La Chaux-de-Fonds.
16. 'On the "Bolshevisation" of the French Communist Party', in *La classe ouvrière française et la politique*, 1980.
17. *Manifestes, theses et resolutions des quatre premiers congrès mondiaux de l'Internationale communiste* (1919–1923), Maspéro reprint, 1969. This particular passage does not appear in the English edition, though of course parallel statements do. See 'Resolution on the Russian Revolution', 5 December 1922, *Theses, Resolutions and Manifestos of the First Four Congresses of the Third International*, London, 1980, p428.
18. In June 1923, the Peasant Union government of Alexander Stambulisky was overthrown in Bulgaria by an army and right-wing coup. The Bulgarian Communist Party refused to take any part in the fighting on Stambulisky's side, and General Tsankov set up a military dictatorship. Censured by the Comintern, the Bulgarian party then attempted an uprising of its own in September, which was easily smashed. Having held its fire during the crisis of the mark and the French occupation of the Ruhr in the spring and summer of 1923, the German Communist Party first decided upon, and then cancelled, an insurrection in October. Unfortunately, the cancellation failed to reach Hamburg, where the local organisation launched an insurrection, which was put down by the Reichswehr. See *Revolutionary History*, Volume 5, no 2, Spring 1994, pp74–129.
19. Quoted by Trotsky in *The Third International after Lenin*, New York, 1970, p320.
20. *Pravda*, 25 January 1924.
21. VI Lenin, 'The State and Revolution', 30 November 1917, *Collected Works*, Volume 25, Moscow, 1966, p455.
22. LD Trotsky, 'Rapport au 4e Congrès mondiale', 1 December 1922, in P Broué (ed), *La Mouvement communiste en France*, Paris, 1967, p221.
23. 'A Militant Programme of Action for the French Communist Party', 5 December 1922, *Theses, Documents and Manifestos of the First Four Congresses of the Third International*, op cit, pp422–7.

24. LD Trotsky, 'Preface to The Communist Movement in France', 25 March 1923, *The First Five Years of the Communist International*, Volume 2, London, 1974, p340.
25. Percentages calculated according to the figures given in *Le PCF, étapes et problèmes*, 1981.
26. V Delagarde, P Monatte and A Rosmer, '2e lettre aux membres du parti communiste: La réponse des trois exclus', *Révolution prolétarienne*, no 1, January 1925, reprinted in *L'Exclusion du PCF de Rosmer, Monatte, Delagarde: Articles de Rosmer dans La Révolution prolétarienne*, supplement to *La République prolétarienne*, no 2, p8. Below, pp91–2.

Part Two

Boris Souvarine and Alfred Rosmer, 'Bolshevisation'

How I Came to be Regarded as a 'Trotskyist'

Boris Souvarine

From the Introduction to the reprint of *La Critique sociale*, Paris, 1983, pp9–15

I enjoyed very friendly relations with André Breton,[1] who was particularly attracted by the personality of Trotsky, then in exile on a Turkish island, which didn't help matters.

In his essential memoir on surrealism (*Révolutionnaires sans révolution*, Paris, 1972) André Thirion[2] attributes to me some influence on the 'Trotskyist' leanings of André Breton and his closest friends. This prompts me to provide more precise details, and a correction that seems necessary. André Thirion wrote about me:

> The influence of this brilliant mind, one of the founders of the French Communist Party, who had had personal links with all the great October revolutionaries, who had been expelled in 1924 [I have corrected the date – BS], the editor of the *Bulletin communiste*, the best written and most widely read organ of the opposition, carried much weight with all the surrealists in favour of Trotsky's theses. Souvarine's intelligence, culture and character captivated Breton. Souvarine forewarned him against the party and against the International, and Breton had to agree, during his

> short stay in the organisation, that Souvarine's warnings were well founded.

André Thirion adds in a note: 'Before the expulsion of Souvarine, the *Bulletin communiste*, founded by Souvarine and edited by him, was the sole theoretical publication of the PCF.'

In fact, I did not attempt to dissuade Breton and his friends from joining the party, though I made no secret of my own feelings. They came to me as a sort of delegation *in partibus* to consult with me and talk in a friendly manner with this in mind (I cannot be exact about the date). There were seven of them: Breton, Paul Eluard, Pierre Naville, Louis Aragon, Raymond Queneau, Benjamin Péret and Robert Desnos.[3] I told them in substance that since I myself had been expelled from the party, I was ill qualified to give objective advice: and that everyone must behave according to his own intuition, even if it meant testing it for himself. And that is what happened.

The surrealists were therefore in the same position as Simone Weil,[4] who intended to join the party herself, but who hesitated when she saw the most respected comrades, in her judgement, excluded on Moscow's orders. She therefore refrained from doing so. However, she did collaborate with *La Révolution prolétarienne*, and then *La Critique sociale*, that is to say, with those on the margins of the official communist movement who had been expelled and who published independent magazines.

'A few weeks after the publication of the *Legitimé défense*, Breton joined the party', Thirion notes next. Other surrealists followed his example. Their stay was of short duration, as I had foreseen, apart from three of them: Paul Eluard, Tristan Tzara[5] and Louis Aragon, who submitted to Stalin and his GPU, praising the atrocities of the knouto-Soviet regime, approving of the pact with Hitler, and therefore justifying its horrible consequences. Only Pierre Naville became involved with the 'Trotskyism' that Trotsky had always denied, disavowed and repudiated, but which he ended up acknowledging. As for André Breton, he 'admired Trotsky', as André Thirion says, and 'the fate that Stalin meted out to the Opposition, the expulsions and the deportations, no doubt hastened the change in position of the surrealists towards leaving ...' Breton always remained faithful to Trotsky, who fascinated him. He paid him an extended visit in Mexico in 1938, and took up the cudgels in all circumstances for the man himself as much as for the historical personality who incarnated the idea of the 'permanent revolution'. Whereas in 1929 an exchange of letters between Trotsky and myself sealed our intellectual and political break,[6] as well as my progressive distancing from the stereotypes that had for so long sterilised the socialist or communist thought we had inherited from our 'great forbears'.

❖ ❖ ❖ ❖

The references made by André Thirion to the *Bulletin communiste* and its influence over the surrealists in a direction favourable to Trotsky call for a minimum of explanation on my part. In 1920, I had been the founder of this *Bulletin*, which exercised a decisive influence over the orientation of the Socialist Party in a direction favourable to the Third International. I was its editor until 1924, when the 'Bolshevisation' that followed the death of Lenin suppressed its publication, as if to mark the break with the original communism.

After my removal from the party and the International, I attempted to revive the *Bulletin* in 1925, without taking any account of the 'Marxism' or 'Leninism' in the sense in which they were understood by the devotees and hypocrites of official communism. My scant resources relying on declining subscriptions prevented it from being published regularly from 1928 onwards. The last issue ended the series in 1933, when *La Critique sociale* had already been coming out for two years.

Such as it is, with its 33 irregularly appearing issues, the files of the *Bulletin* contain a unique documentation on the crises that changed the Communist International and its sections into servile instruments of the Soviet state, manipulated by the secret services of that state, on the orders of Stalin and his henchmen. My friends Pierre Pascale, Amédée Dunois, Pierre Kaan, Lucien Laurat, Aimé Patri, Jacques Mesnil, and Jean Soudeille[7] in particular collaborated with it, as well as Max Eastman, Karl Korsch and Joaquím Maurín[8] from abroad.

In this new series of the *Bulletin*, I published Lenin's

Testament, whose very existence the Stalinists flatly denied, as well as Adolf Joffe's last letter to Trotsky explaining his suicide.[9] There were important texts of the Soviet Communist Opposition, from Trotsky, among others, as well as letters from Russia necessarily signed with pseudonyms (the most important being from Pierre Pascal); in a word, texts of real documentary value, that could not be found elsewhere.

The so-called 'Soviet' regime, set up by the sincere and convinced, but fanatical and narrow-minded Lenin in the service of his socialist utopia, whose real soviets had disappeared from the first year of the revolution in 1917 onwards, transformed itself into an oligarchic regime of oppression and of 'the exploitation of man by man' (to use Saint-Simon's expression)[10] at an alarming speed, arousing increasingly bitter and well-founded criticism from its disenchanted supporters, from within as well as without. This is what was reflected and conveyed in the *Bulletin communiste* from one year to the next, and from one instalment to the next.

On the occasion of the tenth anniversary of the 'October Revolution', the *Bulletin* for October–November 1927 published my article entitled 'Black October' in which there was a passage that very much startled some comrades and encouraged several of them to leave us and go over to a 'Trotskyism' that relied on its reputation for optimism:

> The [Soviet Communist] Party constitutes a new privileged class whilst including within it several other classes of a secondary rank: a proletariat of lowly militants restricted to laborious work and an unnoticed daily heroism; an intellectual, or pseudo-intellectual aristocracy that occupies the top positions; and several intermediate categories spread over various ranks in the public or economic administration. This patriciate[11] enjoys modest but guaranteed living standards; more or less guaranteed against unemployment, it benefits from various advantages standing out from the mediocrity of life in general; but its essential privilege is its monopoly over political life. The party is no longer a division of the proletariat; it is above it. Its interests are no longer those of the class. There is the party, and there are the rest.

Thirty years afterwards, I had to smile when Milovan Djilas' book *The New Class* appeared (Paris, Plon, 1957),[12] to be greeted by a chorus of praise in the press as a whole captivated by its discovery. I was, however, not the first to realise that a new exploiting and privileged class had been set up in the USSR, for Karl Kautsky had noticed or foreseen it before I did,[13] but I did not know that when I wrote 'Black October'. In any case, my very nuanced conclusion was very quickly overtaken by the rapid transformation of the more and more bourgeoisified exploiting class, increasingly stuffed with material advantages, that came in the following years to make up the shameless 'nomenklatura' more and more alien to the labouring plebeians.[14] This was the work of Stalin, who denounced the 'egalitarianism' preached by Lenin (inspired by the example of the Paris Commune) as a petit-bourgeois and reactionary prejudice.

The same anniversary article denounced the 'ersatz Marxism' invoked by the Soviet patriciate to justify its deception, as well as 'the new term that corresponds to the new official ideology: Leninism'. This was to mark a break with an incurably degenerate Bolshevism, as well as with an opposition that called itself 'Bolshevik-Leninist' that had Trotsky as its oracle.[15]

❖ ❖ ❖ ❖

It may seem paradoxical that the *Bulletin* influenced the surrealists in favour of Trotsky, and then turned against Stalin's most prestigious adversary. But this happened, nonetheless. Until 1927, the solidarity between the communist oppositionists seemed evident. Soon things and ideas became clearer, and relations deteriorated and ended in a split. The explanation for this split is well formulated in a short remark made by the historian Michel Heller in *L'Utopie au pouvoir* (Paris, 1982) when dealing with the 1930s: 'Trotsky created the impression of being a clock that had stopped in 1917.'

Imbued with a pseudo-Leninist orthodoxy that he took to be authentic 'Marxism', and which he even held to be 'scientific' but which verges on the laughable, we may well ask why Trotsky in fact did his utmost to make a show of his strict fidelity to ideas that were contradicted by obvious facts. On several occasions, Lenin was not afraid to admit 'we were wrong', and even came to recognise 'the fault is mine'. Trotsky never did.

His unfortunate ideas about the creation of 'labour armies' or the final suppression of money did not, however, resist the test of experience for very long. We cannot read or re-read without amazement his categorical statements of 1919 and 1920 on the 'militarisation' of manual labour, and of the entire Soviet economy, implying the permanent mobilisation of the working population under the authority of Dzerzhinsky, the chairman of the Cheka,[16] and with a rigorous system of fines and rewards, such as severe punishments for failing to fulfil prescribed tasks. 'The labour state considers itself empowered to send every worker to the place where his work is necessary', he wrote in his *Terrorism and Communism*.[17] Thus a working-class family in the Crimea, by a decision of some Stalin or his understudy, must obey an order to move to the Arctic circle.

Nor does anything remain of his famous theory of the 'permanent revolution', implying that in the great industrial countries social conditions were almost identical with those of Russia and peasant China, a theory canonised as 'Trotskyism'. In 1925, he had accepted that Trotskyism had been 'liquidated long ago', and admitted that the theory of the permanent revolution 'applies wholly to the past' (*Letter to the Central Committee*, 15 January 1925).[18] The following year, in agreement with Zinoviev and Kamenev, he declared before the Communist International that Lenin had always been right, particularly against the idea of 'the permanent revolution',[19] and that Trotskyism no longer existed. Yet in exile he wrote an entire book justifying his 'permanent revolution' for today, and explicitly reaffirming his Trotskyism, which became the leitmotiv of his supporters.[20]

He seems to be stricken with amnesia when we recall, in all objectivity, and even without comment, some episodes from his Soviet past, for example the suppression of the Kronstadt popular revolt in 1921. He allowed himself to write:

> The truth of the matter is that I personally did not participate in the least in the suppression of the Kronstadt rebellion, nor in the repressive measures following the suppression ... The rebellion broke out during my stay in the Urals ... I came

> directly to Moscow for the Tenth Congress of the party. The decision to suppress the rebellion by military force ... was adopted with my direct participation. But after the decision was taken, I continued to remain in Moscow and took no part, direct or indirect, in the military operations ... I stepped aside completely and demonstratively from this affair.[21]

Now it is sufficient to consult the collection of his military writings (*How the Revolution Armed Itself*, Moscow, 1923–25) to find the proof of his presence there before Kronstadt and the signed text of his ultimatum to the insurgents which preceded by a short space of time the bloody repression that followed under his orders.[22]

To any serious objection, and to any probing criticism, he thinks he can reply by treating the objector as 'petit-bourgeois'. He sets himself up as the guardian of the absolute truth as the exclusive interpreter of 'Marxism', as opposed to the thinking of Marx, who was notoriously hostile to this insulting 'ism' in his own time, which has become mendacious and odious in ours. Like Lenin, he ascribes to this pseudo-Marxism the principle according to which the party is alone capable of leading the proletariat, whereas Marx on the contrary said, wrote and repeated that it was the 'real movement' of the working class that mattered. And when Stalin concluded his monstrous pact with Hitler, when he invaded Poland and the Baltic countries, and when he carried out aggression against Finland, the Mexican exile justified these 'progressive' measures, and came out in favour of the unconditional defence of the Stalinist pseudo-Soviet state.[23] At that time, this implied favouring the victory of Hitler, Stalin's ally.[24]

Trotsky wisely explained Stalin's rise to personal power, to begin with by the overwhelming influence of the kulaks (rich peasants); but when Stalin cruelly exterminated these unfortunate kulaks, the Trotskyist explanation did a complete about face, and it was the burgeoning bureaucracy that Trotsky blamed. But he claimed at the same time that the Soviet state was proletarian, and that the Communist Party was a working-class party, refusing to admit that this state and this party were precisely the incarnation of this same dominant, privileged and parasitic bureaucracy. And he always draped himself in the toga of pseudo-Marxist infallibility. We can understand all too well why Marx was right to repudiate in advance, very explicitly, and on several occasions, all types of 'Marxism'.

Trotsky's irrational behaviour in the extreme and decisive crisis that accompanied Lenin's decline and end revealed the extent to which he still did not understand the essential realities of the revolution, state and party, one of whose main leaders he was. Obsessed with erroneous ideas, while believing himself to be infallible, he was mistaken at every important step he took. To begin with, in 1924 he considered that 'Stalin is the most eminent man in our party, and its most important militant: without him we could not make up the Politbureau'. He told Max Eastman that Stalin was 'a sincere and brave revolutionary', before explaining to his close collaborator Sklyansky that 'Stalin is the most eminent mediocrity in our party'. He took over as his own the dogmatic Leninist fiction that the party was identical with the proletariat, and the Politbureau represented the party. On two occasions, Stalin proposed to give up his post as General Secretary in accordance with Lenin's *Testament* and Trotsky opposed it, just as his colleagues did. He only changed his mind in 1926, when it was already too late.[25]

But in 1924 he had felt the incomprehensible need to discredit Zinoviev and Kamenev by blaming them for 'wavering' in October 1917 when they opposed the seizure of power by the Bolsheviks alone.[26] He therefore needlessly made them his remorseless enemies, since he encouraged them to ally with Stalin against him in the Politbureau, the real seat of power. By criticising their past, he encouraged them to recall his own, his violent attacks upon Lenin in particular. What need did he have to revive so futile a quarrel? Moreover, Zinoviev and Kamenev did not waver in 1917, they thought about it, and their thinking was entirely justified by history. They had the courage to contradict their boss Lenin, and along with tens of other leaders of their tendency, had the courage to predict that without a coalition between the main socialist parties, the only way forward would be 'maintaining a purely Bolshevik government by means of political terror'. And it was in fact by terror alone that the new regime was to be imposed, which then went on to destroy its founders.

Having thus needlessly aroused the hostility of Zinoviev and Kamenev, Trotsky then allied himself with them, his worst enemies, in order to combat Stalin, as if the three of them did not know, as I did, that the General Secretary had an 'apparatus' of repression at his disposal capable of torturing and murdering anyone whosoever. (Had they not, on their part, contributed to building up this apparatus?) By 1927, at the time of the tenth anniversary of the October coup, these most acclaimed 'Bolshevik-Leninists', Lenin's close companions, were dealt with by the GPU, like ordinary Soviet citizens.

Arrested, deported, exiled and proscribed in 1929, Trotsky took refuge in Mexico from 1937 onwards, surrounded by completely reliable yes-men, among them several GPU agents. Why did he welcome into his room such a run-of-the-mill Trotskyist (soon to become his murderer), whose prose, so devoid of interest, he had agreed to correct?[27] From all the evidence, this was where the clock had stopped in 1914: Trotsky was behaving as he had done in Europe at the time of Zimmerwald and Kienthal, as if everything had to be started again in circumstances that had not changed. We know what followed, and how it ended.

However, when Trotsky had gone he left an inheritance, not of the Trotskyism invented by Stalin, his cowardly, perfidious and lying assassin, but a sort of Trotskyism of a more recent date, followed by Trotsky himself and his disciples. We cannot deal with it here, for to do so would be to go into an anachronism without being able to clarify the subject under discussion, that of a magazine published before the founding of the more or less mythical so-called Trotskyist International, to which I never paid the slightest attention. What is important is to take account of how faithful Trotsky was to his past mistakes, which then became present ones, and made his final efforts, literary activity, and political action sterile.

If he had been wise enough to reread his works that appeared during Lenin's lifetime (several of which were published by me in French), whose analyses and prognostications have been contradicted by the course of history today, he would perhaps have been able to trace out for communism a new path, or begin fruitfully to revise it. But we cannot imagine him writing, inspired by Benedotto Croce, a *Contribution to Self-Criticism*.[28] Moreover, he seemed stricken with amnesia as regards obvious facts that contradicted his certainties. This is demonstrated by his version of the revolt of the Kronstadt sailors, denying his direct rôle in repressing it and his signed and dated ultimatum to the rebels, which obliged him to deny the obvious evidence.

Again, in 1939, in his pamphlet *Their Morals and Ours*, he still affirms that everything comes down to the class struggle, that morality necessarily has a 'class content', and that the principle that 'the end justifies the means' (attributed, perhaps unfairly, to the Jesuits) has nothing immoral about it.[29] He invokes 'dialectical materialism' (an expression that does not exist in Marx, but was one of Plekhanov's inventions) to back it up. He believes that anyone who disagrees is an 'obtuse and slothful shopkeeper' (why do intelligent and hardworking shopkeepers not exist?). He asserts that the bourgeoisie has 'class consciousness'. (One would not say this knowing that for half a century it has been supplying the USSR with all the modern technology that it lacked, and accorded exceptional bank loans for it). He repeats that the Stalinist state is a 'workers' state', however 'backward and isolated' (isolated why, how, and by whom?). All this is barely convincing and quite disturbing hollow rhetoric.[30]

I took up Trotsky's defence alone in 1924, mainly for moral reasons, because he had been slandered, vilified and then condemned to an unjust and cruel repression. I published his pamphlet *The New Course* in French so that it might not be condemned without being read: that was the reason for my disgrace, and my expulsion from the communist movement. I went to the rostrum in Moscow in front of a hostile audience, the congress of the sole party there, to say that the public denigration of Trotsky was discrediting the Soviet regime itself: half a century later, reading Giuseppe Fiori's *Life of Antonio Gramsci*, I learned that in 1926 my Italian friend had written to the Kremlin leaders to express the same arguments as mine (his letter was intercepted by Togliatti, obedient to the GPU's orders).[31] Finally, I published in the *Bulletin* the articles by Trotsky that made such a strong impression on André Breton and those close to him.

Ignorant and indiscreet politicians and journalists have freely charged me with 'Trotskyism'. That did not exist at the time of the conflict in which I took sides, in Moscow, against lying and arbitrary official behaviour. Trotsky and his supporters were then vociferously and sincerely repudiating any

Trotskyism. I have since re-read, for the first time for half a century, chapter eight of my work on Stalin entitled 'The Heritage', where the events following the death of Lenin and ending in Trotsky's exile are explained, with my carefully critical comments. There is nothing to take back, or to alter there.[32]

Second Letter to the Members of the Communist Party: The Reply of the Three Expelled

Victor Delagarde, Pierre Monatte, Alfred Rosmer

From *La Révolution prolétarienne*, January 1925

Rosmer read out the following statement in our name at a special conference held on 5 December (a veritable council of war convened in haste to condemn us) after the two prosecuting counsels Doriot[1] and Treint had eloquently stated their case:

> We are at a loss to understand the agitation that has gripped the leadership of the party since the sending of our *Letter to the Party Members*. To us it seems to indicate a total lack of the detachment that is indispensable to the leadership of a communist party.
>
> What, then, is it all about?
>
> A party congress was to be held in January, in other words, in six weeks' time. Wasn't it necessary for a discussion to take place before the congress about the various points at issue, just as had always taken place in all the parties?

Isn't it the right of every party member to speak? And is it not indeed his duty if he thinks that danger is threatening the party? The discussion will show if he is mistaken, and the party members might then be able to judge the matter in the full knowledge of all facts/opinions.

We spoke out because we thought we had something to say, and it was our duty to do so.

So where is the indiscipline here?

Resolutions and theses are circulating in the sections and cells which do not necessarily bear the imprint of the party leadership.

For months we looked for this leadership, and failed to find it.

The Executive Committee has been closed down without anyone daring to tell the party. Its meetings have become more infrequent, and when they have taken place, since there was only a derisory number of members present, they were reduced to petty chit-chat, and the fixed agenda was not even started on.

The criticisms we directed against this secret elimination of the Executive Committee induced one very experienced comrade to make the following interesting observation: 'For the first time since the Fifth Congress the French Party has an homogeneous Political Bureau, and although it does not rest on the Executive Committee, which is composed of a majority of right-wingers, it has carried out considerable and intensive work.'

So the Executive Committee, which minus three votes voted overwhelmingly for the theses of the Left, has now been disqualified from above as made up of a majority of right-wingers. We do not know what ordinary party members can make of these strange transformations of left and right; the latter, as the occasion demands, being described as an infinitesimal and contemptible minority, then suddenly inflating to become the majority of the Executive Committee.

We shall restrict ourselves to noting that the Executive Committee has been closed down without the party being informed, and to asking if those who, on their own authority, have caused such disarray in the party leadership, are qualified to talk about indiscipline.

But if the leadership is not in the Executive Committee, is it in the Political Bureau?

On the contrary, the Political Bureau is not the leadership of the party, it is the leadership of a faction, a clique that has substituted itself for the proper leadership.

This clique leadership does not deign to reply to the letters sent by those comrades who have been labelled 'right-wingers', and when it makes promises to them, it does not keep them.

It reserves to itself the right to slander the so-called right-wingers in the worst possible way, to misrepresent their thinking quite radically, and to ascribe to them actions they have not engaged in, and never dreamed of. And after imparting a personal note to the discussion, when these comrades object, they are told: 'Of no interest ... petty personal matters ...'

When they challenge us, and ask us to state publicly our opinion as regards the decisions of the Fifth Congress of the Communist International, and we give it, they suppress it.

This is a situation we will not accept.

We are not asking, and we have never asked, for privileges. Nor are we people who stick like glue to their positions, and disrupt the party when they feel they run the risk of being removed from their positions. We very much accept that we are in a minority, and ordinary party members. But what we will never accept is to be belittled, openly insulted and demeaned.

But there is at the root of this matter a question that must be faced frankly. The party leadership decided to expel us, and all it has been doing for the last few months, is only a manoeuvre to make our expulsion appear to come from below; and to ensure that it had been announced before we spoke.

It is this manoeuvre that we wanted to thwart. As far as we are concerned it is no longer only a question of our expulsion, but of crucial matters that dominate the entire activity of a communist party. And if by our letter we have drawn the attention of communists to these questions, to the necessity for a personal and serious study of the facts, to the necessity of being people who want to know, to discuss and to decide, and not pawns shoved around by an irresponsible leadership which is above all obsessed with avoiding all control and all criticism, then we will have done the party a real service.

One day Lenin spoke these words when talking to young people: 'If a communist took it into his head to boast about his communism because of the cut-and-dried opinions he had come by, without putting in a great deal of serious and hard work and without understanding facts he should examine critically, he would be a deplorable communist indeed.'[2]

The present party leadership in no way likes this individual effort. It completely discourages criticism. Its only preoccupation is to provide ready-made arguments.

We are with Lenin against the poor imitations of Leninism.

To those tempted to follow us, and to those who, disgusted, are thinking of leaving the party, we say: 'Comrades, remain within the party. The party belongs to you, and not to those who are kicking us out. Stay there to accomplish the crucial task of reorganising it on the basis of cells: make the cells really live and not just exist on paper, so that they will not operate in a vacuum and end in failure like that of the trade union commissions.'

❖ ❖ ❖ ❖

> As for those of us who have been excluded from the party, far from thinking of setting up another party, we are turning to the great mass of communists who are not party members, and will no doubt be in it when it becomes a real communist party. We will work outside to hasten the day which the present crisis only postpones.
>
> As we said in our letter of 5 October, we return from whence we came, in other words to where we were when we were only a nucleus for safeguarding internationalism in France in 1914, for disseminating the Zimmerwald slogans in 1915, for defending the new-born Russian Revolution in 1917, for joining the Third International at its foundation in 1919, and for defending the tactic of the united front in 1922.

The verdict was then pronounced. It was more or less what we expected. We did not even hope that the two federations of Drôme and Vosges, and a department in the Paris region would abstain; it is true that the Vosges delegate understood that night what it meant to abstain, to remain silent when the conductor of the party orchestra gave the signal for a unanimous chorus.

So here we are, expelled.

Let us give here the text of the sentence pronounced against us:

> Since the Fifth World Congress, the Political Bureau, enjoying the support of the party and the International, has successfully undertaken a formidable task: political campaigns against the Dawes Plan, for the eight-hour day, for wage rises, for the independence of the colonies and an amnesty; reorganising the party on a cell basis, and Bolshevising and creating cadres, particularly by opening the Lenin school.
>
> If the Right had only expressed the backward point of view of some elements in the working class, and if it had limited itself to struggling for the point of view of the international Right and defending the errors of Trotskyism against Leninism, the party would have accepted this

important political struggle and carried it on to the complete triumph of Leninism.

But the Right, which in fact led the party a year ago, and by struggling against the Seine Federation and the CGTU, had dispersed the revolutionary forces, the Right, a real leadership of failure, has today developed into an enemy of the party and the International.

At a time when aggressive fascism, with the support of the Left Bloc, is seeking by means of social demagogy today to prepare anti-proletarian attacks tomorrow, at a time when the entire bourgeoisie inspired by Daudet and Millerand[3] has made an alliance, stretching from the Action française to *Le Peuple* via *Le Libertaire* and *Le Quotidien*,[4] against communism, the proletariat's true defender, the Right, an infinitesimal faction in the party, barely a group, has from within joined the common enemy of the working class and peasantry in order to deliver yet another blow to the party in the middle of the battle.

The arms acquired by Monatte and Rosmer from the arsenal of Pioch and Frossard have at the present time been taken up by the whole of the bourgeoisie and directed against the party and the International.

Thus Monatte, Rosmer and Delagarde have taken part in the anti-proletarian and anti-communist offensive led by the combined forces of demagogic fascism and the fascistic Left Bloc.[5]

This special conference has decided to expel Monatte, Rosmer and Delagarde as enemies of the proletariat, the party and the International, and to carry on within the party as well as among the working masses a bitter struggle to persuade every worker, every peasant and every toiler to rally around his Communist Party more strongly united than ever under the banner of Leninism.

The National Congress found itself faced with a fait accompli, a definitively pronounced condemnation. The party apparatus had got what it wanted. Now it could truly pride itself on being unanimously supported.

But was this unanimity real?

If it was real, how can we explain that one of our chief prosecutors has since been forced to admit that 'there are a good number of comrades in the party ranks and among its sympathisers who sincerely regret the departure of Monatte'? In addition, how do we explain that the leadership's agents went all over the place moaning that it was deplorable that our expulsions had not been understood by the bulk of the party?

A great number of comrades, and in fact the best of them, the first supporters of adherence to the Third International were opposed to our expulsion. The remainder did not understand it.

Someone once said that Austria was made up of two great parties, those who were intimidated and the intimidators. Much the same could be said of the French Communist Party. Will the intimidated put up for long with all that the custodians and accomplices of the party apparatus intend to inflict on them?

❖ ❖ ❖ ❖

'I agree with everything that you say in your letter', one party and trade union comrade told us, 'but you should not have published it. You have therefore laid yourself open to being expelled. You have allowed them to charge you with indiscipline and factionalism.'

But we have not committed an act of indiscipline nor of factionalism, nor, even less so, a crime against the party, the International or the working class.

As far as our expulsion goes, it was not provoked by the publication of our first letter at the end of November. It was decided a long time ago. On 21 September last, at the conference of the federal secretaries, did not Monsieur Cadeau[6] say, with his finger pointing at us, 'You who are nearly outside the party ... ?' Enough of hypocrisy! Ever since the Fifth World Congress our expulsion has been plotted in the dark.

'We should have asked for permission to publish this first letter.' But who should we have asked? The very people who kept in their drawer our letter of 5 October to the Executive Committee? Don't make us laugh!

Moreover, by speaking directly to the party by means of our *First Letter*, we were only making use of the right of any party member to defend himself against disgraceful attacks and to discuss the agenda of the party congress. If there was one or even many acts of indiscipline, the leadership should take the responsibility.

'Our reply would fall into the hands of people alien to the party.' Tell us then, did not the attacks that gave rise to this reply fall into the hands of people alien to the party, since everyone could read them in *L'Humanité* and *Le Bulletin communiste*?

'We should have tried to set up a faction, and organise a "workers' left" within the party by asking the comrades who shared our point of view to help us cover the printing costs of this letter and those that were to follow it, since we were proposing to examine the main questions of the congress in a series of successive letters.' But how would we have been able to cover these unavoidable costs, since the party press was closed to us and we had no access to Sémard's drawer?

We have only our workers' wages to live on. It is only natural that we should have turned to our comrades. They have not responded all that badly.

But, unfortunately, nothing enables us to say that we have organised a 'workers' left'. We have taken seriously the anti-factional resolutions of the International. Nonetheless, if we had infringed them, we would have done the party a great favour. There is scarcely a federation in which working-class consciousness is not stifled by vulgar political attitudes in Blanquist guise. We would have been able to put a curse on that! By forming a faction, we would only have been following the example of the so-called 'Left'. But what we would not have done is to identify our faction with the party, and take over its apparatus to use it in the interests of a tendency, in order to indulge in factional hatred, and muzzle, slander and expel the others.

We feel as if we are repeating the story of what once happened to us. It was a few years ago, with other Treints and other Suzanne Giraults. They were then called Besnard and Verdier. Their field of operations was the CSR [Comités syndicalistes révolutionnaires].[7] There was the same fanatical dogmatism, the same indulgence in abstraction, the same blindness in the face of reality, and the same conviction that they were geniuses selected by destiny to lead. They weakened the CSR as Treint has weakened the party. They concluded an agreement with the intention of taking over positions in the CSR and the CGT such as Treint has agreed with some of the Calzans[8] and Cadeaus to take over the party apparatus. One fine day they were the all-powerful masters of the CSR. But they had done so much and so well that from that day onwards the agony of the CSR began. Treint and his faction are the all-powerful masters of the party. Will they be able to smash it totally, and forever? Will they be content with making it ridiculous for a few months by making a caricature communist party out of it?

Let no one say that we were expelled for an act of indiscipline, or for factional activity: we were expelled because we had committed a crime of high treason. We had spoken ill – and thought even more ill – of the party apparatus. The apprentices of French Bolshevism wanted to apply to the French Communist Party, which had not carried out a revolution, the methods adopted by the Russian party in the period of the dictatorship. Incapable as they were of adopting from the Russian party what was great about it, it was perfectly natural that these apes would copy its excesses and mistakes.

The Real Reasons

Lack of respect for Treint, Suzanne Girault and other like comrades is now called making an attack upon the party and the International, and those guilty deserve to be pilloried as enemies of the proletariat, the party and the International.

And to say that we thought we were helping the proletariat, the party and the International by committing a crime of high treason! And to say that we still think so!

Our disagreement with the leaders of the so-called 'Left' does not date from today. From the time of the struggle against Frossard, we already felt the need to distinguish ourselves from them, and for the 'workers' left' to have its own position. But we then thought that there were only secondary disagreements between us, above all as regards understanding organisational questions.

Our first conflict took place over the Ilbert affair.[9] We believed then, just as we do today, that we cannot serve the revolution with dirty hands, as Lenin's expression has it.[10]

Behind the different organisational conceptions, between those who had a feeling of respect for the organisation, and those who looked upon the organisation as a passive instrument in their hands, there were, as we were forced to recognise in the end, important, deep and irreconcilable disagreements.

We set ourselves apart from the so-called 'Left' on three important points:

1. On our concept of the party.
2. On the prospects for revolution.
3. On Leninism, or what is called Leninism.

Two Concepts of the Party

Their concept of the party is based upon contempt for the masses, the working masses as well as the party masses.

The whole policy they impose upon the party in no way lies in developing the class consciousness of the proletariat, but in creating the greatest possible number of conformists, bootlickers and sluggards. But since they need the masses nonetheless, they want to make them stir by brainwashing.

We, on the other hand, think that such men will never be revolutionaries, that such a party will break in one's hand at the first hard blow, that we must develop thinking people and not reciters of the catechism if we really want to prepare for the revolution.

The French Communist Party is as yet neither the vanguard nor the working-class elite of this country. It has to try to be. But to do that, it has to win its stripes in proletarian battles before boastfully putting them on.

To want to lead and to command at any cost. Is this not the natural right of the bourgeoisie, both small and great? Was it not created and sent forth into the world to dominate, command and despise the workers? Treint and Girault are typical products of the petite-bourgeoisie. The present personal conflict is basically only a phase in the eternal conflict between the proletariat and the petite-bourgeoisie. The working class labours in subjection, but other classes command and live like noisy parasites. But the working class intends to work, and not to serve: it intends itself to be in command in the factory one day, and from today henceforth in its party and in its struggle for its emancipation.

We are told: You have now had the leadership of the party for a year. What have you done with it? You have been a bankrupt leadership.

That's a joke, that is!

Who then, was in the secretariat at the head of the party a year ago? There were two secretaries, Treint and Sellier. That is how we became leaders of the party.

A year ago, we were struggling against the CGTU. This was no doubt when Monatte, who had taken over the 'Social Life' column in *L'Humanité*, was told: 'You surely don't think that you are going to make the journal of the CGTU here?'

We are the new Frossards. The Paris correspondent of the Rosta agency went so far as to telegraph the Moscow *Pravda* on 3 December with truths of this nature: 'Finally Monatte and his supporters, condemning the expulsion of Souvarine, *regretted the expulsion of Frossard, Méric and Verfeuil*,[11] and ascribed the political crisis the party was going through entirely to personal conflicts.'

Those who have not suddenly suffered an attack of amnesia, either in Moscow or here, must find these lies particularly bizarre. When Frossard made the decision to bring about a break of the party with the Communist International, and of the CGTU with the Red International of Labour Unions, it was Monatte who started the first fight-back by bringing about the resignation of the editors of *L'Humanité* who had remained faithful to the [Socialist] International. It was the 'nucleus of the workers' left' that cried 'knock it off' to the syndicalists in a manifesto. It was at this time that Sémard threw out Chambelland from *La Vie ouvrière* for having denounced Frossard's betrayal. Once this same Sémard became the party secretary, he had the cheek to throw Chambelland out of the party.

Two great tasks beckoned to the party leadership, this now at last homogeneous leadership, so very capable.

The first was to reorganise the party on a factory cell basis. It was carried out in such a way that we might well wonder how many cells exist other than on paper. Their first concern was to hold up a great flag; there was nothing yet behind it. But as expected, the flag did have the effect on the bosses of a red rag to a bull. It swooped down on the flag and on those comrades suspected of being communists. What it meant was a hunt to root out the secretaries and members of cells and the reinforcement of the resident company and government police in the factory. Bitter blows and the dispersal of the best elements of the party were the most obvious results obtained by a leadership which, completely ignorant of the factory, could build nothing durable or serious there.

What remains of the party, if it does not yet have cells, and no longer has sections?

The other great task, of preparing a current of opinion favourable to international trade union unity, was sabotaged even more.

Those militants in the working-class movement who were not communists, but sincerely won over to the cause of international trade union unity, were stupidly compromised, and their influence from then on must have been markedly diminished.

Those who are happy with this have a funny idea of communist work among the masses. We hoped a few months ago that they would not play about with the cells as they had played with the trade union commissions. But when they have broken one toy, they pick up another. The petite-bourgeoisie can amuse themselves with this game, because they do not have to foot the bill. But the workers cannot do that. When the Bolshevisation of the parties is understood in this way, it quite simply means they are disintegrating.

Revolutionary Prospects

According to Treint, the prospect of revolution is not far off: the revolution will spread in the very near future. Wake up, chaps!

Appearing to be less revolutionary than your neighbour, or even more so opposing him, is badly received. But since we know that the real spirit of revolution does not consist of getting drunk on illusions, we would say that the world revolution has had a setback with the retreat of the German revolution.

Germany, which for a long time was the battlefield where the revolution and capitalism confronted each other, without knowing which of them would win, has passed completely under the control of capitalism since the autumn of 1923.

Russia remains alone. It must now expect an attack from the coalition powers united under the leadership of Wall Street, and what ought to concern us is to make sure it is defended.

The Dawes Plan means a large-scale offensive to draw the Western powers into America's orbit and stamp out their proletariat's revolutionary plans.

Treint and others believe that the existing antagonisms

within the capitalist world are so deep at the present time that the revolution is able to maintain a policy of offensive.

One question arises to begin with: are they expressing a sincere opinion here, or are they rather, after the manner of Hervé,[12] bluffing?

If they are bluffing, it is a sign of weakness, and we prefer the attitude of Trotsky, which was that of Lenin, when he admitted his tactical errors fair and square, and did not hesitate to make the necessary U-turns.

But if they are sincere, they are leading us into a putsch, whether knowingly or otherwise, a let-down similar to that of the Germans, a putsch or let-down for which Treint would be the scapegoat after its defeat, but the damage that had been done would remain.

And the prospect of revolution would have been put back a little more.

It is impossible to discuss these things in the French party with the seriousness that they deserve. Loriot has just experienced this. The thesis that he submitted to the Seine Congress along with Berthelin[13] was immediately described by Treint in the *Cahiers du bolchèvisme* of 26 December as 'an incoherent thesis sprinkled with opportunistic errors', a 'miserable thesis' repeating the accusations of the bourgeoisie, a 'thesis alien to communism', showing 'a loss of all serious contact with the party and the International'.

It was described by *L'Humanité* as a 'social-fascist' thesis for having dared to make the perfectly natural remark that fascism is not a democratico-anarcho-bourgeois united front. For our idiots, everything that is not communist is fascist. The senate refuses an amnesty – so the senate is fascist. A bourgeois printer refuses to print a communist paper – yet another fascist act. According to this reckoning, fascism has been going on for a good long time. By going on in this way, announcing fascist aggression every morning, there is a strong risk of doing as Guillot, the shepherd of unhappy memory, did when he cried wolf so often that on the day the wolf really did come nobody bothered to help him.

Leninism

We are committed to the Communist International: we are not acquainted with 'Leninism' or 'Trotskyism'. While Lenin was alive the International was big enough to embrace

Trotsky and so-called Trotskyism, as well as the Russian Workers Opposition and numerous elements who had come from revolutionary syndicalism in the rest of the world.

Leninism without Lenin frightens us. It comes under the guise of a name we obviously look up to, all the more, and perhaps even more so, than those who claim to follow him completely but trample on his last pieces of advice, and labour to undo and dismantle the revolutionary international structure that Lenin was determined to build.

In all countries the symptoms of malaise and abstentionism are showing themselves. If we take no notice, we will, under the banner of Leninism, be on the road towards a retreat of the International, a weakening of its forces, and a stifling of its thought.

The Party's Self-Criticism

We are convinced that by saying this fair and square, we are helping the party, the International and the working class. The Communist International may well say of those who have thrown us out of the party, 'O God, save me from my friends!'

The bourgeois press, from *Le Peuple* and *Le Quotidien* to *Le Matin*, has swooped upon our letter. Whose fault is that? It is obvious that the Political Bureau, with its repeated advertisements, has drawn attention to it. Without this furore, our letter would have passed unnoticed by the general public. But then the members of the party would have read it with detachment, and this would never do.

Neither the bourgeoisie nor the government have been able to find in this letter anything whatever that would justify their persecution of communism. And as for the gentlemen of *Le Peuple*, *Le Quotidien* and *Le Matin*,[14] they know better than anyone that we have been, are and will remain their implacable enemies. And they know from their own experience that we are more of a danger to them than the loudmouths who today have excommunicated us. The bourgeoisie and its parties fear a real workers' movement more than battalions led by some little overexcited Blanquists.

If we had doubted for a minute the validity of our actions, we would have been assured by these words of Lenin:

> One more word to the opponents of Social-

> Democracy. They gloat and grimace over our disputes; they will, of course, try to pick isolated passages from my pamphlet, which deals with the failings and shortcomings of our party, and to use them for their own ends. The Russian Social Democrats are already steeled enough in battle not to be perturbed by these pinpricks and to continue, in spite of them, their work of self-criticism and ruthless exposure of their own shortcomings, which will unquestionably and inevitably be overcome as the working-class movement grows.[15]

Unfortunately, the French party has shown that it is incapable of carrying out its work of self-criticism. It attracted more discredit than we threw on it when it opened everyone's eyes as to how it interpreted its members' right to debate.

It was said that we are elements adhering to syndicalist prejudices, whom the party always had to drag along. But it was we who dragged the party towards its internationalist duty in 1914, dragged it later to Zimmerwald, then to the Russian Revolution, then to the Third International, and then to the united front: and it is we today who have said out loud what the best French revolutionary workers are saying under their breath.

And we are as convinced that we have done our revolutionary duty today, in 1924, by writing our first *Letter to the Party Members*, as Monatte was able to be in 1914 when he wrote his letter of resignation from the Confederal Committee.[16]

We are treated as enemies of the proletariat, the party and the International. Being described as enemies of the proletariat by the Treints and Ilberts heaps more of the usual ridicule on these individuals. Lenin taught us to react to extravagant stupidity with laughter. And we are confident that this will be the attitude of the proletariat.

On that note, goodbye, and thank you!

V Delagarde, P Monatte, A Rosmer

About the 'Final Warning' Given to Trotsky

The Myth of Trotskyism

Alfred Rosmer

From *La Révolution prolétarienne*, February 1925

If it was possible, when the crisis erupted within the Russian Communist Party last winter, to wonder what it really meant and where it might lead to, today such doubt is no longer possible.

After a lull that was more apparent than real, at the first opportunity, at the first pretext, the discussion has resumed with increased brutality, and the aim of Trotsky's opponents has been starkly revealed by the resolution – monstrous but hybrid, mean-minded, contradictory, incoherent, the model of a vulgar polemic – which was voted almost unanimously by the Central Committee on 17 January.

Now that we have had more than a year to follow and judge events, everyone can see the successive phases of the campaign being waged against Trotsky, and draw out its meaning.

For the conflict which broke out in the autumn of 1923 must not be reduced to a clash of personalities, or a quarrel between leaders: if it is about individuals, it is even more about the methods which these individuals represent.

To begin with, it was said that it was merely a temporary difference, which could easily be settled. Nonetheless, the turn which the discussion took showed the aim being pursued; this was not to concentrate all efforts and pool forces in order to resolve the crisis which was appearing dramatically and dangerously in the country, but to block Trotsky's influence. When we said so at the time, and claimed that the aim was to get rid of Trotsky, and, at the same time, to get rid of the methods he advocated, we were told: 'What nonsense! Who could dream of attacking Trotsky and detracting from his rôle? His strength is necessary for the revolution.' Zinoviev himself stated: 'Trotsky is mistaken, but his co-operation is indispensable. We cannot conceive of the Political Bureau without him. He remains one of the most authoritative leaders.'

Now today, less than a year after such statements – which were made insincerely, because they were necessary to delude the mass of workers – it appears that after all Trotsky can very well be done without, and that his co-operation is so little indispensable that he has been excluded from the Commissariat of War with which he was so fully identified. As for being a highly qualified leader, we are told that he is a Menshevik, who wants to revise Leninism, to substitute 'Trotskyism' for Leninism; he is said to be the hope of the counter-revolution, and that 'the social fascists[1] of *Avanti*,[2] the mercenaries of the German bourgeoisie on *Vorwärts*,[3] the Renaudels[4] and Grumbachs[5] of the *Quotidien*,[6] etc, are seeking to make common cause with him'. (This is said in so many words in the Central Committee's resolution.)

Doubtless in the intervening period, Trotsky's enemies have not remained inactive. They have manoeuvred endlessly, striving to conceal the real issues with various expedients. They have revived all the old internal discussions in the Russian party, and thrown them into the International. They are piling up article on article and resolution on resolution. The purpose of all this is to create such an atmosphere that when a meeting or congress is held, it is no longer free to discuss or to express its thought. The unanimity which is sought at any price, and which is obtained, is manifested in discontent, muffled criticisms and unease.

The origin of this serious conflict is from now on completely out of sight. It is buried and has disappeared beneath a heap of texts of all sorts. It is worth trying to dig it out and reconstruct it. That leads straightaway to the heart of things, to the reality of the crisis.

The 1923 Debate, its Origin and Causes

How did the 1923 debate arise? Was it in an arbitrary and artificial manner because it suited a comrade who spoke with great authority to stir up a real upheaval in the party? By no means. The debate was provoked by two causes which were profound and all too visible: the economic situation in the country (the condition of the workers and peasants), and the state of the party.

The economic situation was serious, and was causing acute discontent among both workers and peasants. Workers received their wages weeks and even months late, in a currency which was losing its value every day. There were strikes, and even strikes led by communists, by party members. The peasants could not buy anything because of the ridiculous ratio between the price of grain and that of manufactured objects. According to a sound Leninist method, Trotsky characterised this crisis by a striking image, that of the scissors whose blades are opened as wide as possible and which at all costs must be brought closer together. Thereafter everyone had this image before his eyes; all attention was constantly directed to this vital problem, and all wills exerted themselves in trying to solve it.

Trotsky indicated his solutions: the concentration of industry for a better organisation of factories and higher output, and a state plan to replace chaos with order and method.

Within the party, the trouble lay in the extreme passivity of the members, and in the worrying bureaucratic development which resulted from this.

These are unquestioned and unquestionable facts.

A Picture of the Russian CP in 1923

The passivity reigning among the members and throughout the party bodies was such that one of the seasoned leaders of the party denounced it in these terms at the general meeting of one of the largest branches in Moscow:

> Comrades, it seems to me to be indispensable to draw a concrete picture of the concerns perturbing our party. There is no point speaking here of *a priori* premises, of differentiation, etc, etc: we must clearly pose the question of the origin of what is tormenting the body of our party and of

the source of the discontent of the bulk of non-party workers, a discontent which we must all take into account, from the CC [Central Committee] to the bureaux of the party cells: a countless number of faults have provoked a certain state of semi-crisis within our party, a state which is obvious above all as a result of the economic crisis which our country is currently passing through; these faults can all be classified under specific headings.

What is the root of the problem? Observe the life of a party cell, and, to begin with, the mechanics of how it works, for each cell has its own. To judge by the Moscow organisation, cell secretaries are normally appointed by district committees, and note that the districts don't even try to get their candidates accepted by these cells, but simply appoint such and such a comrade. Generally, votes are taken according to a method accepted once and for all. The meeting is asked: 'Who is against?', and as people are more or less afraid to declare themselves opposed, the appointed candidate becomes elected secretary of the committee of the group. If we were to do a survey to establish how many times the voting has consisted of the questions 'Who is for?' and 'Who is against?', we should observe without difficulty that among us, in most cases, the elections of party officials are purely passive, because not only does the voting take place without prior discussion, but also according to the formula 'Who is against?'; and since one is not well looked upon if one speaks against the 'hierarchy', the affair is settled automatically.

Now let's speak of our party meetings; how are they conducted? I have myself spoken more than once in numerous meetings in Moscow, and I know how so-called debate is practised in our party organisations: elections for the chairing of the meeting. One of the members from the district committee presents their list and asks: 'Who is against?' Nobody is against, of course, and the

> matter is settled. The same comrade then declares the bureau unanimously elected. After that comes the agenda; same procedure. In the course of recent years I can only remember isolated and extremely rare cases where the party meetings added new points to the agenda. In general the meeting finishes with the reading of a resolution prepared in advance, which is adopted as the rules require. The chair again asks: 'Who is against?', and nobody is against. The resolution is adopted unanimously. This is how our party organisations normally function. So how can we fail to understand those of our most active elements when they express their dissatisfaction about this question, for they cannot be happy with such a way of operating.
>
> Very often the lower layers of our organisations even put up the barrier: 'No discussion', 'Who is against?', etc, and this system reduces the internal life of the party to nothing. It goes without saying that the result is a great wave of discontent. I have quoted a few examples taken from our internal cells; the same thing can be observed in somewhat modified forms in all the other sections of the party hierarchy.[7]

Who spoke these words? Was it Trotsky or some other member of the opposition? No, it was Bukharin.[8]

The remedy is an unremitting struggle against the pernicious bureaucratism which is atrophying the party and pushing it into decline; it is the establishment of democracy in the party which will restore life and activity in all the party bodies, from top to bottom, and will enable the party to remain equal to its enormous task. That is what Trotsky is pointing to. Is anyone in disagreement? Nobody. Quite the contrary; they are arguing about who said it first. Everyone claims to have discovered it before Trotsky, and everybody is talking about the need for a radical change, a 'New Course' – to use Trotsky's term – a new orientation. I could give 10 typical quotations. A single one will suffice. It is taken from *Pravda*'s reply, and is formulated as follows:

> We don't know a single member of the Central

> Committee who, in the course of the discussions, did not declare himself in agreement with the critique of the 'old orientation', a critique which the Central Committee resolution contains first and foremost. Trotsky could not name a single member of the CC who spoke in favour of the 'old orientation'.

On 5 December, the Central Committee voted unanimously for a resolution embodying the new course.

The debate should therefore have stopped at this point. Nonetheless, it was to resume with new enthusiasm and in the form of a violent polemic after the publication of a letter from Trotsky (written on 8 December, but which appeared in *Pravda* only on 11 December). Why? That is the question we have asked here, and to which we can find no reply. We did indeed believe that our comrade had not written his letter lightly, without serious reasons. But we could not discover these reasons. A comrade who is well known in the workers' movement, and who led the fight for the opposition in a Moscow branch, has explained them to me.

The bureaucratic apparatus of the party, defeated and censured, was obliged to accept the Central Committee resolution. But it was already contemplating revenge. It immediately went out into the Moscow party branches and, taking on the job of publicising the CC resolution itself, it clearly showed its determination, not to implement it, but to bury it. Trotsky, informed of this sabotage which was endangering all the gains made in the debate and the 'New Course' itself, decided to denounce it without delay. Being sick, he could not visit the branches. He wrote a letter which he demanded should be published in *Pravda*. Immediately the debate moved onto a completely new path.

Trotsky showed in his letter how and in what circumstances the old generation could degenerate. The old guard of the party, or more precisely the troika[9] took this suggestion of the danger of degeneration as a reference aimed at itself. Wounded, it lost its coolness and all sense of proportion. From this point on, it completely abandoned the object of the debate, although this was of capital importance, and launched into a bitter polemic against Trotsky who, out of action due to illness, had to stand by impotently and watch the 'monstrous distortion' of what he thought and what he had written, and found himself prevented from bringing the debate back to its proper ground. Everything was discussed: factions, relations between old and young, and even a so-called plot to arrest Lenin.

The bureaucrats were saved, and the 'New Course' was buried.

The Scissors

The debate on the economic crisis took a less harsh turn. Just as the remedy for the crisis of the party proposed by Trotsky was accepted by the Central Committee in its entirety, so those he proposed to overcome the economic crisis did not find any opponents. Everybody recognised the need to concentrate industry and draw up a general plan for production. Once these principles had been accepted, it remained only to undertake their practical application urgently. It did not seem that there was any cause there for violent controversy.

So why did the debate drag on and on? Because while it was not possible to make a frontal attack on the essential principles of the necessary improvement of production, it was very possible to obstruct their application. Some did it by local demagogy; others by idleness, by inertia, or by routine. Now Trotsky wanted to *achieve* something. He was an embarrassment to them all. Hence the furious attacks against him and, as always when bad causes are being defended, the radical distortion of his thought and his proposals.

It is well known how this first phase of the debate ended. The opposition was, to begin with, very strong, and it controlled Moscow; it was undermined and then progressively weakened as the debate shifted away from the questions which had given rise to it and on to others which had been artificially raised and pushed to the fore. The International was mobilised. The recalcitrant branches, which refused to declare themselves blindly on key questions of which they knew little or nothing, had their meetings disrupted. Emissaries from Zinoviev were given this responsibility. By shouting very loudly 'Down with factionalism!', they manufactured factions. It was a golden age for narrow-minded and vulgar careerists who poisoned the working-class movement in the postwar period, and thus had the possibility of pushing themselves into the front ranks.

The Russian party, at its Thirteenth Congress, condemned

the opposition as Menshevik, petit-bourgeois, counter-revolutionary, etc. The Communist International did the same at its Fifth Congress. There was no longer any mention of the original problem, of the observations on which, at the outset, everyone had been in agreement. Lenin's death, which occurred in the thick of the debate, enabled them to be shoved into the background. The disappearance of the unchallenged leader of the revolution had brought the party 200,000 new members, workers. There was no longer any need to be concerned about the apparatus. In the economic sphere it had been possible, by means of short-term solutions, to achieve a temporary abatement of the crisis which was consolidated by monetary reform, with the main result a relative stabilisation of the cost of living. But a quotation will suffice to show that the problem of production remains entirely unresolved to this very day. It is, moreover, only too clear that a short-sighted policy will not enable it to be resolved.

The general situation has, in fact, just been characterised as follows by Rykov in his report to the Sixth Congress of the Trade Unions of the USSR in Moscow:

> Our industry cannot at present satisfy the peasant market. There is a shortage of commodities. The remedy must be an expansion of industrial production. This may be insufficient, because of the weakness of our resources. Therefore this year, as last year, we may have to use part of our gold currency reserves for purchases abroad. Last year, we bought cotton. Other purchases will have to be made this year. Finally, if industry does not develop fast enough, we can envisage for a certain period the introduction of some foreign goods. This question is under consideration.[10]

This brief summary includes all the essential facts, and allows us to discover the origin of the crisis, to follow its development, and to draw out the characteristics of the two groups which formed. The one group, out of laziness, demagogy and routinism – for there is already a very dangerous governmental routine – advocates and defends superficial, short-term solutions which will be valid for a week or a month. To supplement their inadequacy, they will resort to the usual means at the disposal of any government. The others want to attack the problem frontally, following Lenin's example. They are proposing radical measures, asking that they should be considered, and that they should be discussed with the intention of applying the decisions taken, and are calling on the entire party to put them into practice and to explain them to the workers and peasants, seeking above all to convince, and resorting to constraint only when persuasion has failed. That is also the example left by Lenin.

Behind all the noise of the debate, two concepts were coming into conflict. And if the workers were immediately sympathetic to the opposition, it is because they felt that the opposition expressed their aspirations to active participation in Soviet life.

Trotsky, for his part, has always been deeply aware of the need for serious achievements in the sphere of production. He faced up to the fundamental problems of the revolution. He concerned himself with the individual, family and social life of men, women and children.

It is an extraordinary thing that it is precisely for this that he is criticised. It is claimed that it is too early, that the time has not yet come for such achievements to be planned for, that the revolution above all must still think about its defence, and devote all its strength to it.

Those who speak like this, who do not understand that the best way of defending the revolution is to consolidate it, and to ensure that its base becomes every day broader and more solid, are party people wrapped up in politics in the narrow meaning of the word. The party naturally plays a major rôle, especially in Russia, but for the revolution to survive, the trade unions must also exist and be capable of carrying out their functions, and the soviets likewise. Otherwise a dangerous distortion will erupt inside the party itself, which will no longer have any real life, and will fall into the passive state described by Bukharin, and finally find itself reduced to being nothing more than its own apparatus.

A few years ago, when these questions could be discussed in the International, when the respective rôles of the party, the unions and the soviets were considered, we generally came to the conclusion that the party seemed to be the most temporary organism, and that it was either the soviets or the unions which would take the dominant rôle in building a communist society.

With Lenin, who was so attentive to reality and to revolutionary necessities, a balance was established between these different forces.

Now the party people have come out on top, and their day-to-day policies have triumphed. They concoct congresses and unanimous decisions with great skill. Anyone who resists is immediately discredited as being right-wing, Menshevik, petit-bourgeois, (objectively) counter-revolutionary, etc. But where, in all this, is communism?

October

Beaten at his party congress, beaten at the congress of the Comintern – the French 'old Bolsheviks' were there to add insult to injury – Trotsky nonetheless continued his work in the Political Bureau, in the Council of Labour and Defence, and in his Commissariat of War, carrying out his responsibilities with the high conscientiousness which characterises him, and nonetheless finding time to prepare and deliver, to various congresses and meetings, substantial speeches on the international situation and on various domestic questions.

Never had his authority been greater. There was even something exceptional and moving in the welcome he received as soon as he appeared at a meeting. It seemed as if the workers, obliged to condemn him by the party machine, were insisting on affirming loud and clear that they still considered him as their guide. The delegates to the congress of the Comintern were somewhat surprised by the demonstrative testimonies of loyalty which emphasised a serious fact: the divorce between the party leadership and the rank and file. The French, embarrassed and disturbed in their 'Bolshevik' zeal, went to ask Stalin for an explanation.

Trotsky submitted to the party's decision. He had not admitted his errors – as L'Humanité claimed, dishonestly, as though by chance – since he had not committed any. He considered the debate closed, and it can easily be understood that he had no desire to reopen it. After his defeat, the opposition had been decimated, and its most representative figures were dispersed to the four corners of Russia and of the world. Nobody had any interest in reopening the discussion, and Trotsky less than anyone else. Moreover, it could be rightly thought that the facts would prevail, and that they would do the job of modifying the absurd positions adopted in the course of the debate. Rykov's statement, taking up a suggestion made by Ossinsky, is a striking example of this.

But The Lessons of October appeared, and genuine fury was unleashed by the troika. The book was a collection of studies and previously published articles by Trotsky, and was hence all material that was already known. Even the notorious Introduction merely took up ideas already expressed by Trotsky in the party press without having given rise to any scandal.

In fact, if Trotsky had completely ceased hostilities, it was not the same as far as his opponents were concerned. They had pursued their campaign methodically and by use of insinuation. First of all, there had been a pamphlet by Kanachikov,[11] entitled *History of a Deviation*. When this was mentioned to the Russian comrades, they said in embarrassment: 'Don't talk about it. It was a mistake. We're going to withdraw it from sale.' At that very moment, it was being reprinted. Then a special journal was set up to prove that Trotsky had never been a communist. They noted in great detail all his disagreements with Lenin, and all the words that Lenin had been able to write against him since 1903. The two men had also been in agreement at times, in particular at decisive moments; of these no more mention was made.

The ground was well prepared and when *The Lessons of October* appeared, they seized the unexpected opportunity frenetically. They could not have imagined such a splendid excuse!

Trotsky had edited his book and written his Introduction with the sole concern of drawing out the lessons of the Russian October for communists in all countries. At the time of the Fifth Congress of the Comintern, during an interview with Spanish comrades, he had already dealt with this subject. In his view, since the war, revolution had come knocking at the door in three countries: Russia in 1917, Italy in September 1920, and Germany in 1923. This made one victory and two defeats. Why? It was a problem, the greatest of all, which must be studied seriously. He also spoke that evening about American imperialism, not merely in order to note its increased strength, but to show the weak points where it could be wounded, and to draw out in detail a practical task for the Spanish comrades: liaison with communists speaking the same language in South America, where the United States was in process of establishing its influence.

In writing his Introduction, he knew very well that he would offend the Russian comrades who did not share his evaluation of the situation in Germany, while agreeing with him on domestic questions. He was therefore disarming himself in advance in the face of the troika. That should suffice to show that there was no trace of calculation or manoeuvring in the publication of his book.

He was the first to be astounded by the furious attack that was unleashed. Admittedly, the account of the events which led to the Russian October scarcely showed Kamenev and Zinoviev in a favourable light. But is that any reason to abandon study of this period? And did they treat Trotsky tactfully when, in order to attack him immoderately, they had first monstrously to falsify his thought, words and writings?

But once again the opportunity was too good; it was what Zinoviev had hoped for, and he grabbed it and decided to clinch his victory. On this ground, Trotsky would be isolated, and could be destroyed. The first debate paled into insignificance alongside that which was going to begin, in which, moreover, Zinoviev and his friends would be the only ones to speak. Trotsky gave the reasons for his silence in the letter which we publish below.[12] They now said what they had hitherto not dared to say. In the field of military organisation, he seemed to be untouchable. He had always been presented as the man who had saved Petrograd from Yudenich, and who had raised, equipped and trained the victorious Red Army. Now all this was dismissed as mythical. The victories against Kolchak, Denikin, Yudenich, etc,[13] had apparently been won, not by him, but against him. It was Stalin who said so. It was Gussiev who wrote it, in a pamphlet secretly prepared months before, and served up at the appropriate moment.

These characteristics suffice to indicate the fury of the attack. As far as the position of Zinoviev and Kamenev was concerned, it was Bukharin who took on the job of justifying it. He did so in an anonymous and embarrassed reply in *Pravda*, which understandably he was not keen to sign. It was only, he claimed, a secondary disagreement lasting a few days, and, moreover, the comrades had recognised their mistake. And he entitled his reply 'How Not to Write the History of October'. If he had been the only historian of October, we should have a very poor history. Does he think we are so ignorant? Enough documents have already been published for us to be quite certain about the nature and duration of this disagreement. There were others, which he knows about and which we know about too. And he knows very well that Lenin always said that this disagreement was no accident.[14]

As for the way in which Kamenev has recognised his error of 1917, our position is confirmed by the statement he made four years later, at the time of the adoption of the NEP by the party, when he said: 'Well, weren't we right in October?'

Lenin and Trotsky

In accordance with the usual tactic, the debate was shifted onto different ground, that of the disagreements between Lenin and Trotsky.

But even if the former controversies are recalled, it merely brings out the fact that they did not prevent the two men from working together and collaborating closely throughout the period of the revolution. This collaboration is not spoken of. However, it is more relevant than what can be discovered in trawling through the archives.

It is well known what importance Lenin attached to the national question. He brought it to the fore as early as the Second Congress of the Comintern. In 1923, various events had put this question on the agenda of the Russian Communist Party. Out of action due to illness, Lenin was nonetheless following the debate closely. Fearing that he would be unable to intervene himself, he thought about who could replace him. To whom did he turn? To Trotsky. He did so in the following terms:

> 5 March 1923
>
> Dear Comrade Trotsky
>
> It is my earnest request that you should undertake the defence of the Georgian case in the party CC. This case is now under 'prosecution' by Stalin and Dzerzhinsky, and I cannot rely on their impartiality. Quite to the contrary. I would feel at ease if you agreed to undertake its defence.[15]

I am reproducing this document because it is in the public domain. There are others. All indicate the absolute confidence shown by Lenin in Trotsky and the agreement between the two men on all essential current questions. Moreover, is it not a fact known by everyone in Russia that Lenin, prevented from working by ill-health, insisted that Trotsky should take his place on the Council of People's Commissars and in the Council of Labour and Defence?

Revolutionary Prospects and Revision of Leninism

The question of revolutionary prospects is not a new one. Obviously it was constantly on the agenda of the International. Trotsky often dealt with it – at the Third and Fourth Congresses of the Comintern, when he was appointed to report back by the Russian party, and then, more recently, in various speeches and writings.

Those who wish to know Trotsky's thought before they criticise it can take the trouble to read these texts – they have almost all been published in French; they will be struck by two things. First of all, there is an absolute continuity in the point of view. What Trotsky said in 1924 is what he said in 1921, in 1922, in full agreement with Lenin. Then they can grasp in action the way in which his thought is being distorted, on this point as on others. If there has been a revision of Leninism, they will see who is doing the revising.

The Third Congress of the Comintern met just after the insurrection of March 1921 in Germany. At the time, in relation to this insurrection, there existed in various sections of the International a strong tendency in favour of the tactic of the offensive at any price. Lenin and Trotsky considered this tactic extremely dangerous for the labour movement in all countries, with the sole result that leading communist parties would be periodically massacred and decimated. They were instructed by the Russian party to oppose it exhaustively at the congress.[16] After debate, they had their position adopted: the so-called tactic of the offensive was definitively rejected.

Returning to this question in the course of a debate during the Fourth Congress, Trotsky expressed himself as follows:

> I welcome the opportunity ... to oppose – most resolutely – the mechanical, fatalistic and non-Marxist conception of revolutionary development

> which continues, despite the truly salutary work of the Third World Congress, to find a haven in the minds of some people, obviously convinced that they are of the Left.
>
> At the Third World Congress, we were told that the economic crisis would endure without interruption and get worse until the proletariat seized power. This mechanistic outlook was at the bottom of the revolutionary optimism of some of those 'of the Left'. When we explained that cyclical ups and downs are inevitable in the world economy, and that it is necessary to foresee them and take them into account tactically, these comrades imagined that we were engaged in a revision of well-nigh the entire programme and tactic of the International. In reality, we were engaged only in a 'revision' of certain prejudices.

The practical consequence of this evaluation was as follows:

> For us the bourgeoisie is not a stone dropping into an abyss, but a living historical force which struggles, manoeuvres, advances now on its right flank, now on its left. And only provided we learn to grasp politically *all* the means and methods of bourgeois society so as each time to react to them without hesitation or delay, shall we succeed in bringing closer that moment when we can, with a single confident stroke, actually hurl the bourgeoisie into the abyss.

At this time – November 1922 – Trotsky foresaw the coming to power of the Labour Party in Britain[17] and the Left Bloc[18] in France. It seems that his opponents resent the fact that he foresaw exactly what was to happen in these two countries, and to attack him they assert that he stated that this reformist era would last for a long time. Now here is what he said on the subject:

> In power, Clynes[19] or Caillaux-Blum[20] or Turati[21] would not be able to pursue a policy essentially different from the policy of Lloyd George, Bonar Law,[22] Poincaré or even Mussolini. But when they

> come to power the position of the bourgeoisie will be rendered even more difficult, even more inextricable than it is today. Their complete political bankruptcy – provided, naturally, we pursue correct tactics, that is, revolutionary, resolute and at the same time flexible tactics – can become laid utterly bare *in a very brief span of time. In a ruined and completely disorganised capitalist Europe after the illusions of war and victory, the pacifist illusions and the reformist hopes can come only as the ephemeral illusions of the death agony of the bourgeoisie*.[23]

The same debate is beginning again today, but with the key difference in the outcome that now it is the 'ultra-lefts' who are coming out on top, those 'ultra-lefts' who were defeated at the Third and Fourth Congresses of the Comintern, and who were more roughly treated by Lenin than by anyone else.

Trotsky persists in the method which consists of analysing the situation precisely and in detail, of determining the various trends working within the bourgeoisie, and of taking account of the facts so as to be in a position to elaborate the appropriate tactic for the struggle.

Now the two major facts dominating the present situation are the failure of October 1923 in Germany, and the massive development of American imperialism and a change in its policy of remaining an observer with regard to Europe.

For the ultra-lefts, these facts are unimportant. To take note of them implies that one no longer believes in the Revolution. It is enough to ignore them and to proceed by unsupported assertions. A revolutionary wave has been broken in Germany: so we must say that we are closer than ever to the Revolution. As for American imperialism, it is a harmless apparition which will soon vanish of its own accord. Everything that is not communist is fascist. The practical conclusion from these maunderings is that there is no other tactic but the putsch. All forms of positive, fruitful work which prepare the working class for the struggle and arm it solidly against the bourgeoisie are sabotaged, for example, the action taken to achieve trade union unity. This self-styled Leninism is the most vulgar, clownish parody of Leninism. It is a simplified communism, for the use of unsophisticated robots. And even if that is not the conscious intention, it can lead to nothing other than a putsch.[24]

The leadership of the Comintern seems to be aware of this danger. It wants to put on the brakes. But it is too late. It has been outflanked by the 'ultra-lefts' which it was responsible for putting in the leadership of its own sections. And the language it speaks is not always very different from theirs.

So who, on this key point, has revised Leninism? Who has provoked a brutal split in the tactic of the International? Who disowned the position taken by Lenin and Trotsky at the Third and Fourth Congresses? Who destroyed the fruitful work of these congresses?

One of the most notorious 'ultra-lefts', Béla Kun, was so roughly treated by Lenin at the Third Congress that it was believed that his rôle in the International was finished. He was definitively discredited. Now not only did he reappear at the Fifth Congress, but the leadership of the Comintern went so far as to give him the job of explaining what is Leninism, and producing propaganda for it!

Before closing this section on revolutionary prospects, I want to give a short extract from a speech Sokolnikov[25] has just delivered in Moscow on this subject. Sokolnikov is an opponent of Trotsky. He spoke as follows:

> When studying the present situation in Europe, it must be said that in the countries of Central Europe there has been a lull, which means an undoubted setback for the possibility of the proletariat seizing power. Until now, as a result of the antagonism prevailing between Germany on the one hand and France on the other, the situation was such in Central Europe, that it appeared that power could pass immediately into the hands of the proletariat. Now that there has been a temporary agreement between France and Germany, not only has the latter country's currency been stabilised, but also its entire economic situation, which has been followed by a certain industrial recovery. Wages are rising and workers, weary of the struggle, are repeating: 'We shall wait and see what we get from the Dawes Plan; perhaps we shall eat bread with butter on it, whereas hitherto we have eaten only crusts.' Thus there has been a certain relaxation of tension in Central Europe; the differences between Germany and France

> have been temporarily assuaged, and as a result the hopes of a revolution in Germany are on the retreat.

If Sokolnikov were a member of the French Communist Party, it is certain that as soon as he had spoken those words he would have been expelled as a Menshevik, a defeatist, a right-winger, etc.

As soon as you abandon the territory of hysterical demagogy, you speak as Trotsky does. But the conditions in which you do so deprive this belated agreement of any value. Only incoherence remains.

The Attitude of the Counter-Revolution to the Crisis

It is said that Trotsky, by his attitude, is providing ammunition for the bourgeoisie against the Russian Revolution; the counter-revolution is making common cause with him. That is stated in the resolution of the Central Committee.

As soon as a crisis breaks out in Soviet Russia, it is clear that the bourgeoisie is rejoicing. Not having succeeded by armed intervention, it can expect deliverance only from internal struggles which will weaken and then endanger the revolution.

Hitherto, it has always been disappointed, because Soviet Russia has emerged from debates and crises stronger and more united. If today its hope persists, it is solely because the crisis is continuing, and because it is resulting in a division and dispersal of forces. Now the revolution cannot allow itself the luxury of squandering its forces. It will only triumph for as long as it succeeds in pulling them together. That is what we tried to say, in a resolution, early in 1924, and if there had been an International it would have said the same thing. Those who didn't want to use such language, and who, on the contrary, demanded that the International should endorse the division of forces, are entirely responsible for the present situation. It is their policies which are reviving and maintaining, among the counter-revolutionary forces, the hope which they had lost.

Two European journals, among the most dogged and persevering enemies of Soviet Russia, express this attitude very well. The *Morning Post* writes in its editorial of 20 January: 'In the best interests of European civilisation it is, perhaps, a satisfaction to learn at last definitely that the triumvirate has won.'

It does not side with Trotsky, but with the troika against Trotsky, in 'the interests of European civilisation'.

The *Daily Mail*[26] notes with joy, on the same date, that 'Trotsky's summary ejection from the office of Soviet War Commissar shows that if "dog does not eat dog", Bolshevik devours Bolshevik'.

But what is much more serious than the bourgeoisie's estimate of our disputes, about which it can understand nothing, is the fact that reformist newspapers can write that in Soviet Russia, in order to increase production, it has been necessary to introduce piece-work, that coal is piling up on the ground at the pit-heads, that it is necessary to buy wheat abroad when it had been hoped to export it, that the number of unemployed is substantial, that the murders of party representatives by peasants are increasing in number, and that finally it has just been decided, in order to balance the budget, to re-establish the vodka monopoly – as in the days of Tsarism.[27]

That is what can disturb workers. That is what puts a dangerous weapon in the hands of the reformists, and it is insane to believe that it is enough to deny these facts in order to suppress the danger which they represent.

Neither Trotskyism nor Trotskyists

Trotskyism was invented against Trotsky, in order to fight him. His opponents have drawn up a detailed list of all the controversies which took place between Lenin and him since 1903. In vain, Trotsky replies that all that has been settled, has only an historical interest, and that it caused no problems for collaboration after 1917. It cuts no ice. Long articles are devoted to the theory of Permanent Revolution, and it continues to be asserted that Trotsky underestimates the rôle of the peasantry. The first point only interests those who have spare time and an interest in historical research. The second, however, is so immediately relevant that there will certainly be an opportunity to return to it. Stalin has just drawn attention to its seriousness, by defending the political concessions made to the peasantry, against criticisms emanating from working-class quarters. The peasants are irritated by an unbearable and stupid bureaucratism, and they want to be able to buy the manufactured items which they need. In the last resort, we are thus brought back to the problem of production, and to the struggle against the bureaucrats in the apparatus whose 'official optimism makes you feel sick', to quote Stalin's words. It therefore seems difficult to make Trotsky responsible for this state of affairs.

We decided to give our journal[28] the double hallmark 'Communist Syndicalist'. At a time when the conceptions which were at the very foundation of the International have been called into question, it is a good thing to make one's position clear.

We are not Trotskyists, since there is no such thing as 'Trotskyism', and I am quite sure that our 'Communist Syndicalist' position will not please Trotsky, and that he will criticise it severely.

We are not pessimists about the Russian Revolution and its propagation throughout the world. Even if the revolutionary upsurge has slowed down for a time in Europe, the influence of Soviet Russia in the East remains enormous and is increasing, and this significant fact continues to have ever more consequences.

But when our Russian comrades offer us nothing – us to whom they have given and taught so much – but a reminder of their old outdated polemics, plus the monopoly of vodka; at a time when a new offensive led by British imperialism is unleashed against Soviet Russia, they find nothing more urgent to do than to divide their forces and tear themselves to pieces; when, in the International, they want nothing but instruments to be manipulated, then we are alarmed. And there is no need to be a Trotskyist to think that such policies are a crime against the revolution.

David King Collection

Alfred Rosmer (1877–1964)

A Ridiculous Gesture

The Central Committee of the French Communist Party addresses a demand to Trotsky

Alfred Rosmer

From *La Révolution prolétarienne*, May 1925

Even though the leadership of the Communist Party has subjected them to a harsh regime, the readers of *L'Humanité* must have experienced real stupefaction on encountering, on 16 July last, over three columns of small text devoted to Eastman's book *Since Lenin Died*.[1] It concerns a book published in English in London three months ago. They had not read it and cannot have read it, and the members of the Central Committee of the French party who condemn it today have not read it either. So why this violent attack? The Communist Party really does not have all that many forces to defend the French proletariat and the Moroccan peasants against the shameless onslaught of banditry – just after the Great War for Justice! – prepared by the bankers' and military clique, or to protect the lowly militants on whom falls the vindictiveness of the government. The attack on the Rif is only a police action, but it has got to be particularly audacious for our imperialists to dare to attempt it at present, and it a shows great contempt for the working class' capacity for struggle.

However uninteresting in itself this diversionary move of

the French party might be, we must therefore look for its reasons. Has it perhaps seen in it a means of getting out of a seriously compromising situation? It has been discredited by its repeated mistakes, its inexperience, and its incapacity. The entry of three CGTU secretaries into the party at so badly chosen a time can only be explained by the need and urgency for a reinforcement. It describes how the bourgeois press confronted with Eastman's book 'has immediately understood all the benefit and all the use it could make of it [sic]'. Now it is a fact that the American and English bourgeois press has hardly spoken about our comrade's book. There were 'bolshevised' British and Americans who thought it necessary to kick up a fuss about it, beginning their shouting even before the book had appeared. Yet again the leadership of the French party has shown that anything it says is wrong and at cross purposes. It also claimed that we had put *Révolution prolétarienne* under Trotsky's patronage, which is quite simply absurd. We have already explained this in the second issue of the journal, and the communist syndicalist position we have taken up is in itself enough to rule out this fantasy, in which we see only too clearly its bad faith.

This resolution of a Central Committee talking about a book with which it was not acquainted proves only one thing: that the party leadership was lying when it denied the existence of Lenin's *Testament*. It is now proven that such a document exists, that the Central Committee of the Russian Communist Party did not think it wise to publish or communicate it to the sections of the Communist International, and that the entire discussion from now on must be about, not its existence, but its content.

But it is only too clear to us in the present case that the Central Committee of the French party does not act on its own volition. We are experiencing the same methods, the same means, and the same people as when the crisis in the Russian Communist Party was brought before the leadership of the French party. It is a new manifestation of 'Bolshevisation'.

The Pretext

In fact, Eastman's book is only a pretext. When the French comrades have a French translation at their disposal, they will see that it provided nothing new to those who had followed the debate in *Inprecorr* provoked by the crisis in the Russian Communist Party, which started two years ago. What they will find there is a methodical demonstration of the development of the crisis and an analysis of its causes, written by a man deeply attached to the Russian Revolution, who saw the crisis unfold before his own eyes. To make his analysis Eastman used official texts and documents as well as information he had collected in Russia that allowed him to clarify some points that remained obscure. It is true that the Central Committee of the Russian Communist Party, for very understandable reasons, has decided to keep secret some of its documents. A party which is in charge of and responsible for a revolution cannot hand over its archives to its enemies. But for this to be so, the leaders of this party must not be the first to place their archives in the public domain, and even more so they must not ask the sections of the Communist International to pronounce upon problems that only they can pass judgement on if they know everything about them. As things stand, Eastman's revelations cannot harm the Russian Revolution; they can only assist it, and that is the main motive behind his decision to publish the book.

The Real Reason

When we have Eastman's book in our hands, we very quickly understand why it has given rise to such violent anger within the Zinoviev-Kamenev group. Its account of the crisis, even with the new facts it provides, should have left them completely unmoved. Once again, all this has already been said, and since this group succeeded in taking over in the Russian Communist Party and the Communist International it could rest securely on its laurels. But the book provides in an appendix a hitherto unpublished letter by Lenin relating to the events of October 1917,[2] and it is the publication of this letter that is the real cause of the Zinoviev-Kamenev group's new outburst. The best thing, in the interests of the discussion itself, would be to reproduce the letter here. This is it. [We have omitted the text of Lenin's letter.[3]]

Readers of Lenin's book entitled *On the Road to Insurrection* published by the *L'Humanité* library,[4] have obviously noted that it turns out to be a little foreshortened, and leaves the impression that it is somehow incomplete. They can now finish it off with this letter – along with an article from *Pravda* of which Eastman also provides the text.[5] The decisive discussions which then took place within the Central Committee of the Bolshevik Party between those who supported the insurrection, led by Lenin, and its opponents, are in full daylight from now on.

'Bolshevisation' and Its Consequences

Some comrades might say: 'Why go over these debates again now? Would it not be better to devote all our efforts to organising the working class and putting it in a position to resist successfully the capitalist offensive that is threatening it on all sides?' Obviously that would be better. But when people have not hesitated to denounce Trotsky and all those siding with him in the Russian Opposition as Mensheviks, petit-bourgeois and (objectively!) counter-revolutionaries – which they obviously are not, there can be nothing wrong here, but on the contrary, a necessity, to show Zinoviev and Kamenev for what they are.

We have done everything on our part to prevent the crisis in the Russian Communist Party from being brought before the sections of the Communist International, and particularly before the French section. We said so in a resolution, the wisdom of which can now be recognised by anyone. Our position, which was required by the interests of the Russian Revolution and the entire workers' movement, was deemed unacceptable. It appears that the time for 'Bolshevising' had come, even though it had not been carried out while Lenin was alive, and had to wait until his death.

Today 'Bolshevisation' can be judged by its results: the 'Bolshevik' Germans have shown themselves quite capable of getting Hindenburg elected,[6] and their French co-thinkers, by their repeated stupidities, have succeeded in creating the impression that the strength of the working class was visibly weakened at a time when it was possible to organise it in a compact and resolute manner against the banditry in Morocco. Anyone can see who is helping the bourgeoisie – objectively!

The set-up in the Russian Communist Party and Bolshevisation in the Zinoviev manner are inseparable, and since disastrous methods are always being put into operation, Max Eastman's book comes at an opportune time. This is why the leadership of the French party does not want it to be read.

Its resolution, passed in complete ignorance of the case, smells from one end to the other, as if it is to be put on the *index prohibitorum*. It should not be read, and it should not be known.

Eastman's book should obviously be discussed. Different conclusions from his can be drawn on the basis of the facts he has collected. One can go much further. This is an inevitable consequence of the nature of the crisis of the Russian Communist Party. Those Russian comrades who still do not understand that the way they have carried on their discussions, and the conclusions they have given them, have been disastrous for the indispensable prestige of the Russian Revolution and the Communist International, are very short-sighted.

A Rosmer

The Reply of the 'Nucleus' to Trotsky's Two Requests

From *La Révolution prolétarienne*, no 10, October 1925

Under the heading of '*La Révolution prolétarienne*, condemned by Trotsky', *L'Humanité* for 1 October has published a 'Reply by the Central Committee of the Russian Communist Party to the Question Asked by the Central Committee of the French Communist Party Concerning the Monatte-Rosmer Journal'. You will find the text of this reply further on, just as it appeared in *L'Humanité*.

Trotsky asks two things of us at the end:

1. To close down *La Révolution prolétarienne* immediately.
2. To address an appeal against the decision to the Executive of the Communist International.

This is not the first time that such requests have been made of us. Communists from various countries, as well as Russian communists, have on several occasions urged us to appeal against our expulsion from the French Communist Party to the Executive of the Communist International. We replied with a refusal to one and all, and we have given them reasons, to our mind conclusive, for a well-considered decision.

Naturally, we attach a quite different importance to the criticism that Trotsky has made of our present position. We knew Trotsky in the difficult times of the Great War; he was with us from the end of 1914 to the end of 1916, the time when he was deported from France; we struggled together against the imperialists who had run amok, and his far-sightedness, his rare knowledge of the workers' movement in Europe, his intrepid courage and his revolutionary faith were of great help to us. Along with him we prepared the French proletariat to take part in the Zimmerwald and Kienthal conferences, which at the height of the war allowed working-class internationalism to be heard amid the bankruptcy of the Second International, and heralded the formation of the Communist International.

So when it is he who asks us to close down *La Révolution prolétarienne* and appeal to the International against our expulsion, we are obliged to examine yet again and more deeply the reasons that dictated our previous decision, as well as the criticisms he has made of us.

❖ ❖ ❖ ❖

So why have we not made an appeal to the International?

We could limit ourselves to replying that if we thought it useless to take our case before the International, it is because we thought that our expulsion was not an accidental or an isolated act; that it was part of what is called 'Bolshevisation'; that it could only take place by forcing the French communists to chose between the International and ourselves; that if it was a major error, it was perfectly possible for the International to come back to the affair without our having to ask for it; that by not intervening itself, it reinforced our conviction that our expulsion was desired by the Communist International itself, as some statements allowed us to understand; and finally that members of the French Communist Party had appealed in great numbers to the Communist International for it to recognise the dangers that the present leadership of the party was bringing to the French workers' movement, and that, whilst they received not the slightest response from Moscow, they have been threatened with expulsion by the same party leadership against whose malpractices they had appealed to the International.

But we think that these are only secondary matters, however important they may be, and that it would be much better to go straight to the heart of the matter.

We did not make an appeal because we are convinced that the cause of the serious mistakes made by the sections in the course of the last two years lies with the policy and methods pursued by the Communist International itself: and that this policy and these methods signify a break with the previous policy and methods, putting in question even the principles upon which the Communist International was based, and showing the beginning of a turn back towards Social Democracy.

Denunciations of an 'international Right' and the slogan of 'Bolshevising the Parties' made their appearance at the beginning of 1924, at a time when two important events – the October defeat in Germany and Lenin's death – coming at a time when his party was going through a serious internal crisis, weighed heavily upon the international workers' movement. It was a time when the greatest coolness was necessary.

Now it was after these two important events that we saw men trusted by the leadership appear in the International's sections, bearing the slogan of 'Bolshevisation' and denouncing an 'international Right'.

It seems that a state of panic had gripped the leadership of the Communist International, or was created by it. There was a new and serious situation that needed to be studied, and decisions that had to be taken after examining it. But study, discussion and examination were not wanted. It was necessary to condemn without delay the opposition that had appeared within the Russian Communist Party as counterrevolutionary, to place all the responsibility for the German setback upon some men who were identified as scapegoats, and to denounce the 'international Right', not the real one, which we know all too well, and which has been tolerated within the Communist International until now, and which is still there, but an imaginary 'Right', especially created for the occasion.

There was a state of siege in the International, and anyone who refused to give in to or share in this panic was broken. And it was no accident that the men who were removed from the leadership of the various parties were to be found among the very first workers to belong to the Communist International. Obviously, all of them disagreed with each other over more than one point. The only thing that united them was that they refused to be mere tools of the leadership of the Communist International, and wanted to examine the situation as communists, as had always been the case in the past.

The Fifth World Congress ratified this regime of a state of siege. It accepted as true Bolsheviks the leaderships of the parties assembled in the course of the crisis by overturning those that had been regularly elected by their congresses. To reinforce this Bolshevisation, however summary and rapid, it was decided to reorganise the communist parties on a factory cell basis.

The Third Congress had already voted for a resolution on this subject, a resolution concerning which Lenin had come up with some strong criticisms at the following congress. 'The resolution is an excellent one', he said, 'but I am sure that no foreigner can interpret it ... even if they read it, they will not understand it because it is too Russian. Not because it is written in Russian – it has been excellently translated into all languages – but because it is thoroughly imbued with the Russian spirit.'[1] And turning to the delegates, he called out, 'Do not imitate servilely. Study our revolution, disentangle its lessons, and incorporate its experience into your own respective movements.'[2]

Now what has been done at the Fifth Congress and since in all the various sections is only a servile copy of the organisation and practices of the Russian Communist Party. This is how you become a Leninist. Since it is difficult to understand deeply the two movements, the Russian and our own, and since it is a difficult task that requires ability and knowledge that these entirely new Leninists barely possess, they simply copy. They even take over the language, which leads them to use laughable jargon and a caricature of Leninism which is not only ridiculous, but a permanent menace to the working-class movement.

❖ ❖ ❖ ❖

We have just seen what has happened in Germany. After a year of intensive Bolshevisation, there has been an enormous decline in the influence of communism over the masses of workers and the well-nigh total elimination of communist influence in the trade unions. The neo-Leninists were shouting that the so-called Right wanted to liquidate Bolshevism. We can see that they have done it all too well themselves, not only in words, but in deeds.

The catastrophic situation created in Germany by the Ruth Fischer-Maslow group[3] has forced the Communist International to intervene and to undo, after an interval of a year, what it had done. This is already very serious. But what is much more so is that they had no right to ignore what was the policy of this group, and the results it produced. Ruth Fischer and Maslow are well known. We know what they represent, personally and politically. Their opposition to the united front tactic has been determined, and their ignorance of trade union work absolute. In the Berlin-Brandenburg organisation, where they had their influence, communists deserted the reformist trade unions, and since before the Fifth Congress the percentage of organised communists had fallen to a derisory figure.[4] It is therefore impossible to have any illusions about them, and even if all the same the Fifth Congress was a congress of fools, that is all the more reason why the workers should demand some explanation from the leadership of the Communist International.

Why, therefore, did the leadership of the Communist International put Ruth Fischer and Maslow at the head of the German Communist Party? Because it needed them to combat Radek and Brandler. The finishing off of these two comrades by Ruth Fischer at the Fifth Congress, with the approval and encouragement of the French delegation and the majority of the delegates who came there, not as communists, but as lackeys, was the linchpin of the essential work of the congress – a nauseating display of scalps.

And it did not stop there. Ruth Fischer was sent into several sections of the International, where, after the pre-eminent rôle she had played at the Fifth Congress, she appeared to be the ideal type of the new model Leninist. *L'Humanité* greeted her as a new Rosa Luxemburg.[5] And it is we who are accused of being enemies of the International, and of bringing its prestige and influence into disrepute!

Today, forced by an alarming situation, the Executive of the Communist International has taken away the leadership and central organ of the German Communist Party from the Ruth Fischer-Maslow group. But the damage they have done remains, and their successors will only find ruins, and an exhausted party, with what remains of it torn apart by internecine struggles.

Since the war, Germany has been by far the most susceptible country, where events move rapidly and have more resonance than elsewhere. And that is where the results of 'Bolshevisation' were to show themselves most rapidly. But they have also appeared elsewhere.

❖ ❖ ❖ ❖

Trotsky claims that our methods are tending to discredit the French Communist Party and undermine its authority and influence.

As for discrediting it, and undermining its authority and influence – and that of communism at the same time – the leadership of the French party is doing that. No declared enemy can ever equal them. There are no errors it has not committed, no true principles it has not badly applied, no good tactics it has not sabotaged, and no absurd slogans it has not launched.

Today's mistake makes one forget those of yesterday. But someone must have the patience to pull this leadership back to the beginning and cast a sharp eye over its illogical actions. He will find the lot: the most 'leftist' leftism and the shallowest opportunism, a rudimentary Blanquism and a sophisticated reformism, even when it does not acquire the dim justification of success: he will find the lot, apart from communism and an understanding of the workers' movement.

And by denouncing some of its mistakes, is it we who made them, or have we revealed them?

They are all too obvious, and the bourgeoisie, like its reformist allies, has not failed to notice them without our needing to tell them. If, for example, a great workers' demonstration is announced and nobody turns up, it is only too obvious, and there is no need to point out the setback for the bourgeoisie to work out its significance.

And it is no accident that this 'Bolshevisation' coincides with an obvious strengthening of the socialist and reformist trade union organisations. For it is an indisputable fact that in the course of this last year the Socialist Party has experienced a growth in the numbers of its supporters to the point at which its strength has overtaken that of the Communist Party, to which it had been inferior ever since the Congress of Tours. The Lafayette[6] CGT has also revived its declining influence and won back the ground it had lost, allowing it all the more effectively to fulfil its baleful rôle of bringing over part of the working class to the side of the left bourgeoisie. The newspaper of this social group, including state employees, artisans, petty traders and small peasants, which in

France amount to a serious political force, for so long lagging behind *L'Humanité*, has now completely overtaken it and has double its print run. It is now the most read and the most widespread political journal, which had been the position of *L'Humanité* ever since the war. The reformist leaders might well be scum. But they are not idiots, and they know all too well how to take advantage of our mistakes.

This decline of communism to the advantage of its opponents goes side by side with the reorganisation of the party on the lines of factory cells, allowing us to take stock of the way this operation has been carried out. There are a large number of cells – on paper. But bluff cannot paper over setbacks: on the contrary, it shows them up all the more clearly.

How was such a leadership able to continue? It is only because from the very beginning, soon after setting it up, the International put it under glass with a 'Do Not Touch' sign! Furthermore, it has understood only too well the advantages of the state of emergency. The nuisances were thrown out while others were tolerated but rendered impotent, denounced as counter-revolutionaries, and threatened with expulsion. Nobody had the right or the possibility of speaking, apart from itself. It is a long time since we heard that 'the first imbecile to come along can govern with a state of emergency': all this has provided a new and shining confirmation of this celebrated proverb.

The necessity of justifying the state of emergency they were in, and of making the members of the party accept an intolerable internal régime, has led the party leaders to absurd lengths. One day they are announcing the revolution: the next day it is fascism. Now the French workers have witnessed neither the revolution nor fascism. But they have experienced a new rise in banditry in Morocco which the government has easily been able to indulge in at its leisure, accumulating men, artillery, planes, tanks and ammunition. Merely by using despicable laws, it was able to control the anti-war propaganda that again showed the courage and devotion of ordinary party members.

❖ ❖ ❖ ❖

We know all too well that the work of the Russian Communist Party is being carried on amid enormous difficulties, and that it is a hard and immense task to cut a way through for the revolution. But it heaped up difficulties for itself the day it asked the sections of the Communist International to pronounce upon the crisis it was going through without their understanding it, whilst dictating to them the response they should make. And being the dominant party in the International, as is natural, the responsibility for the policy followed by the Communist International, carried out in the sections in its name, which it certainly never wanted, devolves upon it, along with 'Bolshevisation', with its disastrous consequences. And having done more by its example than any theoretician could to reconcile the revolutionary syndicalists with the idea of the political party, it is now in the process of once more driving them away. We once saw it in a heroic light, as a sure and capable guide for the working class. But this latest crisis, by laying bare the shady tricks, the wire-pulling and the manoeuvres, has cast a baleful light on its hitherto invisible internal structure. It has shown its bad side, and the caricatures of Bolshevik parties that have begun to be set up everywhere in the International have only aggravated the disquiet and the unease.

Here we are touching upon a most important point, at least as far as France is concerned, of the present situation.

We ought to remember that France is an example of a country where before the war the revolutionary workers' movement was organised and developed, not only without the help of the political parties, but against them. The workers were able to gain valuable experience during that time. They saw political parties of all sorts and colours developing, from the reddest to the palest.

When the various socialist sects poisoned the life of the trade unions, they and the anarchists were rather rudely requested to take their arguments and behaviour elsewhere. That was at the Amiens trade union congress.[7] If Ruth Fischer has shown that she understands nothing of the trade union movement, then Treint and his ilk understand it no better, and are no better acquainted with it. We have just seen what they have done with the unity of the trade unions. They sabotaged a movement that stood out in their favour and have messed up the exceptionally favourable situation created by the formation of a left within the Amsterdam International,[8] just as they had previously completely compromised the tactic of the united front. They have now, by their stupid methods, awoken the old suspicions among the workers as regards political parties. And if nothing changes, we can see that the time is not far off when a sort of mood not very different from what existed about 1906 will show itself in the trade unions, and one fine day the angry workers will cry out 'To hell with your political party. Go and make your criticisms elsewhere, and leave us to get on with our work.' So then we will be back to the prewar position, and all the advantage that could and should have been gained from the Russian Revolution will run the risk of being completely lost.

The present situation in France may be different from the one so starkly revealed in Germany, which provoked an intervention from the Executive of the Communist International. It may appear to be less catastrophic. But it is no less serious.

The cases of both France and Germany are quite enough to show, in deeds, the results of 'Bolshevisation'. Other countries provide similar examples, and if we examine the situation in its entirety, we must recognise a weakening of the sections of the Communist International, and an evident decline in the prestige and influence of the Communist International among the European working class. On the other hand, the social democrats and reformists are consolidating and reinforcing their positions by skilful tactics, by taking advantage of all our mistakes. The bourgeoisie, demoralised and almost desperate in the aftermath of the war, has recovered the initiative, brought under control the inflation that gave rise to so many troubles, and succeeded in creating a state of relative stabilisation. Obviously we do not want to say that it is saved. As long as the Russian Revolution exists, it created by its very existence a threat to the bourgeoisie of every country, and fresh revolutionary opportunities can still arise. We are limiting ourselves to sketching the picture as it is at present. And if we are not inclined to offload the entire responsibility for this setback on the leadership of the Communist International, we are still convinced that it has some responsibility.

'Bolshevisation' was the departure point for a break with the previous policy of the Communist International, and it amounts to a return to social democracy. It has substituted a sickly and extravagant boastfulness for revolutionary realism. Social democracy was not short of revolutionary rhetoric. So we get things written like this: 'It is necessary to distinguish between the right, the so-called right, and the elements of which it is composed.' If a revolution could be made with words, we would certainly have seen several of them in the course of last year.

At the end of a flamboyant speech delivered by Ruth Fischer in the Reichstag, one of her supporters said to one of us: 'Well and good, there is something changed in Germany. There is now a real Bolshevik party, as you can see!' Mouthing off in parliament and sabotaging trade union work, that too is a manifestation of pure social democracy.

The man best qualified, at least by his position, to speak in the name of the Communist International,[9] writing to a French communist, said that he was not surprised by the attitude of Monatte and Rosmer, due to the fact that they had only come late to the party, but that he did not understand a similar attitude on the part of a man who had belonged to the Socialist Party before the war. If it is an original sin having been a revolutionary syndicalist, and it is better to have had a long stay in the social democracy, then we must admit that our expulsion was justified. This new cast of mind has just surfaced at the congress of the American Communist Party, where Foster and his friends have been accused of wanting to 'trade unionise' the party.[10] This open warfare on comrades who came from revolutionary syndicalism nearly provoked a split, only avoided with some difficulty.

Social democracy possessed, and still possesses, imposing 'apparatuses'. Those of the communist parties are no smaller, and what is worse in their case is that they are out of all proportion to the real membership of these parties. The number of full-timers is growing at an alarming rate, and the meetings, conferences and as a result the entire life of the party are completely warped.

❖ ❖ ❖ ❖

All these questions merit a much longer treatment. We can only point them out in all too cursory a way. But we have said enough to allow the reasons for our attitude to be understood, why we did not appeal to the International yesterday, why we will not appeal to it today, and why we cannot close down *La Révolution prolétarienne*.

At the beginning of this change in the Communist International, it was said that 'this is a passing folly, an accident: it will end with the cause that gave birth to it. It cannot last.' But it has continued, and it is still going on. The German affair, like the brake put on expulsions, only marks a brief pause. We are not too happy to have been right, and nothing would delight us more than to see the International return to the creative policy typical of it and which so powerfully helped the working class of every country. If we allowed ourselves to be influenced by anger and false pride we should very much be lowering ourselves to the level of those who desired our expulsion from the Communist Party. Every time the Communist International gives us the opportunity, and every time it proposes a correct tactic we will give it our utmost support, as we have done for trade union unity.

We laid out our position in a perfectly clear way in our second letter to the Communist Party members. We did not for a minute envisage creating a new party: on the contrary, we immediately asked our friends to remain in the Communist Party. As for ourselves, who have been expelled, we will continue the work outside that we were doing inside the party, as we have always done. We did not come to the working-class movement yesterday, and to the extent to which the past can guarantee the future, we can provide this guarantee. And if anybody says that it is not possible to be outside the International and the party without being against them, we reply that many examples prove that this hasty judgement is baseless.

The Communist International was set up by a regrouping of the revolutionary forces under the impact of the war and the inspiration of the Russian Revolution. Social democrats, revolutionary syndicalists and anarchists, who had to revise their previous views, came together around a common platform. Lenin said: 'Let us discard our dirty social democratic linen!' But today no one wants to be a communist any more, but an 'Old Bolshevik'. The structure that was constructed in 1919 and consolidated in 1920 has been broken, and the forces that went up to make it have been dispersed. The natural consequence is that today there is room for a revolutionary outside the Communist International. And another consequence is that a magazine like *La Révolution prolétarienne* is a necessary organ. Since we cannot speak out in the party or the International, we must speak outside, for there are things that must be said, not out of any desire for empty polemics, but in the interests of the working class itself. *La Révolution prolétarienne* is a refuge for sincere revolutionaries who can no longer bear the stifling atmosphere in the party, and a defence against the sabotaging of the working-class movement.

We are as committed today as we were yesterday to the Russian Revolution, and just as keen to understand its lessons and profit from its teachings, and we know that we have not deviated from the line of conduct that we marked out for ourselves. We did not abandon the working class during the hard test of the war; we struggled with it against the leaders who betrayed it. We will be with it tomorrow, on the right side of the barricades: but we are not sure that we will find there all those who have expelled us.

The Nucleus of *La Révolution prolétarienne*[11]

PS: The party leadership has not failed to supply a comic note to these important matters. In a short cover note to Trotsky's reply, it announced that it was going to correct some mistakes in understanding committed by him as regards the rôle played by Monatte and Rosmer during the war and in the development of the Communist Party. No doubt a latecomer might be prepared to accept that it was better to be sent on an official mission to Mussolini than to have gone to Zimmerwald, and that to become a perfect Leninist in this way it was the best thing out to have helped Frossard's intrigues against the Communist International from the very start, or only to have come over to the Russian Revolution in 1924, which, happily, would have able to wait until then.

Notes

How I Came to be Regarded as a 'Trotskyist' – Boris Souvarine

1. André Breton (1896–1966) was a poet, critic, Dadaist and founder of the surrealist movement. On his visit to Coyoacan, see *Revolutionary History*, Volume 7, no 2, 1999, pp203ff (translator's note).
2. André Thirion (1907–?), a surrealist during the 1920s and 1930s and Communist Party organiser in Nancy and then Paris, was expelled from the French Communist Party in 1931, and later became a Gaullist (translator's note).
3. Eugène Grindel, known as Paul Eluard (1895–1952) was a surrealist poet, and a staunch defender of the Moscow trials, although he did not join the PCF until 1942 (*Revolutionary History*, Volume 7, no 2, 1999, p208). Pierre Naville (1904–1993) was a surrealist in the 1920s and later leader of the French Trotskyist movement (see LD Trotsky, 'Fighting Against the Stream', April 1939, *Writings of Leon Trotsky, 1938–39*, New York, 1974, p255; *Revolutionary History*, Volume 7, no 2, 1999, pp140–5). Louis Aragon (1897–1982) was a poet who joined the PCF in 1927, and defended the enormities of the Stalinist regime throughout the 1930s. Raymond Queneau (1903–1976) was a well-known writer. Benjamin Péret (1899–1959) was a surrealist poet who became a Trotskyist, and later fought in the Spanish Civil War (translator's note).
4. Simone Weil (1909–1943) was a philosopher who supported various oppositional groups in the 1930s (translator's note).
5. Samuel Rosenstock, called Tristan Tzara (1896–1963), was a Dadaist poet and essayist and apologist for Stalin (translator's note).
6. These letters were published in *Contributions à l'histoire du Comintern*, edited by Jacques Freymond, Librairie Droz, Geneva, 1965 (author's note). See LD Trotsky, 'Six Years of the Brandlerites', 25 April 1929; 'The Basic, Fundamental Question', 10 May 1929; 'A Man Overboard', 3 July 1929; 'To the Marx and Lenin Circle', 22 August 1929, *Writings of Leon Trotsky, 1929*, New York, 1975, pp111–6, 128–9, 188–9, 246 (translator's note).
7. Pierre Pascal (1890–1983) spent 17 years in Russia. He was later Professor of Russian Literature and Civilisation at the Sorbonne. Pierre Kaan (1903–1945) had assisted Souvarine in editing *L'Humanité* before his expulsion from the PCF. He was deported to Germany during the Second World War, and never came back. Othon Maschl, known as Lucien Laurat (1898–1973), was an Austrian Communist who had been appointed as a professor of economics at the Communist University of the National Minorities of the East due to Souvarine's influence. He continued to be a well-known Marxist writer in the 1930s. Albert Georges Aimé, called Aimé Patri (1904–1983) was a philosophy student active in the Trotskyist movement in the 1930s. He later became teacher of philosophy in secondary schools. Jean-Jacques Dwelshauvers, known as Jacques Mesnil (1872–1940), was an anarchist and later a communist journalist and art historian who collaborated with the *Bulletin communiste*, *Vie ouvrière* and *Révolution prolétarienne*. Jean-Jacques Soudeille (1899–1951) was a commercial employee and left-wing activist (translator's note).
8. Karl Korsch (1889–1961), a prominent Marxist theorist, was expelled from the German Communist Party for 'Trotskyism' in 1929. See his *Marxism and Philosophy* (London, 1970) and *Three Essays on Marxism* (London, 1971). Joaquín Maurín (1876–1973) was the leader of the Spanish Bloque Obrera y Campesino, and later of the POUM. Cf Manuel Grossi, *The Asturian Uprising*, London, 2000, pp26–9 (translator's note).

9. Cf below, p239, n145 (translator's note).
10. Claude Henri de de Rouvry, Comte de Saint-Simon (1760–1875), was a French utopian thinker (translator's note).
11. The ruling class of ancient Rome (translator's note).
12. The English edition was published by Thames and Hudson in 1957 (translator's note).
13. Karl Kautsky (1854–1938) was the foremost theoretician of the Second International. See *The Dictatorship of the Proletariat*, Michigan, 1964, p85 (translator's note).
14. The lower classes in ancient Rome (translator's note).
15. A reprint of this *Bulletin communiste* was published in 1967, by Feltrinelli Reprints, Milan (author's note).
16. Felix Edmondovich Dzerzhinsky (1877–1926) was a Polish revolutionary, and head of the secret police after the Russian Revolution. He died of a heart attack after denouncing the Russian Opposition (translator's note).
17. LD Trotsky, *Terrorism and Communism*, London, 1975, p153 (translator's note). And to think that it was I who published this book in French in 1920. But as Michelet said when writing the preface to the republication of his *Histoire romaine* in 1866: 'I am not among those who blush at having been young.' (author's note)
18. LD Trotsky, 'Letter to the Plenum of the Central Committee', 15 January 1925, *The Challenge of the Left Opposition, 1923–25*, New York, 1975, p305 (translator's note).
19. LD Trotsky, 'Speech to the Seventh (Enlarged) Plenum of the ECCI', 9 December 1926, *The Challenge of the Left Opposition*, 1926–28, New York, 1980, p176 (translator's note).
20. LD Trotsky, *The Permanent Revolution*, New York, 1931 (translator's note).
21. LD Trotsky, 'More on the Suppression of Kronstadt', 6 July 1938, in VI Lenin and LD Trotsky, *Kronstadt*, New York, 1979, pp95–7 (translator's note).
22. LD Trotsky, 'A Last Warning', 5 March 1921, *The Military Writings and Speeches of Leon Trotsky*, Volume 4, London, 1981, p285 (translator's note).
23. See below, pp214–20 (translator's note).
24. Trotsky has doubtless not read his books again, such as *Europe and America* (1926) and *Where is Britain Going?* (1926). He would have found something there to make him more modest (author's note). *Europe and America* consists of two speeches delivered in 1924. It was reprinted as a pamphlet in 1926 (English edition, New York, 1971). *Where is Britain Going?* takes up pages 6–123 of Volume 2 of *Trotsky's Writings on Britain*, London, 1974 (translator's note).
25. On this subject, cf my more explicit article, 'Staline et Trotsky', *Le Contrat Social*, no 3, Paris, May 1960 (author's note). See I Deutscher, *The Prophet Unarmed*, Oxford, 1978, pp137–8; 'Trotsky and the Suppression of Lenin's Testament', *Solidarity*, Volume 6, no 6, pp17–25. Trotsky's remark to Sklyansky about Stalin is reported in *My Life*, New York, 1960, p512. On Trotsky's failure to propose Stalin's resignation as General Secretary, see *Inprecorr*, no 64, 17 November 1927, pp1428–9; Max Eastman, *Love and Revolution*, New York, 1964, p351 (translator's note).
26. LD Trotsky, 'The Lessons of October', 1923, *The Essential Trotsky*, London, 1963, pp152–5 (translator's note).
27. The reference is to Ramon Mercader. See below, pp 25–28 (translator's note).
28. Benedetto Croce (1866–1952) was a historian and humanist, as well as being Italy's leading philosopher and a symbol of the Italian opposition to Mussolini (translator's note).

29. Souvarine is being dishonest here. Trotsky actually wrote: 'Permissible and obligatory are those and only those means ... which unite the revolutionary proletariat, fill their hearts with irreconcilable hostility to oppression, teach them contempt for official morality and its democratic echoers, imbue them with consciousness of their own historic mission, raise their courage and spirit of self-sacrifice in the struggle. Precisely from this it flows that not all means are permissible.' (LD Trotsky, *Their Morals and Ours*, London, 1974, pp36–7)
30. Op cit, especially pp6, 9, 13, 21–3, 36–7 (translator's note).
31. Giuseppe Fiori, *Vita di Antonio Gramsci*, Bari, 1966. Togliatti's interception of the letter is also described by Alberto Pozzolini, *Antonio Gramsci: An Introduction to His Thought*, London, 1970, pp45–6 (translator's note).
32. See *Stalin: A Critical Survey of Bolshevism*, Plon, Paris, 1935. Expanded edition, Champ Libre editions, 1977 (author's note).

Second Letter to the Members of the Communist Party. The Reply of the Three Members – Victor Delagarde, Pierre Monatte, Alfred Rosmer

1. Jacques Doriot (1898–1945) had been leader of the Communist Youth, and as mayor of St Denis in the 1930s broke with the PCF over its refusal to offer a united front to the SFIO. He later set up a semi-fascist organisation and collaborated with the Germans in the Second World War.
2. VI Lenin, 'The Tasks of the Youth Leagues: Speech Delivered at the Third All-Russia Congress of the Russian Young Communist League', 2 October 1920, *Collected Works*, Volume 31, Moscow, 1966, p288.
3. Léon Daudet (1868–1942) was a royalist writer, and Alexandre Millerand (1859–1943) was notorious for being the first French socialist to sit in a bourgeois cabinet, along with Gallifet, the butcher of the Commune.
4. *Action française* was a royalist journal, *Le Peuple* was the newspaper of the Socialist Party, *Le Libertaire* that of the Anarchists, and *Le Quotidien* was a Paris newspaper during 1923–26, which supported the Cartel des Gauches in 1924.
5. See above, p50.
6. Paul Léon Cadeau (1890–1978) was secretary of the CGTU in 1922, and a member of the Executive Committee of the PCF in 1924. A supporter of Treint and Girault, he left the PCF some time between 1928 and 1930.
7. Eugène Pierre Besnard (1886–1947), a member of the railwaymen's federation, replaced Monatte as General Secretary of the Comités syndicalistes révolutionnaires, the main left opposition to Jouhaux in the CGT. Guillaume Jacques Verdier was a metal workers' leader who was also on the CSR executive. He opposed the First World War, and afterwards joined the PCF, but was expelled in 1921.
8. Claude Joseph Calzan (1876–1939) was Secretary of the Rhône federation of the SFIO, and an opponent of the First World War. He continued in this capacity in the PCF, and as a supporter of Treint and Girault he replaced Souvarine as editor of the *Bulletin communiste* in 1924.
9. Léon Ilbert was secretary of the Seine Federation of the PCF. He had been found guilty of embezzling money by a control commission, and removed from his post. The verdict was quashed due to the intervention of Suzanne Girault.
10. When Parvus, who had supported Germany during the First World War, applied to join the Bolsheviks in November 1917, Lenin instructed Radek to reply that 'the cause of the revolution should not be touched by dirty hands' (ZAB Zeman and WB Scharlau, *The Merchant of Revolution: The Life of Alexander Israel Helphand (Parvus), 1867–1924*, London, 1965, p246).

11. Victor Méric (1876–1933), a journalist who opposed the First World War, and Raoul Verfeuil (1887–1927), a postal worker and journalist, were supporters of the right in the PCF, along with Sellier and Fabre. They were expelled in the autumn of 1922. See LD Trotsky, 'Letter to Comrade Kerr', 6 June 1922, *The First Five Years of the Communist International*, Volume 2, London, 1974, p141.
12. Gustave Hervé (1871–1944) was a socialist of the extreme left, famous for his anti-militarism and his verbal extravagances. He became an extreme patriot in 1914, and later moved in the direction of fascism.
13. Pierre Berthelin was a schoolteacher and an active trade unionist in the Paris federation of the PCF. Treint attacked him in 'Lutter sans cesse pour la bolchèvisation', *Cahiers du bolchèvisme*, 26 December 1924. He was expelled in January 1925.
14. *Le Matin* was a bourgeois paper with a right-wing bias.
15. VI Lenin, 'One Step Forward, Two Steps Back', May 1904, *Collected Works*, Volume 7, Moscow, 1961, p208.
16. Reproduced in full in A Rosmer, *Le Mouvement ouvrier pendant la première guerre mondiale*, Volume 1, Paris, 1993, pp177–80.

About the Final 'Warning' Given to Trotsky – Alfred Rosmer

1. The notion of 'social fascism' was developed, well before the 'Third Period', by Zinoviev in 1924 (see P Broué, *Histoire de l'internationale communiste*, Paris, 1997, p381).
2. The paper of the Italian Socialist Party.
3. The paper of the German Social Democratic Party.
4. Pierre Renaudel (1871–1935) was the leader of the right wing of the SFIO.
5. Salomon Grumbach (1884–1952) was a supporter of the right wing of the SFIO.
6. A Paris newspaper during 1923–36; the organ of the SFIO-Radical electoral alliance in 1924.
7. This statement by Bukharin is quoted in Max Shachtman's 'The Struggle for the New Course', in LD Trotsky, *The New Course*, Ann Arbor, 1965, pp172–3.
8. In his speech to the Thirteenth Congress of the Russian Communist Party, Trotsky cited these statements by Bukharin. *Correspondance Internationale*, 19 July 1924, gave the text of Trotsky's speech and *Bulletin Communiste*, 4 July, reproduced it (pp639ff). But look for Bukharin's comments in the *Bulletin Communiste*. You won't find them. Doubtless they were considered too embarrassing. [Rosmer's note]
9. I am using this term because it is current in the International. It indicates the triumvirate of Zinoviev, Stalin and Kamenev, who, having three votes out of seven settled in advance, have a preponderant influence in the Political Bureau. [Rosmer's note]
10. It will be recalled that during the debates in 1923, Ossinsky had already proposed a similar measure. He was immediately described as a Menshevik, petit-bourgeois, 'objective' counter-revolutionary etc, etc. [Rosmer's note]
11. SI Kanachnikov (1879–1940) was a violent polemicist, a supporter of Zinoviev, and later ambassador to Prague; he was shot by Stalin.
12. LD Trotsky, 'Letter to the Plenum of the Central Committee', 15 January 1925, *The Challenge of the Left Opposition, 1923–25*, New York, 1975, pp304–8.
13. Nikolai Yudenich (1862–1933) was a Tsarist general who attacked Petrograd during the Russian Civil War; Admiral Alexander Vasiliyevich Kolchak (1873–1920) advanced upon the Bolsheviks along the Trans-Siberian Railway; and General Anton Ivanovich Denikin (1872–1947) marched north against them from the Crimea.

14. A reference to Lenin's 'Testament'; *Collected Works*, Volume 36, Moscow, 1966, p595.
15. VI Lenin, *Collected Works*, Volume 45, Moscow, 1970, p607.
16. We should note in passing the methods used at that time in the Comintern, in absolute contrast to those resorted to today. Lenin never dreamt of 'preparing' the sections in order to guarantee the unanimity of the congress in advance. The delegates came to Moscow, where they had time to defend their point of view in the course of a full debate. [Rosmer's note]
17. The general election on 6 December 1923 gave Labour 191 seats against 259 Conservative; on 22 January 1924, Labour formed a minority government.
18. In May 1924, the Bloc (or Cartel) des Gauches, based on an alliance of the SFIO and Radicals, was successful in the French elections, and Edouard Herriot became Prime Minister.
19. Joseph Robert Clynes (1869–1949) was the leader of the Gasworkers Union and later a right-wing Labour MP, an ally of Ramsay MacDonald.
20. Joseph Caillaux (1863–1944) was a French right-wing politician and Finance Minister; Léon Blum (1872–1950) was a leader of the SFIO and leader of the Popular Front government of 1936.
21. Filippo Turati (1857–1932) was the leader of the right wing of the Italian Socialist Party.
22. David Lloyd George (1863–1945) was coalition Prime Minister in Britain for the second half of the First World War. Andrew Bonar Law (1858–1923) was leader of the Conservatives in the House of Commons, and briefly 'the unknown prime minister' after Lloyd George had been ousted from power.
23. These extracts in fact come from a text called 'Political Perspectives' published in *Bolshevik* after the Fourth Congress (LD Trotsky, *The First Five Years of the Communist International*, Volume 2, New York, 1953, pp297–303).
24. A secondary but significant fact is characteristic of the method of working of our 'Leninists'. To attack Trotsky on the question of prospects and of American imperialism, they criticised a report he made to the congress of veterinary surgeons. They made the criticisms first, and then finally published the text of the speech. Now the text that they published was not that of the report to the veterinary congress. It was a speech delivered two weeks later, to a meeting called by the Society of the Friends of the Faculty of Sciences, as is indicated in the speech itself. So they have not even read the text which they are criticising and publishing. [Rosmer's note]
25. Grigorii Brilliant, known as Sokolnikov (1886–1938) was an economist and a Bolshevik from 1905 onwards, and a supporter of Zinoviev. He was executed after the Trial of the 17.
26. Under the headline 'TROTSKY OF THE EVIL EYES'.
27. The Tsarist authorities abolished the vodka monopoly during the First World War, before the revolution. But as Trotsky wrote: 'The circumstance that the "drunkards" budget was abandoned during the imperialist war does not alter the fundamental fact that the abolition of the system by which the country encouraged people to drink is one of the iron assets of the revolution.' (LD Trotsky, 'Vodka, the Church and the Cinema', 12 July 1923, *Problems of Everyday Life*, New York, 1973, p31)
28. *La Révolution prolétarienne*, which was founded in January 1925 by Monatte, Rosmer, Delagarde, Chambelland, Louzon, Charbit and Godonnèche.

A Ridiculous gesture – Alfred Rosmer

1. Max Eastman, *Since Lenin Died*, Labour Publishing Company, London, 1925. Eastman's reply to Trotsky's repudiation of his book, 'A Response to Trotsky', was published in *The Plebs*, Volume 17, no 10, October 1925, pp393–8.
2. Eastman, op cit, pp137–40.
3. It would take up space needlessly to reproduce it here. It can be consulted in VI Lenin, 'Letter to Bolshevik Party Members', 18 October 1917, *Collected Works*, Volume 26, Moscow, 1964, pp216–9.
4. A collection of Lenin's articles from 1917.
5. Eastman, op cit, pp140–1. See VI Lenin, 'From the Central Committee of the Russian Social-Democratic Labour Party (Bolsheviks)', 5–6 November 1917, *Collected Works*, Volume 26, Moscow, 1964, pp304–6.
6. Field Marshal Paul von Beneckendorff und von Hindenburg (1847–1934) was the titular head of the German army during the First World War. He was elected president of the Weimar Republic in 1925, in spite of being an opponent of both democracy and republics.

The Reply of the 'Nucleus' to Trotsky's Two Requests

1. VI Lenin, 'Five Years of the Russian Revolution and the Prospects of the World Revolution: Report to the Fourth Congress of the Communist International', 13 November 1922, *Collected Works*, Volume 33, Moscow, 1966, p420.
2. No such remark appears in the text of the speech as printed (n1, above), nor in Rosmer's eyewitness report in *Lenin's Moscow*, London, 1971, p170. But it has all the marks of an extempore statement, and may well be genuine. It certainly conveys Lenin's sense.
3. For Fischer and Maslow, see above, p64 n14. In Berlin, they encouraged communists to leave the reformist trade unions and set up their own red unions. All Brandler's supporters, who were the party's trade union activists, were removed from their positions in the party.
4. There were 88 KPD delegates at the ADGB congress of 1922, but only four in 1925. KPD membership itself fell from 300,000 to 121,000 between April and December 1924.
5. This was the image projected by Radek. See Rosa Leviné-Meyer, *Inside German Communism*, London, 1977, p65. This is doubly ironic, as Luxemburg herself thoroughly detested him.
6. Marie-Joseph-Paul-Yves-Roche-Gilbert du Motier, Marquis de Lafayette (1757–1834) was commander of the National Guard in the French Revolution, and controlled the police. His guard fired on a crowd in the Champ de Mars in 1791 demanding the abdication of the king, since he had entered into secret intrigues with the royalists. His name is used here to imply that the CGT of Jouhaux was acting as a police force for the employers.
7. The CGT Congress of Amiens in October 1906 adopted a charter which declared its independence from 'all political schools'.
8. The International Federation of Trade Unions, to which belonged the British TUC, was re-established after the war at a conference in Amsterdam, and so is generally called the Amsterdam International, as opposed to the communist-dominated Red International of Labour Unions (Profintern). The reference to a left developing in the IFTU is to the formation of the Anglo-Soviet Trade Union Committee in May 1925.
9. Obviously Guralsky. See above, p61 n17.
10. The Foster-Cannon faction took control of the American Communist Party in 1923, in opposition to the Labor Party orientation of the Pepper/Pogany group.

Pepper, who was assumed to enjoy the support of the Comintern, sought to label his opponents as syndicalists, since part of their faction was made up of the previous Trade Union Education League.

11. 'Nucleus' is the term given to those revolutionary syndicalists around *La Vie ouvrière* led by Rosmer and Monatte who had opposed the First World War in 1914.

Part Three

On the Planet Without a Visa (1929–1940)

Alfred Rosmer

Trotsky in hunting outfit at Samanli, Turkey, November 1931

Chapter One: In Turkey

On this inhospitable planet Trotsky was to live for 11 years an always threatened existence under the surveillance of governments which never accorded him any more than temporary residential rights, whilst Stalin in person directed a numerous special police force which included ordinary secret agents reinforced by provocateurs and spies in the opposition groups and professional killers who were to carry out murders in Switzerland, France, Spain and America. Trotsky noted and recorded this combination of repressive measures without ever complaining. He had chosen a merciless and unyielding struggle, and he knew what it meant.

The decision that imposed exile upon him had remained secret until the time Stalin judged it necessary to prepare working-class and socialist circles to receive news that would leave opinion incredulous. The campaign began whilst the train carrying Trotsky from Alma Ata to Istanbul halted in the region of Kursk. It was developed fully in France: Trotsky had spent the first two years of the First World War there, and had gained some personal support among socialists, syndicalists and anarchists who had met him in groups opposing the war and had appreciated his qualities as a militant. The task of watching the development of the French Communist Party had been his particular responsibility in the Communist International.[1]

It was only three days after he had left Alma Ata on 25 January 1929 that the first news report was put out by *L'Humanité* in the shape of a long dispatch from Moscow published under the heading '*Pravda* Reveals the Reasons for the Measures Taken Against the Trotskyists'. In the course of 1928, the report said, they had transformed their illegal anti-party group into an illegal organisation, hostile to Soviet power; and, in order to rule out any discussion in advance, the question was posed in this way: either with Trotsky, or with the proletarian dictatorship. The first article appeared on 1 February as an unsigned editorial: it obviously came from Moscow. 'Socialists and Trotskyists', it read, 'are at the service of the counter-revolution.' Short reports appeared in the following days; in accordance with their customary method they reported that 'resolutions have been passed throughout the Soviet Union against the Trotskyist Opposition'. However, other reports confirmed the existence of the grain crisis that this same opposition had constantly shown would inevitably happen if the Stalinist leadership continued with its agricultural policy. And at the same time that the press was made to say all was well, the government had to restore bread rationing. Finally, on 17 February, a short report appeared in the corner of the third page of *L'Humanité*; it was dated 16 February, Constantinople: 'Trotsky, who arrived with his family in Constantinople during the evening of the 12th, has been greeted by the personnel of the Soviet Consulate. He will be the guest of the Soviet Consulate, where he is at present staying with his family.' One would think that it was not a question of deporting a 'counter-revolutionary', but of an official visit of a the Soviet leader. The first signed article published by *L'Humanité* on the 22nd was by Maurice Thorez, which was not accidental, because Thorez had been a Trotskyist in 1924, and had backed the French edition of *The New Course*, a collection of Trotsky's main articles.[2] The tone was to change considerably as things went on, but it was still necessary then to write that 'Trotsky was one of the revolution's good workers'. The events concerned were still too close and the habit of using the enormous and unbelievable lie had not yet taken over.

But the preparations were complete when Trotsky arrived in Istanbul; the Tass Agency broadcast to the four corners of the world the Stalinist explanation for his exile: the Trotskyists were allies of the counter-revolution. What could we reply, and where could we reply? The various oppositional groups that then existed barely managed to publish monthly bulletins. An unhoped-for opportunity was to allow Trotsky to give an immediate reply that was to be widely broadcast; an American press agency proposed that he write a series of articles, which was to give him the opportunity to reach those whom the Tass Agency had deceived about the meaning of the events. And there was something else: all sorts of rumours about his exile were going round, among others the claim that it was only a stunt by the leaders to spread Soviet propaganda in the east. Trotsky therefore accepted the proposal made to him, but he placed conditions upon it: that the articles he would write had to be printed without any changes and omissions, just as he wrote them, or not at all. The agency's 'dollars' incidentally allowed the family to take up residence in the land of their exile. Trotsky had left Russia without any money. The 'foreign gold deposits' are a myth; it had been a long time since he had seen either gold or silver. His life had always been simple, sometimes difficult, and he did not know the prices in America for these types of articles, and accepted what was offered him without debate.

However, the agency was not the 'hit' he was counting on, at least in Europe: there were fewer buyers there for the articles than he had envisaged, and some of the newspaper editors who had taken out an option on them gave them up when they became acquainted with the articles. Seeing Trotsky above all as a polemicist, they expected a scathing denunciation which, by including Stalin, would attack the regime itself. But the articles were as impersonal as possible; it appeared as if their author was determined in them to keep to a tone of dialogue, obviously not Platonic, but always on the level of ideas.

It was a detached exposition, a reply to the question 'How could this happen?', in which the sensational aspect of the events was played down from the first line: 'Sensation is the inevitable shadow of politics', the author observed, and added: 'in the matter of my expulsion from the Soviet Union this shadow has, however, acquired dimensions that are too grotesque. Moreover, sensationalism is inimical to the kind of politics that is directed towards great ends. My object in writing these lines is not to create more of a sensation but, on the contrary, to undercut this by providing public opinion with objective information – so far as objectivity is attainable in political struggle in general.' And to put everyone immediately in the picture, he declared:

> Our attitude toward the October Revolution, Soviet power, Marxist doctrine, and Bolshevism remains unchanged ... I am now resorting to a communication with the public that is rather

> exceptional from the standpoint of the methods to which I have been accustomed during my political life. But this flows from the exceptional nature of the conditions in which I am now placed.[3]

The reasons that led to the formation of an opposition, the meaning of the deportations, the intellectual activity of the opposition – and with very few exceptions, they were the most eminent men in the party – a portrait of Stalin, who was still barely known, and the reasons for his victory, were set out in a series of six articles couched in general terms to be accessible to the general public, but without cutting corners. So much for the past. And now? Where is the Russian Revolution going? Trotsky replied: 'The course of the revolutionary process is much more complex than that of a mountain stream.'[4] And he poses all the problems that he would later deal with more fundamentally – how a bureaucracy came to be formed, at first only functional, which later became social – 'Thermidor', etc. Let us merely note the following important passage, because it gives the reasons for the tactic followed by the Opposition, and by Trotsky in particular, a tactic that surprised both his opponents and supporters:

> This is not the place to discuss whether it was correct to try to maintain some common ground for collective work at the price of very great personal concessions, or whether I should have taken the offensive all along the line, despite the absence of sufficient political grounds for such action. The fact is that I chose the first way and, in spite of everything, I do not regret it.[5]

And to conclude:

> The very fact of our struggle testifies also that we are far removed from the so-called attitude of pessimism. We proceed from the conviction that the Soviet system has great inner reserves and resources. The line of the Opposition is not toward the collapse of Soviet power but toward its strengthening and development.[6]

As soon as it was possible to get a place to live, the family left the hotel to get settled. There was on Prinkipo, the main island of the small archipelago of the Princes' Isles, a villa that was sufficiently isolated to allow the maximum desirable security. (Trotsky had already been to Prinkipo at the beginning of 1919, but then as the plenipotentiary of the Soviet government. Being opposed to the armed intervention of the Allies against the Soviet republic, President Wilson proposed to bring together in Prinkipo the representatives of the de facto governments of Russia and the various pretenders; but the Bolsheviks alone accepted the proposal, which had to be abandoned in the face of the underhand opposition of Lloyd George and Clemenceau.)[7] The house was large enough for work to be comfortably organised there. Trotsky set up his office on the first floor; some planks brought together and put on two trestles formed the large table he needed to spread out his always abundant documentation; along the walls were shelves which only filled up gradually, to the extent to which his supporters in Europe and America sent works that would make it possible to reassemble a library. The house was surrounded by a garden, cutting it off from the street on one side, and going straight down to the sea on the other. Of the two large rooms on the ground floor, one was occupied by his eldest son, Lev Sedov, his active collaborator, particularly responsible for the 'chancellery' – for the post was always extensive;[8] the other was the dining room, where the family and occasional secretaries came for their meals, but where there was no hanging around; there was work for everyone to do.

There were numerous visitors during the first weeks: journalists, inquisitive ordinary people, publishers, and members of Communist opposition groups who came as quickly as they could, but for whom it was a long journey. Trotsky very quickly adopted a rule; far from eagerly welcoming them 'out of concern to be talked about', as his enemies stupidly claimed, he only received them with suspicion, and only decided to accord them an interview when he thought it possible to hope for an honest relationship. The aim of journalists in an interview, he said, was to find basic materials for an article, which did not stop them, as so often happened, from distancing themselves from the person being interviewed, nor from rearranging his statements to their convenience, nor from finishing off with ironic or malicious remarks.

The first publisher to appear was the managing director of Fischer Verlag. He came with a very precise aim in view – to ask Trotsky to write his autobiography. Trotsky had many books in mind, but absolutely not this type of writing. The struggle of the Opposition against the leadership of the Russian Communist Party had not involved debate, because Stalin had kept silent, simply imprisoning, deporting and exiling them, but research work, studying the problems of the development of the Soviet Union. All the texts had been collected together in Alma Ata, and Trotsky had succeeded in bringing them with him. Important as they were for the Soviet Union, they were no less important for the sections of the Communist International, where they were still completely ignorant of them – this is what Trotsky was impatient to make public. The publisher did not refuse to do this, but he always came back to the autobiography, and he wanted to begin with this.[9]

A work that was also ready to be printed was entitled *The Deformed Revolution*. It was to come out in Paris in 1929, in Russian in 1931, and in an English translation in New York in 1937 under another title, *The Stalin School of Falsification*. When the book came out in France the Bukharinist 'Right' (Bukharin, Rykov and Tomsky)[10] had just been removed from the party leadership, and the story had to be rewritten for the third time: it had first been tailored to the Triumvirate (Zinoviev, Kamenev and Stalin),[11] then adapted when the first two passed over to the Opposition, and finally when Stalin alone enjoyed absolute power. As Trotsky remarked: 'The lie in politics, as in daily life, serves as a function of the class structure of society ... Every new variant of the past served not only to supplement but also to destroy the preceding variant.'[12] In 1927, the historical section of the Bolshevik party had sent Trotsky a printed questionnaire regarding his rôle in the October Revolution, and he had used this excuse to set up and highlight the grossest of the falsifications that concerned him personally, as well as the more general ones appearing in these successive 'histories'. Then came three speeches delivered by Trotsky before the highest party bodies, the Central Committee and the Central Control Commission, when Stalin was preparing the expulsions. Called as the accused, Trotsky turned himself into the accuser. He could in no way change decisions that had been made in advance, but his speeches allowed the main facts to be fixed in history. These speeches were published here for the first time; they are fine pieces of eloquence, worthy of the times and the great revolutionary struggles.[13] This other book is essential for studying the policy of the Russian Communist Party and the Communist International; all the problems that arose between 1923 and 1929 are dealt with in depth; it is the summing up of the work of the Opposition in this period, specified by Trotsky in these terms: Our way is that of the internal reform of the regime:

> ... after having gone through a series of tests and crises the Communist International will free itself from the yoke of a bureaucracy without ideological principles, capable only of swinging the helm wildly, of describing zigzags, of repression, and of preparing defeats... We continue and develop the line of the Third International which we prepared during the war and in whose foundation we participated with Lenin.[14]

❖ ❖ ❖ ❖

Putting together the autobiography took up a great deal of Trotsky's time, but left him with enough to be able to talk with socialists and communists, whether expelled or still party members, who made the journey to Prinkipo. He was up from seven o'clock and had long days for well-regulated work. He was solidly built, but suffered an affliction all his life – stomach or intestinal? – whose true nature no doctor, from Russia, Germany, France or Mexico, succeeded in identifying. He rarely went out. He only went once to Istanbul during the four years he spent on the island, as for all that he had to see Hagia Sophia.[15] Being close to the sea easily permitted him to take the exercise he needed, which was fishing. This was no peaceable relaxation of fishing with a rod, but an active operation for which the whole household was mobilised and took over a boat; to begin with it was a matter of stretching out a crescent-shaped net 40 metres long and then going to the coast to load on board the necessary stones to throw in the water to make the fish move and get caught in the net. Trotsky directed these operations, dragged along the dawdlers who would rather take an interest in the scenery than the fish, and was particularly proud when he could bring back a load of red mullet for dinner. In the evening after dinner he sometimes allowed himself to relax. Every night from his office balcony, along with Natalia and some friends, he enjoyed the nightly enchantment made by the play of light in the sky and over the water. Then he brought together his current visitors and informed them of some developments in the struggle in Soviet Russia which they only later found repeated in his works; he questioned them about the general situation and the state of the communist parties and of the working-class movement in their respective countries.

We were now on the eve of the great American crisis which was to disrupt profoundly the world economy in the following months. But every country already had its own difficulties; France was experiencing unemployment that the Communists put down to the 'rationalisation' that had been recently introduced into industrial production. Cliques went in for an underhand or open struggle with each other for power in the Central Committee of the Communist Party; the zigzags typical of Stalinist politics made the task very difficult for those who wanted to follow the Moscow 'line'. The 'turn' that had so suddenly thrown the pendulum towards the left was then at its height. The 'Rightists' who were in the leadership after the elimination of Zinoviev were made responsible for the difficulties affecting the grain supplies. They were relieved of their functions or sent on leave – to begin with. And even while success in every sphere was being announced, it had to be admitted that there was a serious grain crisis; there was not enough bread, they had to regulate the sale of it, and reintroduce ration cards. Following the new technique, the press affirmed that it was the workers who had demanded that it should be regulated at the same time as they were voting for the resolutions against the Trotskyist Opposition. But the crisis had been exactly forecast by this same opposition, which had not only foreseen it, but had established its causes and indicated remedies. Stalin struck a double blow by means of the tactic of the scapegoat. The left turn by which he had rid himself of the 'Right' at the same time allowed him in parallel to disintegrate an opposition that until then had been solidly united. In order to combat Bukharin, he spoke with a voice and used formulae which so exactly recalled the language of his opponents that some of them exclaimed: 'Our policy is winning, our opposition has no more reason for its existence.' From the end of February, when Trotsky had only just arrived in Istanbul, the Russian papers noted that 'divisions exist within the Trotskyist group; some of its members are advocating a return to the party'. The movement grew: between August and September 500 oppositionists signed a letter to the Central Committee proclaiming their approval of 'the party's political rectification', but they did, however, insist on the necessity for the restoration of democracy within the party. In spite of Trotsky's warnings the majority returned to the party, even though Stalin required complete submission, ignoring the demand to restore democracy.

Outside Russia, the 'left' turn was based upon 'an obvious radicalisation of the masses'. The formula came from Moscow, and was a complete invention; there was no trace of 'radicalisation', in France possibly no more than anywhere else, for at the same time as they were proclaiming it, *L'Humanité*'s headlines alone were denying it. For example: 'In Clichy the police broke into the hall of the congress of the Paris Region of the Communist Party. It dissolved the meeting and arrested the 120 delegates who were there.' And the next day '*L'Humanité* is seized'. The response can be summed up in a few words: the 'radicalised masses' did not move. This was the start of the tactic of deepening the divisions within the working-class movement by labelling the socialists 'social fascists', which in France was to wreck trade union activity, and in Germany was to help Hitler into power. The culmination of this leftist stupidity was an appeal of the Communist International 'to the workers of Europe to prepare a "Red Day" against war on 1 August 1929'. They had to 'go down into the streets', and 'take over the streets'. As soon as this text arrived in Prinkipo, Trotsky decided to denounce it as a crime against the working class, by sending it stupidly into a massacre. A leaflet was put together and distributed in various countries by agreement with the groups of the Opposition. The Stalinists were obliged to beat a retreat, and to renounce their stupid provocation; they now explained that the 'Red Day' did not mean a day of disturbances, but a day of protest strikes against imperialist war, and for the defence of the USSR.

This event alone showed the dangers of the 'left turn'. To

get rid of it, and to put the working class on its guard, for it could come back under another shape, Trotsky wrote a pamphlet. In Stalinist phraseology this 'leftism' was called 'The Third Period of the Communist International', so the pamphlet was called *The Third Period of the Comintern's Errors*.[16] It went patiently over all the ranting about the 'radicalisation of the masses' and the consequences drawn from them for everyday activity, and how the leaders of the French Communist Party who had applied them had done great damage to the working class. Their lack of comprehension of the elementary principles of socialism made him remind them that 'leadership of the workers' movement is incompatible with ignorance, as Marx once said to Weitling'.[17]

Another pamphlet Trotsky wrote at the same time was aimed at his own supporters, those who were sympathetic to the Communist Opposition. The disastrous events that followed the death of Lenin, from Zinoviev's 'Bolshevisation' to the 'Third Period' had split off the best elements in the working-class movement from the communist parties, and, at least in part, even from communism itself. That was another danger Trotsky wanted to warn against. In this pamphlet, which was called *Defence of the Soviet Republic and the Opposition*,[18] he showed that it would be fatal to abandon the Russian Revolution; that the Stalinist regime was repugnant and threatened degeneration, but all the conquests of the October Revolution were not yet lost; that we must stick with those that remained and defend them against the 'Soviet' enemies within and the capitalist imperialists who never gave up the hope of overthrowing the socialist republic.

Life in Prinkipo went on with this useful toil when one day, as a pleasant surprise, an invitation arrived from the Independent Labour Party. The leadership of this party, the oldest of the British socialist parties, asked Trotsky to come and take part in the discussions at the next party summer school. An acceptance was quickly sent off. The question of a visa remained; for the second time the Labour Party had just got into power, Ramsay MacDonald was Prime Minister for the second time, and he had been one of the leaders of the ILP for a very long time. How could his government refuse the visa under these conditions? We already know that it did refuse it; that can be read in a former chapter, as well as the 'justification' given for avoiding giving a visa.[19]

Just before this invitation arrived dispatches inadvertently published by *L'Humanité* made clear the reasons why the German government, then headed by the social democrat Hermann Müller, had also refused him a visa. When the matter had been debated in the cabinet, the socialists came down emphatically against issuing the visa. Stresemann supported them, basing himself upon a consultation with the main civil servants in his ministry and on a report from the Reich ambassador in Moscow.[20] The socialists 'feared that their left would be strengthened', and Stresemann did not want to upset Stalin. British labourites and German social democrats and bourgeois alike had made themselves into Stalin's assistants.

Trotsky followed very closely the newspapers and magazines published by the opposition groups all over the world. But the publication closest to his heart was the *Bulletin of the Opposition* (in Russian), which in spite of many difficulties came out every month between 1929 and 1940, printed first of all in Paris, and then in New York. His oldest son, Lev Sedov, was in charge of it; organisation and distribution were his responsibility, but he was also able at one time or another to provide articles, and, particularly in the early years, while contact with the Soviet Union was still possible, remarkable information could be found in it on the real situation inside Russia. The Russian leaders feared it, but sought it out at the same time; and if it found its way to Russia (there was no question of sending it there directly) it was because Soviet diplomats, many of whom had now come to Europe, bought it and took it back to circulate on their return to Russia.

In the autumn of 1932, a group of Danish social democratic students invited Trotsky to make a speech in Copenhagen about the Russian Revolution. Visas were granted this time, but it was only a matter of transit visas. I reproduce here Natalia Trotsky's notes about the journey:

> On 14 October 1932, we were at last able to leave Constantinople and pay a short visit to Copenhagen ... With us travelled our young comrades ... When the steamer docked at Athens, Lev Davidovich was cheered, greatly to our surprise. At Naples, we were allowed to disembark, and to visit the ruins of Pompeii. At Marseilles, the police took quite extraordinary precautions. A motor launch came alongside and took us further

down the coast. A plain-clothes detective travelled in our car, first as far as Lyons, and then on to Paris, and the press had no idea of where we were.

After a day in Paris we boarded a ship at Dunkirk, where we were so closely guarded that the police did not even allow the secretary of the stevedores' union to approach us. In Denmark, small groups of Stalinists were waiting at all the stations on our route but they only managed a few shouts and cat-calls. Leon Davidovich addressed an audience of some 2500 at the Copenhagen stadium on the October Revolution. He spoke in German, and ended with a defence of socialism, which represents: 'a leap from the realm of necessity into the realm of freedom in this sense too, that the man of today, with all his contradictions and lack of harmony, will open the road for a new and happier race'.[21]

The Danish government refused to have this lecture broadcast over the radio, on the grounds that the king and court objected. Our visa was for eight days only, and we heard that the king was opposed to any extension. Some 20 political friends, all of them well known and holders of valid passports, had come to talk to Trotsky. This so-called clandestine conference, which was neither secret nor formal, aroused the anger of reactionaries and Stalinists alike ... Stauning's Social Democratic government insisted on our leaving the country the very day our visa expired. As there was no boat, we had to pretend that we had left and spend the next 24 hours travelling about by car. Leon Davidovich had applied for a Swedish visa, and had heard from socialists in Stockholm that Sweden was perfectly willing to allow him to enter the country, but that the Soviet ambassador, Alexandra Kollontai,[22] had raised insurmountable objections ... Our son, Lev Sedov, who was living in Berlin at the time, was refused permission to join us... We had expected to spend some time in France on our way back, but the French authorities demurred.[23]

The travellers had barely got back to Prinkipo when a fire broke out and reached the library, causing serious damage there. The conversion had been so basic that they had to cook on a primus stove heated with very crude Russian paraffin. The most serious and irreplaceable losses were the photostats of documents that Stalin had prevented from being published, and a rare collection of photographs of the revolution was also destroyed. They had to make a fresh appeal to their friends to be able to rebuild a library.

The repression got worse in Russia. Even if some of the comrades, allowing themselves to take appearance for reality in the left turn, had rallied around the government again, there were many others in agreement with Trotsky who refused to give in. Stalin hounded these irreconcilable opponents. Through them he was always targeting Trotsky. On 20 February 1932, the Russian government had made public its decision to withdraw Soviet nationality from Trotsky and those members of his family who were abroad. The Turkish authorities conducted themselves in a proper manner, but Stalin had concluded a secret agreement with Kemal[24] for the exile; another agreement could take place to hand over Trotsky to Stalin, for experience had clearly shown that no government, whatever its political complexion, was prepared to resist the pressure of the Soviet leaders. His friends, once alerted, took up a campaign to obtain a visa allowing him to move away from an area that was henceforth unsafe. Their moves were successful. At the beginning of July 1933, with Daladier as Prime Minister,[25] the French government allowed him permission to stay in France, imposing, however, certain conditions.

Chapter Two: In France

Trotsky, Natalia and the friends who were with them arrived in Marseille on 24 July 1933. The police, fearing that demonstrations would take place at the normal embarkation point in the great port, arranged a landing by patrol boat at Cassis. A police inspector then took them by road to Saint-Palais, near Royan, which was the place chosen for his residence in France. He was banned from the Paris region.

The villa was 'right by the sea', wrote Natalia Trotsky, 'and its name, *Les Embruns* [*Sea Spray*], suited it very well. On our very first day there, when we had only just arrived, it caught fire, entirely by accident. We had to take shelter in a car in the road while the fire was put out. We stayed, incognito, at Saint-Palais for about two months, and our presence was only known to the minister of the interior, the prefect of the Charente-Maritime Department and a fairly small number of friends ... Then he fell ill and we moved to Bagnères-de-Bigorre in the Hautes-Pyrénées, where we lived in almost complete solitude for two weeks.'[26]

Hitler's accession to power was the event that then dominated the international situation. Governments were uneasy, all the more so because American policy complicated the situation and made it worse. Roosevelt's New Deal involved the devaluation of the dollar, and a currency war took place between the hard-line supporters and opponents of stabilisation by means of the gold standard.[27] A new tendency formed among the socialists around the supporters of a controlled economy, of the plan, of the restoration of state control; the word 'dirigism' made its appearance. Austria, cut down to a head without a body, tried to unite with Hungary under a Habsburg. The Little Entente, and Beneš above all, were against it: 'I would rather have the Anschluss than a Habsburg', he said, a rare example of political myopia, for he did get the *Anschluss*, but Hitler along with it.[28] And an international economic conference and a disarmament conference met and talked, yet again without result.

In the midst of these serious events, the French Communist Party persisted in a verbal revolutionarism that ignored reality. Its press claimed that the discontent and anger of the deceived Germans had already seen through the demagogy of Hitlerism. 'Social fascism' remained the slogan, now rounded off with 'radical fascism'. All the parties, apart from the communists, were on the road to becoming fascist; socialists, whether of the right or the left, were both equally preparing the way for fascism. Daladier was then the agent of French imperialism. These verbal excesses only served to emphasise the state of impotence into which the party had fallen; for the time being it no longer counted, either in political life or in the French workers' movement. Not having to bother with it, Daladier could allow Trotsky to live on French soil.

On 23 July, a dispatch from Marseille to a Paris newspaper stated that 'Trotsky arrived in Marseille as an ordinary traveller yesterday; the previous decision to expel him has been rescinded; he has therefore been allowed to land and move about freely on French territory'. But *L'Humanité* immediately launched a campaign of insults and threats whose tone was provided by its editor, who wrote:

> From France, from this hotbed of the anti-Soviet struggle, Trotsky can attack the USSR, and attack the Communist Parties of France, Germany and Spain. It is a strategic position. That is why M. Trotsky has come here. And that is why he has been welcomed. But he and the government are fooling themselves if they think that this abominable work can be carried out with impunity, guarded by a police paid with secret funds voted for it by the socialist MPs. In spite of the police precautions and false communiqués, which are deceptive as to his movements, Trotsky, in his new White Guard lair, is bound to arouse the anger of the revolutionary workers of France, in solidarity with their free brothers in the USSR.

As always, the Stalinists found helpers, sometimes well-wishing and innocent, but most often hirelings, who aimed to stir things up with exaggerated reports. This is why one of these cronies, confusing Royan with Royat, after writing that 'Trotsky has taken refuge in the Auvergne', added that he had requested an interview with Litvinov, who was then in France: 'One last hope inspires him ... the time of forgiveness for Trotsky is not yet.' However, there were journalists who were disgusted by so many crude, despicable acts and base manoeuvres; one of them said: 'Trotsky is being welcomed with insults, and accusations that sicken even the most objective and most neutral. And those who are treating him in this way are those who were so recently praising him to the skies!'

This campaign might have spoiled the pleasure that Trotsky experienced when he found himself once more in France. He knew that the French communists were speaking for Stalin, and consequently what they wrote was not insignificant; it was therefore necessary to take precautions. But this was already the case in Turkey, and now life in France brought with it substantial compensations. His friends sometimes mocked Trotsky for his francophilia, and it was true that outside Russia France had become his favourite country. He liked its literature and language; in his youth studying socialism had brought him to Marx, and its social democracy appeared to be a model, an exemplary party. But to the extent to which he got to know it better, his admiration for its leaders cooled noticeably, and the collapse of 1914 was to justify his doubts. His two years' stay in France during the decisive years of 1914–16 permitted him to understand the working-class movement from within, and he had even taken part personally in its activity. He became close to militants of various tendencies; he obviously remained firmly opposed to certain theories and certain of the movement's ideas, and he was sometimes impatient with its hesitations and caution which were as alien to his ideas as they were to his temperament. But he found unique features and a vitality which he liked in the French proletariat, and he never let an occasion slip to affirm his faith in its future, even when the difficulties in building the French Communist Party caused him some painful disappointments.

Now he could take up the problems he had already studied in Prinkipo, the most important of which concerned Spain, and above all Germany. Although the preparation of his works and a voluminous correspondence would have been quite enough to take up all his time and energy, he found it possible to follow closely what was going on in the world, and within the working-class and socialist movement. His long and exceptional experience as a socialist who had, after leading the struggle against Tsarism, wielded power and led to victory the Civil War, gave him firm points of reference. His worry had been that Prinkipo was too far from the important sources of information, and that the news took so long to reach him. When putting together an article on something important that had happened to the German Communist Party, he had to state beforehand that 'when these lines reach the reader, they will perhaps, in one section or another, be out of date. Through the efforts of the Stalinist apparatus and the friendly collaboration of all the bourgeois labour and socialist governments, the author of these lines is placed in such circumstances under which he can react to political events only after a delay of several weeks.'[29] However, since the articles he wrote to follow events were then collected together into pamphlets, it can be said that there was nothing essential that needed to be changed; they can be picked up on secondary errors of detail; his general assessment showed a foresight that could rarely be faulted. During the period of the threatening rise of Hitlerism in 1929–31, he warned unceasingly against the consequences of the deadly 'leftist' policy of the Third Period. In November 1929, when the threat to Austria had already become serious, he wrote:

> Fascism, unless one wishes to play a senseless game with words, is by no means a feature characteristic of all bourgeois parties. Rather, it constitutes a specific bourgeois party, fitted for special tasks and circumstances, opposed to the other bourgeois parties, and most sharply of all precisely to the social democracy ... to *equate* the social democracy with fascism when social democratic workers have a mortal hatred of fascism and the leaders fear it just as mortally means to act in contradiction to the real political relations ... The first thing, then, is to throw out the senseless formula, so full of bravado and empty of content, equating social democracy with fascism.[30]

The organisation of a referendum in Germany was an opportunity for Trotsky to emphasise another aspect of Stalinism's international policy. He wrote on 25 August 1931:

> A fact remains a fact, in a certain campaign, the Stalinist bureaucracy involved the revolutionary workers in a united front with the national socialists against social democracy ... In the communist fanfare of 1 August, in the very heat of the agitation for the Red Referendum, along with the picture of Scheringer, is printed one of his new apostolic messages. Here is what is said there verbatim: 'The cause of the dead of the world war, who have given their lives for a free Germany, is betrayed by everyone who comes out today against the people's revolution, against the revolutionary war of liberation.'[31]

Thus the Stalinist bureaucracy was more and more attempting to oppose fascism with its own weapons; it borrowed the colours of its political palette and attempted to outbid it in patriotism. It is difficult to imagine a more shameful capitulation of principles than that of the Stalinists, who had replaced the slogan of the proletarian revolution with that of 'people's revolution'.

This disastrous policy created exceptionally important new tasks for the Communist Left Opposition whose forces, as Trotsky recognised, were not great, 'but every current grows together with the growth of its tasks. To understand them clearly is to possess one of the most important guarantees of victory.'[32] For example, when asked about workers' control of production, the factory councils, which were the subject of frequent discussions in the workers' organisations, he explained that 'workers' control thus implies a sort of *economic dual power* in the factory', and two roads lay in front of it: 'if the participation of the workers in the management of production is to be lasting, stable, "normal", it must rest upon class collaboration, and not upon class struggle. Such a class collaboration can only be realised through the upper strata of the trade unions and the capitalist associations. But the more you encroach upon production, "workers'" control through factory councils is conceivable only on the basis of sharp class struggle ... The central body of a city's factory councils can thoroughly fulfil the rôle of the city soviet.'[33]

At the same time, the fall of the monarchy in Spain had created a revolutionary situation. The attitude of Stalinism here was no less alarming than in Germany. After having said that the fall of Primo de Rivera's dictatorship was an event of scant importance,[34] the Stalinist press was full of reports that 'practically the entire working class is behind the Communist Party', and that 'the peasants are already setting up soviets'; *Pravda* even printed that 'Spain is in flames'. In articles, and above all in his frequent letters, Trotsky examined the problems as they arose, insisting all the more on the necessity for providing a correct response; he was worried about what was going on: 'I am very much afraid that the historians of the future may have to accuse the Spanish revolutionists of not having known how to take advantage of an exceptional revolutionary situation.'[35] The situation appeared to be so serious to him that he decided to appeal to the Central Committee of the Russian Communist Party, asking it to place among its highest priorities an urgent proposal aiming at encouraging the organisation of an active unity of all the revolutionary forces in Spain. If not, he wrote on 24 April 1931, 'the defeat of the Spanish Revolution, which is inevitable ... will lead almost automatically to the establishment of genuine fascism in Spain'.[36]

❖ ❖ ❖ ❖

In France, after an imposing start, Premier Daladier found himself in a situation that was becoming more and more difficult. Hitlerite Germany was exerting a growing pressure upon its neighbours, and on France in particular. The consolidation of the Hitler regime was to force Stalin into a new 'turn'. For if his French underlings were still stuck in the policy of the left turn, he was already preparing a turnaround that would steadily push Soviet Russia into the camp of the 'imperialist democracies'. Even if on occasion he also indulged in boasting in the face of Hitler, he could not ignore the fact that Hitler had the powerful industry of Germany behind him, and a military force that made him a formidable neighbour. This is why he dreamed up the policy of the 'Anti-Fascist Popular Front'. Litvinov[37] was put in charge of foreign affairs, and he negotiated non-aggression pacts with the Baltic states, Poland and the Balkan countries; he was ready to sign pacts with every country – except Germany. He made a cautious approach to France, where fear of Germany found him auxiliaries in all political circles. After hesitating for a long time, Laval[38] undertook a journey to Moscow, and after the end of long discussions with Stalin a communiqué was published on 15 May 1935 which read astonishingly: 'Stalin understands and fully approves the measures of national defence taken by France to raise its armaments to the level of its security.' This is what *L'Humanité* had to print; the formula was Stalin's own, said Laval. 'Class against class' was replaced with 'the division between fascists and anti-fascists'.

The new tactic fitted Stalin's policy perfectly. It was launched under the cover of anti-fascism; it would help to encircle Hitlerite Germany, and commit the democratic countries to a road that risked involving them in a fresh war with Germany; it would allow communist infiltration into the civil and even the military administration in every country. The communist parties would thereby provide indispensable help in time of peace, and later on in a war if a conflict broke out; they would become well-placed informants and allies in all circumstances. The naivety of the Western democracies astonished Trotsky; how could they allow themselves to play a game so full of dangers for themselves? Nonetheless, when he wrote that if the present international tension ended up in a general war, Stalin would abandon his partners to make a deal with Hitler, it was generally thought that he was going too far, that his 'hatred' for Stalin had led him astray, and that such duplicity appeared to be inconceivable, to the extent that on this occasion Trotsky's habitual foresight seemed to be at fault, even to the Trotskyists.

When the now famous communiqué appeared, *L'Humanité* was still involved in a daily campaign against the government's military preparations; it was appealing for action against the two years' military service demanded by the war minister. But from one day to the next the communists turned themselves into patriots and democrats, and the anti-fascist union allowed them to emerge from the isolation in which their forces had been melting away. 'When the strategists of *L'Humanité*' were afflicted with barricade delirium,' wrote Trotsky, '"conquered" the streets every day, and stamped as "social fascist" everyone who did not share their extravagances, we predicted: "The moment these gentlemen burn the tips of their fingers, they will become the worst opportunists." That prediction has now been completely confirmed.'[39]

While manipulating the Popular Front, the Stalinists piled up boasting and bluster. At the time of the plebiscite that was to decide the future of the Saar, they boasted that 'the Saar will never be delivered up to Hitler'. 'Unity in action, an unshakeable barrier.' And the result? A total of 477, 119 voted to rejoin Germany, and 46,513 for the status quo.[40] Trotsky became annoyed at such stupid boasting: '"The United Front will not permit" ...; "the fascists will not dare", etc. These are phrases. It is necessary to say squarely to the workers, socialists and communists: do not allow yourselves to be lulled by the phrases of superficial and irresponsible journalists and orators. It is a question of our heads and the future of socialism.' What was necessary to bar the way to the Leagues which originated with Hitler and Mussolini was a serious organisation of workers' militias capable of squashing the first shoots of aggression, for 'if there is no organisation of defence, that is, a workers' militia, *Le Populaire* and *L'Humanité* ... will find themselves defenceless before the first well-prepared attack of the fascists'.[41]

❖ ❖ ❖ ❖

After several months' stay in Royan, Trotsky was authorised to come closer to the centre of France, though the departments of the Seine and Seine-et-Oise remained forbidden to him. Barbizon appeared to be convenient. He settled into a relatively isolated house on the edge of the forest. What Trotsky appreciated here above all was that it provided him with the opportunity to assess all the tendencies that were stirring during this extremely confusing time. In order not to give rise to an unwelcome disturbance around his home, he went to Paris quite frequently to the homes of his friends, where meetings had been laid on for him. Apart from the French, visitors came from Belgium, Holland, Britain and America, as well as genuine Italian and German anti-fascists. Trotsky listened, learned, and offered advice. A general malaise held sway in all the working-class parties. Among the socialists, those who were called Neo-Socialists[42] were preaching the controlled economy and the organisation of economic life in accordance with a plan, rejecting Marx and proletarian internationalism, and demanding a strong government. They were active and incessantly attacked the party leadership, which was itself divided. At times a left wing came close to Trotskyist positions.[43] It was a period of great activity for Trotsky. The numerous meetings and contacts made it possible for him to feel for the first time since he was exiled that he was at the heart of the movement, even if his personal position obliged him to be very cautious. He continued to write on Spain and Germany, taking up and developing the ideas he had already formulated in his writings in Prinkipo, whose correctness was confirmed by the unfolding of events.

A single incident was to compromise everything and even put at risk his permission to stay. The young communist who was responsible for the post – which was collected and sent from Paris in secret – was the victim of a motorcycle accident. The gendarmes asked questions. The secret got out. The news spread in the newspaper offices that Trotsky was in Barbizon. Journalists rushed round, and in their behaviour in these circumstances they sank to the level of the most detestable practices of the American yellow press. They took up residence and camped out, lay siege to the house, and lay in wait for the departure of the trapped and hunted man. However, Trotsky eluded their surveillance, and succeeded in escaping these amateur policemen without being seen. From then on he led a wandering life across France, for as soon as his place of refuge was discovered it was necessary to leave. The government, harassed by the Stalinists as well as by the reactionaries howling in concert, began to lose patience; but since no country wanted the undesirable, it could only show its disapproval by increasing police surveillance.

Work henceforth became more difficult. Trotsky concentrated his attention on the general situation in France. It had changed considerably since he came there; the Radicals had been in power then, and Daladier had gained some parliamentary successes. But new organisations had come into existence in the country, one of them clandestine, carrying on a particular type of agitation.[44] A financial scandal in which some MPs were implicated was the occasion of rowdy demonstrations in Paris looked on indulgently by the police. On 6 February 1934, the Parisian municipal councillors – most of them reactionary – played at insurrection, and mobilised their forces against the Palais Bourbon. People were killed, and Daladier left office in haste. Contrary to constitutional law, on his departure his successors sought out a retired ex-president of the republic who could become the head of a new government. What did this mean? Trotsky wanted to reply to this question. According to him, the new regime was a form of Bonapartism. The workers replied to the Sixth of February of the fascist reactionaries with a powerful general strike a few days later, on the 12th. Trotsky wrote:

> A slight curb had been put on the fascists, and the Radicals breathed just a bit easier. *Le Temps*, which had already rushed to offer its hand and heart in a number of articles to the 'young generation', discovered anew the superior merits of a liberal regime, as the one most in harmony with French genius. Thus the unstable, transitional, bastard regime was established, which harmonises not with the genius of France, but with the decline of the Third Republic. What stands out most sharply in this regime are its *Bonapartist* traits: the independence of power from parties and programmes, the liquidation of the parliamentary legislation by means of emergency powers, the lifting of the government in the guise of an 'arbiter' above the struggling camps, that is, factually above the nation. The ministries of Doumergue, Flandin,[45] Laval, all three with the invariable participation of the compromised and abject Radicals, represented minor variations of one and the same theme.[46]

Finally, after months of wandering about, Norway, where a Labour government had just come to power, agreed to welcome the exile. Trotsky took his leave of France in *An Open Letter to the Workers of France* which was published by several newspapers. I give some extracts from it here:

> Dear Comrades
>
> I leave France today, and this circumstance enables me, at last, to put my case openly before you; so long as I remained on French soil, I was condemned to silence.

Two years ago, the 'left' government of Daladier, in its honeymoon weeks, gave me permission to settle in France, presumably with the same rights as other foreigners. As a matter of fact, I was forbidden to live in Paris, and I found myself immediately under the strict surveillance of the police. Shortly after 6 February 1934, the minister of internal affairs, Albert Sarraut,[47] after a wild campaign in the press, signed a decree deporting me from France. No foreign government, however, could be found willing to accept me. This is the sole reason why the deportation order was not put into effect until now ... Thus, during my last year's sojourn in France I was cut off from the outside world more than when I lived on the island of Prinkipo, in Turkey, under the surveillance of the police of Kemal Pasha. Thus, the visa of a Radical government turned into a trap, after its own fashion ... If, however, I took the liberty to call your attention to so minor a question as my living conditions in France, it was only because this episode is most intimately bound up with the policies of the Communist International ...

Two years ago, *L'Humanité* used to harp daily: 'The fascist Daladier has called the social fascist Trotsky to France in order to organise, with his assistance, a military intervention against the USSR.' There were to be found quite a number of honest but naive and ignorant people who believed in this *canard* ... One should not accuse uneducated and duped people – one must, instead, enlighten them. But one can and one must accuse the enlightened scoundrels who consciously broadcast lies and slanders in order to fool the toilers ... Today, as everybody knows, these gentlemen have made an anti-fascist 'People's Front' with the 'fascist' Daladier. The Stalinists, who call themselves communists, have stopped talking altogether about the intervention of French imperialism into the USSR. On the contrary, at present they perceive the guarantee of peace in the military alliance between French capital and the Soviet bureaucracy ... Right now, Messrs Calumniators are beginning to say ... that the policy of Trotsky and of the Bolshevik-Leninists performs a service not to Herriot[48] and Daladier, but to Hitler, that is, not to the French, but to German imperialism...

Stalinism is today the chief plague of the world working-class movement. This plague must be extirpated, excised, burned out with a hot iron. Once again the proletariat must be united under the banner of Marx and Lenin! ... I depart with a burning love for the French people and with an unwavering faith in the great future of the French proletariat ... the toiling people will sooner or later offer me that hospitality that the bourgeoisie today refuses.[49]

Chapter Three: In Norway

It was the same small group of wanderers, Trotsky, his wife Natalia, and two friends who served as secretaries, who set out for their new refuge. He took ship at Antwerp for Oslo. His wanderings in France had started off well, but finished badly. It was to be the same in Norway, even though the end was to be worse. But their arrival and the early days contrasted so happily with the final months of their lives in France that Natalia was happy enough to jot down:

> Quiet, rugged, handsome Norway! There, during the latter part of 1935 and the beginning of 1936 we enjoyed the illusion of genuine security while staying with honest people who became our close friends. Members of the Labour government had advised us to accept the hospitality of the well-known Socialist Riksdag member, Konrad Knudsen,[50] who lived in the village of Weksal near Honnefoss, some 30 miles from Oslo. The village was small and the house spacious with a huge courtyard in front. The main gate to the road was kept open day and night ... this could only happen in Norway! If we were watched or guarded in any way, we never noticed it. The old leader of the Labour Party, Martin Tranmael, a trade unionist who had served on the Comintern for a brief space,[51] paid us a courtesy call, as did the minister of justice, Mr Trygve Lie.[52] These were our only contacts with the authorities.
>
> We had two comfortable rooms at the Knudsen's. We ate with the family; we had few visitors – several Norwegian socialists and some from abroad. The only way of reaching us was

> through the editorial offices of the labour newspaper in Honefoss, which was edited by Konrad Knudsen ... I used to do my shopping in Honefoss. Sometimes we would accompany the Knudsens to the local cinema where we saw old films ... We began to feel so safe that Leon Davidovich would occasionally go for long, solitary walks through the woods ... He was extremely busy with his correspondence ... and writing a book to which he attached the utmost importance: *The Revolution Betrayed*.[53]

❖ ❖ ❖ ❖

The news from France was of great strikes that were shaking Paris and the whole country; the workers were occupying the factories. The bourgeoisie was frightened, and conceded on everything; in a few days parliament adopted new social legislation – a 40-hour week, a raise in wages, paid holidays, etc.[54] Under the heading of Trotsky wrote on 5 June: 'The rhythm of events in France has become sharply accelerated ... now facts speak for themselves ... the fate of France is being settled in the factories.'[55] And a few days later, on the 9th: 'Never has the radio seemed so precious as during these days. From a distant village in Norway one can follow the pulse beats of the French Revolution ...'[56] 'The February days of 1934 marked the first serious offensive of the united counter-revolution. The May-June days of 1936 herald the first mighty wave of proletarian revolution.'[57] As in the first days of his political life, his revolutionary enthusiasm was always ready to break out; he greeted the June days of 1936 all the quicker because he knew that the salvation of the Russian Revolution depended more than ever upon a revolutionary movement in Europe. The basis of a new start was already there; a revolution in Europe would reawaken revolutionary energies in the Soviet Union, would annihilate the bureaucratic structures and the castes, and would sweep along the German proletariat in its struggle against Hitlerism ... and if not, war. An excess of hope, it might be said, even if tempered by his alternative. But this revolutionary optimism has always been a feature of all socialists, above all when they are obliged to live in exile, and is the very precondition of their activity.

In these favourable working conditions, Trotsky undertook an extensive study of the contemporary state of the Soviet Union, what it had become and where it was going. The study was made more difficult by the continual lack of genuine and precise information and risked being discredited completely by drawing up a picture using already outdated facts. Today is always very different from yesterday, but reliable information only comes later, and the zigzags of Stalinist policy made complicated an already difficult study. To be able to make a valid sketch and to adapt his critique it was necessary to follow the unceasing changes as closely as possible.

We saw that at the beginning of his exile, when he arrived in Istanbul, Trotsky was convinced that 'Soviet rule has profound vitality and great elasticity. Our course is one of internal reform.'[58] And in the preface to *The Third International After Lenin*, written in Prinkipo on 15 April 1929, he said: 'What general conclusion is to be drawn from this book? On different sides attempts are being made to attribute to us the project of creating a Fourth International. That idea is entirely false ... We have no need at all to build a Fourth International.'[59] Four years were enough to bring him to modify his point of view considerably, but they were four years during which he was able to take account of the true position of the sections of the Communist International, reduced from now on to rubber stamping the stupidities of an ignorant and incapable leadership, during which he witnessed the collapse of the German Communist Party, the Communist International's 'model party', which gave up without a struggle in the face of Hitler.

In October 1933, the *Bulletin of the Opposition* published an appeal signed by the German Socialist Workers Party, the Dutch Independent Socialist Party, the Dutch Revolutionary Socialist Party, and the Russian Bolshevik Opposition, in favour of the imminent formation of a Fourth International, whose task was to resume the tradition of revolutionary Marxism abandoned by the Communist International,[60] on which Trotsky commented: 'Now the Bolshevik Party no longer exists ... The policy of reform is exhausted to the very end ... the workers' state can only be saved by the intervention of the world revolutionary movement ... The Comintern is dead for the revolution.'[61] And in the preface he wrote for a new edition of *Terrorism and Communism* (published under the title of *The Defence of Terrorism*) he made his thinking clear:

> After the shameful capitulation of the Communist International in Germany, the Bolshevik-Leninists, without hesitating a moment, proclaimed: The Third International is dead! ... The two Internationals, not only the Second but also the Third are tainted to the marrow ... great events (China, England, Germany, Austria, Spain) have given their verdict ... We are not talking about artificially 'proclaiming' the existence of the Fourth International, but of preparing for it systematically.[62]

This 'proclamation' was only to take place five years later:[63] the period preparing for it would therefore be quite long. This is because it met with resistance. The groups or parties that were inclined to form it were numerically weak everywhere, even if they existed everywhere, in Europe, in America, in Asia, and in South Africa. Those who were against it said that the groups were really too weak, that they had not yet succeeded in demonstrating to the workers that the Communist International had lost all its international and proletarian character, and that it was only an agency of Russian foreign policy. To these, but above all to his socialist and Stalinist detractors, Trotsky replied:

> The Fourth International rises on the shoulders of its three predecessors. It is subjected to blows from the front, the sides, and the rear. Careerists, cowards, Philistines, have nothing to seek in our ranks. The percentage of sectarians and adventurists, inevitable at the beginning, is winnowed away as the movement grows. Let pedants and sceptics shrug their shoulders about 'small' organisations that issue 'small' papers and fling a challenge to the entire world. Serious revolutionists will pass contemptuously by the pedants and sceptics. The October Revolution also began with its swaddling clothes.[64]

So much for the Communist International. But what has

Soviet Russia itself become? Could it still be said that it was a workers' state – without even discussing the Stalinist contention that socialism had already been achieved! This was a topic that provoked lively discussions within the groupings of the Fourth International. The major study that Trotsky undertook was intended precisely to reply to these questions.

To begin with, Trotsky pointed out in his introduction that pro-Soviet works were now abundant. Their authors were of three types: dilettante journalists like Duranty and Louis Fischer, lyrical and pacifist humanitarians, like Henri Barbusse and Romain Rolland,[65] and representatives of economic schematism in the old spirit of German academic socialism like the Webbs: 'Thus there is quietly coming into being an international school which might be described as *Bolshevism for the Cultured Bourgeoisie*, or more concisely, *Socialism for Radical Tourists*.'[66] Was it necessary to discuss their works? It was useless, because 'questions end for them where they really begin'.[67] He then defines the purpose of his work:

> To estimate correctly what is, in order the better to understand what is coming to be ... If you remember that the task of socialism is to create a classless society based upon solidarity and the harmonious satisfaction of all needs, there is not yet, in this fundamental sense, a hint of socialism in the Soviet Union. To be sure, the contradictions of soviet society are deeply different from the contradictions of capitalism. But they are nevertheless very tense. Police repression hushes up and distorts a political struggle, but does not eliminate it.[68]

Starting on his subject, he devotes the first chapter to the subject of 'What has been Achieved', showing the extent of the results already gained in the sphere of the organisation of production. But the book is so rich in information and theoretical discussion and the chapters in it are so dense that there can be no question of summarising them; we have to limit ourselves to listing them: economic development and the leadership's zigzags, socialism and the state, the struggle for productivity, the Soviet Thermidor,[69] the increase in equality and social antagonisms, the family, youth, culture;

foreign policy and the army, what is the USSR?, the USSR as mirrored in the new constitution, and where is the USSR going? But a few quotations will give the essence of Trotsky's thinking and conclusions on these different points:

> 'We are still far from the complete abolition of classes', confesses the official press ... The thousand-year-old caste barriers defining the life of every man on all sides – the polished urbanite and the uncouth muzhik,[70] the wizard of science and the day labourer – have not just been preserved from the past in a more or less softened form, but have to a considerable degree been born anew, and are assuming a more and more defiant character.[71]
>
> From the point of view of property in the means of production, the differences between a marshal and a servant girl, the head of a trust and a day labourer, the son of a people's commissar and a homeless child, seem not to exist at all. Nevertheless, the former occupy lordly apartments, enjoy several summer homes in various parts of the country, have the best automobiles at their disposal, and have long ago forgotten how to shine their own shoes. The latter live in wooden barracks often without partitions, lead a half-hungry existence, and do not shine their own shoes only because they go barefoot. To the bureaucrat the difference does not seem worthy of attention. To the day labourer, however, it seems, not without reason, very essential.
>
> Superficial 'theoreticians' can comfort themselves, of course, that the distribution of wealth is a factor secondary to the production. The dialectic of interaction, however, retains here all its force. The destiny of the state-appropriated means of production will be decided in the long run according as these differences in personal existences evolve in one direction or the other.[72]
>
> Two opposite tendencies are growing up out of the depths of the soviet regime. To the extent that, in contrast to a decaying capitalism, it develops the productive forces, it is preparing the economic basis of socialism. To the extent that, for the

benefit of an upper stratum, it carries to more and more extreme expression bourgeois norms of distribution, it is preparing a capitalist restoration. This contrast between forms of property and norms of distribution cannot grow indefinitely. Either the bourgeois norm must in one form or another spread to the means of production, or the norms of distribution must be brought into correspondence with the socialist property system.

The bureaucracy dreads the exposure of this alternative. Everywhere and all the time – in the press, in speeches, in statistics, in the novels of its *littérateurs*, in the verses of its poets, and, finally, in the text of the new constitution – it painstakingly conceals the real relations both in town and country with abstractions from the socialist dictionary. That is why the official ideology is all so lifeless, talentless and false.[73]

Classes are characterised by their position in the social system of the economy, and primarily by their relation to the means of production. In civilised societies, property relations are validated by laws. The nationalisation of the land, the means of industrial production, transport and exchange, together with the monopoly of foreign trade, constitute the basis of the soviet social structure. Through these relations, established by the proletarian revolution, the nature of the Soviet Union as a proletarian state is for us basically defined.[74]

The Soviet bureaucracy has expropriated the proletariat politically in order by methods of *its own* to defend the social conquests. But the very fact of its appropriation of political power in a country where the principal means of production are in the hands of the state, creates a new and hitherto unknown relation between the bureaucracy and the riches of the nation. The means of production belong to the state. But the state, so to speak, 'belongs' to the bureaucracy. If these as yet wholly new relations should solidify, become the norm and be legalised, whether with or without resistance from the workers, they would, in the long run, lead to a complete liquidation of the social conquests of the proletarian revolution. But to speak of that now is at least premature. The proletariat has not yet said its last word.[75]

The attempt to present the soviet bureaucracy as a class of 'state capitalists' will obviously not withstand criticism. The bureaucracy has neither stocks nor bonds. It is recruited, supplemented, and renewed in the manner of an administrative hierarchy, independently of any special property relations of its own. The individual bureaucrat cannot transmit to his heirs his rights in the exploitation of the state apparatus. The bureaucracy enjoys its privileges under the form of an abuse of power. It conceals its income; it pretends that as a special social group it does not even exist ... All this makes the position of the commanding soviet stratum in the highest degree contradictory, equivocal and undignified, notwithstanding the completeness of its power and the smokescreen of flattery that conceals it.[76]

The October Revolution has been betrayed by the ruling stratum, but not yet overthrown. It has a great power of resistance, coinciding with the established property relations, with the living force of the proletariat, the consciousness of its best elements, the impasse of world capitalism, and the inevitability of world revolution.[77]

Let us assume ... that neither a revolutionary nor a counter-revolutionary party seizes power. The bureaucracy continues at the head of the state. Even under these conditions social relations will not jell. We cannot count upon the bureaucracy's peacefully and voluntarily renouncing itself on behalf of socialist equality. If at the present time, notwithstanding the too obvious inconveniences of such an operation, it has considered it possible to introduce ranks and decorations, it must inevitably in future stages seek supports for itself in property relations. One may argue that the big bureaucrat cares little what the prevailing forms of property are, provided only they guarantee him the necessary income. This argument ignores not only the instability of the bureaucrat's own rights, but also the question of his descendants. The new cult of the family has not fallen out of the clouds. Privileges have only half their worth, if they cannot be transmitted to one's children. But the right to bequeath is inseparable from the right of property. It is not enough to be the director of a trust; it is necessary to be a stockholder. The victory of the bureaucracy in this decisive sphere would mean its conversion into a new possessing class. On the other hand, the victory of the proletariat over the bureaucracy would insure the revival of the socialist revolution.[78]

The Soviet Union is a contradictory society halfway between capitalism and socialism, in which (a) the productive forces are still far from adequate to give state property a socialist character; (b) the tendency towards primitive accumulation created by want breaks out through innumerable pores of the planned economy; (c) norms of distribution preserving a bourgeois character lie at the basis of a new differentiation of society; (d) economic growth, while slowly bettering the situation of the toilers, promotes a swift formation of privileged strata; (e) exploiting the social antagonisms, a bureaucracy has converted itself into an uncontrolled caste alien to socialism; (f) the social revolution, betrayed by the ruling party, still exists in property relations and in the consciousness of the toiling masses; (g) a further development of the accumulating contradictions can as well lead to socialism as back to capitalism; (h) on the road to capitalism the counter-revolution would have to break the resistance of the workers; (i) on the road to socialism the workers would have to overthrow the bureaucracy. In the last analysis, the question will be decided by a struggle of living social forces, both in the national and in the world arena.

Doctrinaires will doubtless not be satisfied with this hypothetical formulation. They would like categorical formulae: yes – yes, and no – no. Sociological problems would certainly be simpler, if social phenomena had always a finished character. There is nothing more dangerous, however, than to throw out of reality, for the sake of logical completeness, elements which today violate your scheme and tomorrow may wholly overturn it. In our analysis, we have above all avoided doing violence to dynamic social formations which have had no precedent and have no analogies. The scientific task, as well as the political, is not to give a finished definition to an unfinished process, but to follow all its stages, separate its progressive from its reactionary tendencies, expose their mutual relations, foresee possible variants of development, and find in this foresight a basis for action.[79]

The socialist culture will flourish only in proportion to the dying away of the state. In that simple and unshakeable historic law is contained the death sentence of the present political regime in the Soviet Union. Soviet democracy is not the demand of an abstract policy, still less an abstract moral. It has become a life-and-death need of the country.[80]

A certain Petrov, member of the party since 1918, participant in the civil war, subsequently a Soviet agricultural expert and member of the Right Opposition, who escaped from exile in 1936, writing in a liberal émigré paper, now characterises the so-called Trotskyists as follows: 'The lefts? Psychologically, the last revolutionists, genuine and fervent. No grey bargaining, no compromises. Most admirable people. But idiotic ideas ... a world conflagration and suchlike raving.' We will leave aside the question of their 'ideas'. This moral and political appraisal of the left from their enemy on the right, speaks for itself. It is these 'last revolutionists, genuine, fervent', that the colonels and generals of the GPU are arraigning for ... counter-revolutionary activity in the interests of imperialism.[81]

This is the first time in history that a state

> resulting from a workers' revolution has existed. The stages through which it must go are nowhere written down. It is true that the theoreticians and creators of the Soviet Union hoped that the completely transparent and flexible soviet system would permit the state peacefully to transform itself, dissolve, and die away, in correspondence with the stages of the economic and cultural evolution of society. Here again, however, life proved more complicated than theory anticipated. The proletariat of a backward country was fated to accomplish the first socialist revolution. For this historic privilege, it must, according to all evidence, pay with a second supplementary revolution – against bureaucratic absolutism.[82]
>
> More than ever the fate of the October Revolution is bound up now with the fate of Europe and of the whole world. The problems of the Soviet Union are now being decided on the Spanish peninsula, in France, in Belgium. At the moment when this book appears the situation will be incomparably more clear than today, when civil war is in progress under the walls of Madrid.[83]
>
> Trying to insure itself by a union with France and a friendship with Germany, the Polish bourgeoisie is incapable of accomplishing anything with its manoeuvres except to hasten the war and find in it a more certain death.[84]
>
> The population of Japan is suffocated under the combined yoke of Asiatic agrarianism and ultra-modern capitalism. Korea, Manchukuo, China, at the first weakening of the military pincers, will rise against the Japanese tyranny. A war will bring the empire of the Mikado the greatest of social catastrophes.[85]

The polemicist in Trotsky is so continually present that after the arguments and theoretical discussions, he usually puts an appendix to his works where he sets about people who have particularly annoyed him by their ignorance, dishonesty, or bad faith. In this case it was a question of the 'new friends' of the USSR, and of Beatrice and Sidney Webb in particular, who had published a volume of 1,200 pages after a visit to Russia entitled *Soviet Communism*. For people of that ilk, accustomed to working only from published documents, the Stalinist leaders had afforded generous assistance. The scandal was that this indigestible compilation was favourably received and taken seriously. Trotsky commented on it in these terms:

> Instead of relating what has been achieved and in what direction the achieved is developing, the authors expound for 1,200 pages what is contemplated, indicated in the bureaux, or expounded in the laws. Their conclusion is: When the projects, plans and laws are carried out, then communism will be realised in the Soviet Union. Such is the content of this depressing book, which rehashes the reports of Moscow bureaux and the anniversary articles of the Moscow press.
>
> Friendship for the Soviet bureaucracy is not friendship for the proletarian revolution, but, on the contrary, insurance against it ... The Webbs speak as of something which goes without saying about the vanity of hoping for a European revolution in the near future, and they gather from that a comforting proof of the correctness of the theory of socialism in one country. With the authority of people for whom the October Revolution was a complete, and moreover an unpleasant, surprise, they give us lessons in the necessity of building a socialist society within the limits of the Soviet Union in the absence of other perspectives ... As late as 1923, the Webbs saw no great difference between Bolshevism and Tsarism (see, for example, *The Decay of Capitalist Civilisation*, 1923). Now, however, they have fully recognised the 'democracy' of the Stalin regime. It is needless to seek any contradiction here. The Fabians[86] were indignant when the revolutionary proletariat withdrew freedom of activity from 'educated' society, but they think it quite in the order of things when a bureaucracy withdraws freedom of activity from the proletariat ... The Webbs swear, for example, that criticism in the Soviet Union is

> completely free. A sense of humour is not to be expected from these people ...
>
> Naivety? Neither Engels nor Lenin considered Sidney Webb naive. Respectability rather. After all, it is a question of an established regime and of hospitable hosts. The Webbs are extremely disapproving in their attitude to a Marxian criticism of what exists. They consider themselves called to preserve the heritage of the October Revolution from the Left Opposition.[87]

Among the other new-found friends of the USSR Trotsky singled out Léon Blum, about whom he wrote:

> Léon Blum, who was an enemy of Bolshevism in its heroic epoch, and opened the pages of *Le Populaire* for the express purpose of publicly baiting the October Revolution,[88] would now not print a line exposing the real crimes of the Soviet bureaucracy. Just as the Biblical Moses, thirsting to see the face of Jehovah, was permitted to make his bow only to the rearward parts of the divine anatomy, so the honourable reformists, worshippers of the accomplished fact, are capable of knowing and acknowledging in a revolution only its meaty bureaucratic posterior.[89]

The editing of *The Revolution Betrayed* was barely finished when everything was about to change suddenly in this fairly quiet life in Norway. Trotsky sent the first two copies of the manuscript to the French and American translators on 5 August 1936. Preparing the book had cost a great deal of effort, made even more difficult by frequent attacks of his illness. He had decided to go and spend two weeks at the seaside with the Knudsens. But the next day, when he was still only on the way, he was informed that fascists had got into the house in Weksal in the middle of the night, with the express aim of stealing his archives. They introduced themselves in the disguise of policemen; but Knudsen's daughter, suspicious of this, had alerted the neighbourhood, and they had to flee taking only a few documents at random during their hasty flight. The police identified them easily and were inclined to treat the affair as an amateur effort. General electo me, had held a meeting on 14 August to protest [against] the fascist attack at Weksal – only a few hours before Tass had allied me to the fascists. The French Stalinist organ, *L'Humanité*, later published a cable from Oslo saying that inasmuch as the fascists had paid me a 'friendly visit', the Norwegian government considered my nocturnal interview with them an interference in the political life of the country ...

We had returned to Weksal for the end of the Moscow trial. Dictionary in hand, I puzzled out the Tass reports in the Oslo papers. I felt as if I were in a madhouse. Journalists besieged us – the Norwegian wire service was still conscientiously publishing my rebuttals, which were spread throughout the world ...

If the accused were not put to death, no one would take the accusations seriously. I was convinced that it would all end with executions. Nevertheless, I could scarcely believe my ears when I heard the Paris announcer report, with trembling voice, that Stalin had had all the accused, among whom were four members of the old Bolshevik Central Committee, shot ...

Little by little, the international slander machine went into operation; it did not suffer any lack of grease ... The Norwegian communist paper, which only the day before had seen itself obliged to defend me against the fascists, suddenly changed its tune. It now demanded my expulsion, and, above all, it demanded that my mouth be closed ...

On 26 August, while eight plain-clothes policemen occupied the yard of our house, Police Chief Askvig[90] and a functionary of the Central Passport Bureau in charge of the supervision of aliens called on us. These important visitors invited me to sign a document accepting new conditions for residing in Norway: I was to agree to write no more about current political matters and to give no interviews; I was to agree to have all my correspondence, incoming and outgoing, inspected by the police ... I categorically refused ...

tions for the Storting were approaching. In spite o
es, Trotsky found himself in the middle of electoral
Making use of the articles he had published abroad
nents of Labour accused him of fomenting revo
disturbing Norway's international relations, and
government on that account for having admitted h
country. The fascist attack embarrassed Moscow
then preparing the first of the great trials; it kn
the scaffolding of accusations it had long conten
chief of the criminal police went from Oslo to We
tion Trotsky as a witness with reference to the a
result he declared to the press that there wa
Trotsky's actions contrary to Norwegian laws a
The incident should be considered 'closed'; but
only beginning. Trotsky could not fail to unders
how he reported the facts marking the start of i

> On 14 August, the Soviet press ager
> announced the discovery of a Tr
> Zinovievist terrorist plot. Our host,
> Knudsen, was the first to hear this
> the radio. But there was no electrici
> island, the antennas were most primiti
> make matters worse, the radio was no
> well that night. '... Trotskyist groups .
> revolutionary activity ... ' was all tha
> could get ...
>
> Toward dawn, a journalist friend
> taken notes of the Tass communiqué, a
> Kristiansand, a small neighbouri
> Though I was prepared for anything ,
> not believe my eyes – so outrageous
> able did the mixture of villainy, imp
> stupidity in this document seem to m
>
> Then and there, I dictated to the j
> first statement on the announced tri
> essary to prepare for struggle – some
> was in the offing. The Kremlin coul
> strong reasons, compromise itself w
> frame-up.
>
> The trial took world opinion,
> Communist International, by
> Norwegian Communist Party, desp

The following morning, police agents conducted me to Oslo to be interrogated – still in the capacity of 'witness' in the affair of the fascist raid. The examining magistrate was hardly interested in the facts. On the other hand, he interrogated me for two hours about my political activities, my connections, my visitors ...

From the courthouse I was taken before the minister of justice, who was surrounded by his highest officials. Again I was invited to sign the document, very slightly modified, agreeing to police surveillance, which I had refused to sign the previous day.

'If you want to arrest me,' I demanded, 'Why do you want me to authorise you to do it?'

'But,' the minister replied, 'between arrest and complete liberty there is an intermediate situation.'

'That can only be an equivocation – or a trap; I prefer to be arrested!'

The minister made this concession to me and gave the necessary orders on the spot ... Four policemen, this time in uniform, brought me back to Weksal. In the courtyard I saw others pushing Van Heijenoort,[91] whom they held by the shoulders, out of the house. My wife, alarmed, came out. They kept me locked in the car while indoors they prepared our isolation from the Knudsen family. Police occupied the dining room and cut the telephone wire. We were thus prisoners. The mistress of the house brought us our meals under the surveillance of two policemen ... On 2 September, we were transferred to Sundby, a village in Storsand about 22 miles from Oslo, at the edge of a fjord. There we were to spend three months and 20 days under the surveillance of 13 policemen. Our mail passed through the Central Passport Bureau – which couldn't see any reason for hurrying. No one was admitted to see us. To justify this procedure, which is contrary to the Norwegian constitution, the government had to pass a special law. As for my wife, she was arrested without even any attempt at explanation.

> It would seem that the Norwegian fascists had a victory to celebrate. In reality, it was not they who were the victors. The secret of my internment was simple. The government in Moscow had threatened Norwegian commerce with a boycott – and had immediately given concrete examples of the seriousness of this threat. Ship-owners besieged the ministries: 'Do what you like, but give us soviet business.'
>
> The country's merchant marine, fourth largest in the world, holds a decisive position in public affairs, and the ship-owners make policy – regardless of who occupies the seats of government. Stalin used the monopoly in foreign commerce to prevent me from unmasking his frame-up. Norwegian financial circles came to his aid. The socialist ministers justified themselves by saying: 'All the same, we can't sacrifice the country's vital interests to Trotsky!' That was the reason for my arrest ...
>
> The autumn was foggy and rainy. it would be difficult to describe the atmosphere at Sundby: a wooden house, half of which was occupied by slow-moving, heavy policemen who smoked pipes, played cards, and at noon brought us newspapers overflowing with slander.[92]

From this peculiar prison, Trotsky attempted to alert the workers and public opinion; he wanted to say that a second trial would follow, as monstrous as the first, and that this time the GPU would transport the scene to Oslo. But in vain; the censorship held up letters and appeals, only letting through allusions to the machinations of the trial. When the fascist attackers were brought before the court, and Trotsky was called as a witness, the government insisted that it take place behind closed doors; Stalin was well protected. As the defending attorney, using his articles as evidence, cried out 'I emphasise that these pages were written in Norway'. 'And *I* emphasise', Trotsky quickly shot back, 'that the Soviet oligarchy finds vigilant defenders – disinterested ones, I hope – in the Norwegian fascists.' And he then pronounced a little-known name that was soon to enter the international vocabulary: 'In any event, Stalin and Mr Quisling have collaborated to have me interned.'[93]

During the long voyage on the ship that was taking him to Mexico, Trotsky kept a sort of diary to place on record the thoughts that his recent experience in Norway aroused in him, but above all to start on his reply to the Moscow trial, which the Norwegian police had not even allowed him to begin. On 28 December, he wrote:

> The Norwegians are justly proud of Ibsen, their national poet. Thirty-five years ago, Ibsen was my literary love. One of my earliest articles was devoted to him.[94] In a democratic jail, in the poet's native land, I once again reread his dramas. A great deal of them seems nowadays naive and old-fashioned. But how many prewar poets are there who have completely withstood the test of time? All of history prior to 1914 appears to be soft-headed and provincial. But on the whole Ibsen seemed to me fresh and, in his northern freshness, attractive. I reread *An Enemy of the People* with particular satisfaction. Ibsen's hatred of protestant bigotry, provincial boorishness and stiff-laced hypocrisy became more comprehensible and closer to me after my acquaintance with the first socialist government in the poet's native land.
>
> 'There are any number of ways of interpreting Ibsen', said the Minister of Justice in his own defence, as he descended upon me in Sundby with an unexpected call.
>
> 'Whatever the interpretation, he will always be found against you. Recall the Burgomaster Stockmann ...'
>
> 'Do you imply that I am Stockmann?'
>
> 'To make out the best case for you, Mr Minister: Your government has all the vices but none of the virtues of a bourgeois government ...'
>
> Notwithstanding their literary flavour, our conversations were not remarkable for excessive courtesy ...
>
> 'We were stupid to grant you a visa!' I was

unceremoniously told by the minister of justice in the middle of December.

'And you are preparing to rectify this stupidity by means of a crime?' I replied, repaying frankness with frankness. 'You are behaving towards me in the same way that Noske and Scheidemann behaved toward Karl Liebknecht and Rosa Luxemburg.[95] You are paving the road for fascism. If the workers of Spain and France don't save you, you and your colleagues will be émigrés in a few years like your predecessors, the German social democrats.' [This was written in 1936 ...]

I did not entertain any great hopes about the possibility of finding a haven in some other country. Democratic countries protect themselves against the danger of dictatorships by this, they borrow certain worse aspects of the latter. For revolutionists the so-called 'right' of asylum has long since been converted from a right into a question of indulgence. Coupled with this were: the Moscow trial and my internment in Norway.

It is not hard to understand how welcome a piece of news was the cable from the New World stating that the government of distant Mexico would extend to us its hospitality. There loomed a way out of Norway and the impasse. On the way back from court, I said to the police officer accompanying me: 'Kindly inform the government that my wife and I are ready to depart from Norway at the earliest possible moment. However, before applying for a Mexican visa I should like to make arrangements for a safe voyage. I must consult my friends ...' The Minister of Justice, who arrived on the following day in Sundby, chaperoned by three of the highest police officials, was obviously staggered by the extremism of my requests. 'Even in Tsarist jails', I told him, 'the exiles were allowed to see their relatives or friends in order to arrange their personal affairs.'

'Yes, yes', replied the Minister of Justice philosophically, 'but times have changed ...' On 18 December, the minister once again made his appearance, but only to announce that I had been refused the visits.[96]

David King Collection

Marguerite and Alfred Rosmer with Trotsky, Natalia Sedova and Sieva in Mexico

Chapter Four: In Mexico (Part One)

The strictness of the internment and police surveillance was maintained to the last minute of his stay in Norway; on the one hand there was absolute secrecy, and on the other press statements were issued to the newspapers in order to mislead public opinion. All this was hardly reassuring. 'Our own security,' noted Trotsky, 'coincided in this instance with the security of the Norwegian vessel and its crew.'[97] The writer Helge Krog was able to find words to convey the indignation of militant workers and intellectuals shocked at such servility.[98] The secretaries were kept away; this time Trotsky and his wife went off alone, with only the policeman Jonas Lie for company.[99] To begin with, the crew only displayed curiosity. The ship-owner himself came to the boat, and in a friendly manner placed his cabin at the disposal of the deportees. Trotsky was therefore able to work for the 21 days' duration of the voyage. His thoughts were totally absorbed in the monstrous trial. However painful it might be to take up the gross lies and falsifications of the indictment and the prosecutor, they had to be refuted one by one; it was a task made all the more necessary because if so odious an intrigue were to be tolerated and allowed to pass, this trial would only be a beginning, and others would follow. It was necessary to reply as quickly as possible.

Trotsky used his long hours of leisure on the voyage to jot down notes that could be published on arrival in Mexico. He concentrated upon the two principal accused, Zinoviev and Kamenev, outlining their essential traits, their political biographies, describing their attitudes during these latest years, and showing how and why they had become Stalin's victims. 'There are no compelling reasons,' he said, 'for me to take upon myself any political or moral responsibility for Zinoviev and Kamenev. Discounting a brief interval – 1926–27 – they were always my bitter adversaries. Personally, I did not place much trust in them. Each of them, to be sure, was Stalin's intellectual superior. But they lacked sufficient character.'[100] It was nonetheless necessary to understand that when these two men came before the court, they were completely different from the Bolshevik leaders they had once been: 'For 10 years they had been enveloped by clouds of slander paid for in heavy gold. For 10 years they had been suspended between life and death, first in a political sense, then in a moral sense, and lastly in a physical sense. Can one find in all past history examples of such systematic, refined, and fiendish destructive work upon the spines and nerves, upon all the elements of the human spirit?'[101] That was why 'unintelligent in the extreme are the comparisons, so widespread in intellectual circles, with the conduct in court of Danton, Robespierre,[102] and others. Those were cases of revolutionary tribunes who came directly from the combat arena to face the knife of justice, still at the height of their powers, with their nerves almost unaffected, and ... without the slightest hope of survival.'[103]

But the big question remained: why did they confess to crimes they had not committed? For those who refused to go deeper into it, and for those who were inclined to avoid the question, this was a decisive argument. Trotsky provided some penetrating explanations of it, after noting that 'the tanker's two sirens suddenly blared tonight; the alarm gun fired twice; the *Ruth* was greeting the New Year. No one answered us. During the whole crossing we met, I think, only two ships. We are indeed taking an unaccustomed route. However, the fascist police officer accompanying us received from his socialist minister, Trygve Lie, a telegram of greetings. All he needed were greetings from Yagoda and Vyshinsky!'[104] To respond to this question, it was necessary to follow the development of events since the formation of the Opposition in 1923. In the course of the years following, for a variety of reasons and at different times, some oppositionists gave in, finding the new policy resulting from a 'turn' to be correct. But pure and simple approval of the new policy was judged to be insufficient for their readmission into the party; they had to accuse themselves publicly of 'deviations', and to affirm that they had been mistaken previously; that Stalin had always been right, and that they declared him to be infallible. The 'confessions' and 'admissions' of the future trials were present in embryo in these abjurations. Beginning with the assassination of Kirov on 1 December 1934,[105] there was a constant progress in this degradation.

> Simple people ask, 'Isn't Stalin afraid his victims will denounce the falsifications to the audience?' The risk is negligible. The majority of the accused tremble not only for themselves but also for their closest ones. It is not easy to decide what the effect will be on an audience when one has a wife, a son, a daughter in the hands of the GPU. Besides, how can one denounce the falsification? ... The confessions 'freely given' by each of the accused only continue his preceding denunciations. How can one make the audience and the whole of mankind believe that one has done nothing but slander oneself for 10 years?
>
> Smirnov tried to denounce to the audience the 'confessions' to which he had agreed at the preliminary examination. Immediately, his wife's testimony was brought against him, with his own depositions and the affirmations of all the other accused ... Everything has been foreseen. The parts have been studied. The accused, who, at the preliminary examination, had resigned himself to this dishonourable task, sees no reason to change his attitude in public session.[106]

The Norwegian tanker entered the port of Tampico on 9 January. The voyage had been arranged in such a way that Trotsky had informed Jonas Lie that he would not agree to embark unless there were some friends there to receive him at the port.

'Then a launch drew up and all our fears evaporated,' Natalia Trotsky wrote. 'We were greeted by honest and smiling faces.' Diego Rivera, who was unable to move from hospital, was not able to come, but his wife, Frida Kahlo,[107] was there, along with 'journalists, Mexican officials, and comrades, all friendly, warm, open and welcoming':

> There was a great deal of encouraging news from New York; the whole New World seemed to have been incensed by the Moscow crimes. We gulped in the air of freedom ... A train provided by the Mexican government took us through sun-baked country, scattered with palm trees and cacti ... We were shown a car ... we arrived in a suburb of Mexico City, at a low house painted blue, it had a patio filled with plants, fresh, airy rooms, a collection of pre-Columbian objets d'art, and a vast number of pictures we had come to a different world, the house of Frida Kahlo and Diego Rivera.[108]

'Backward' Mexico was giving a sharp lesson to Norway and the great nations of the West. It then had a president of exceptional quality, General Lazaro Cardenas.[109] Continuing and deepening the work of his predecessors, he was undertaking a great plan of basic reforms, freeing the peasant from the semi-slavery in which he had been held for so long, and increasing the numbers of 'rural schools' which an educationalist was able to say were models of socialised schooling. These reforms were going to strengthen his regime and allow him to create a new society, beyond the reach of the pressures of international capital, because an audacious measure to reclaim the petroleum resources for the nation had succeeded in expropriating the powerful British and American companies. London had recalled its ambassador and had broken off diplomatic relations, and the oil companies were carrying on an undercover struggle, attempting to intimidate the government, but without success.

Trotsky soon set to work in this sympathetic atmosphere. He knew that time was pressing; a second trial was sure to be on the way, precisely because, among other reasons, the first had been received with incredulity in the West, even by those who wanted to believe it. Stalin wanted to give these people a double dose. This trial was brought forward quicker than could be expected, and still using the same method. The first telegram announcing it reached Mexico on 19 January – exactly 10 days after they had arrived in Tampico – and it began four days later in Moscow on the 23rd. Trotsky wrote on the 21st:

> Tass announced that ... a new trial of 'Trotskyists' (Radek, Piatakov,[110] and others) would take place. It has been known for a long time that such a trial was in preparation, but there was no certainty that they would really dare go through with it in view of the extremely unfavourable impression created by the Trial of the Sixteen (Zinoviev and others). The Moscow government is now repeating the same manoeuvre as in the Trial of the Sixteen. International working-class organisations cannot intervene in just four days'; dangerous witnesses cannot reply from abroad, and undesirable foreigners cannot even attempt to get into Moscow. But as far as the tried and tested 'friends' ... are concerned, naturally they have been invited to the Soviet capital in time ... so that they may later sing paeans to the justice of Stalin-Vyshinsky. When these lines appear in the press, this new trial will probably be over. The sentences will have been imposed and perhaps carried out. So far as this angle is concerned the design of the backstage directors is absolutely clear: to catch public opinion unawares and to commit rape upon it.[111]

It could be said at any rate of this 'justice' that it was quick; it did not allow those under the death sentence to await the hangman for too long, any more than it allowed the necessary time for an appeal or a possible reprieve, or for recognising an error; like its head of state, it was infallible. But it was no more than a pretence of justice, for the accused had been condemned a hundred times before the 'judges' pronounced the sentence dictated by the boss. The best defence against this gross travesty of justice was to take the offensive. When the trial of Zinoviev was being organised and developed, Trotsky had defied Stalin from Norway to ask for his extradition, a request all the more natural since the whole trial had revolved around Trotsky, the instigator of these murder attempts which had not even begun to be carried out, but for which the accused had been condemned. The challenge had not been taken up: a request for extradition would have to come before a proper court, conducted in accordance with the law, and would provoke a public and contradictory debate, precisely what Stalin did not want at any price. The same demand, and the same challenge, were repeated from Mexico, with the same avoidance.

It was nonetheless necessary to force the debate feared by Stalin. Committees had been spontaneously formed in various countries after the first trial; in Britain and America under the name of 'The Committee for the Defence of Leon Trotsky', in Czechoslovakia 'For Justice and Truth', and in France it was 'The Commission of Enquiry into the Moscow Trial'. They in no way included great numbers of people, for the majority of the intellectuals avoided them; they admitted their unease in private, but publicly they even refused to associate with what was only a request for an investigation. They were 'anti-fascists', and Stalin had just placed Russia in the camp of the democracies. It was fruitless to remind them that at the time when the Franco-Russian alliance was at its height the 'anti-fascists' then were not afraid to denounce the crimes of Tsarism, and that French governments, even the most reactionary ones, had granted asylum to the authors of 'real' assassination attempts, and had refused the extradition demanded by the government with which they were allied. These committees had only scant resources at their disposal; they published duplicated bulletins, and a pamphlet from time to time, and organised public meetings. Trotsky's eldest son, Lev Sedov, who had been accused alongside his father, refuted the charges of the indictment in a weighty study on the trial published as the *Red Book*.[112] After the Zinoviev trial, Trotsky had remarked in his note of 21 January, that another trial of 'Trotskyists' had taken place at the end of November, supplementing the former and preparing that of Piatakov-Radek; this trial must be regarded as a rehearsal in the provinces before coming back to Moscow. The main stress in the indictment was no longer terrorism, but the sabotage of industry, preparation for a war in the interests of Hitler and Japan.[113] Trotsky recalled that he had written in a message to the press on 15 September the previous year:

> Viewed in the mirror of world opinion, the Moscow trial has been a terrible fiasco ... The 'leaders' cannot quietly let the matter rest there. Just as the GPU was forced, after the miserable failure of the first Kirov trial in January 1935, to prepare the second trial (August 1936) ... they now have no other choice than to discover new 'assassi-

> nation attempts', new 'conspiracies', etc. Although the Norwegian government confiscated my statement, it has not thereby lost any of its force. The new trial is above all necessary to reinforce the old one, to fill in its cracks, to mask the contradictions already laid bare by criticism.[114]

The indictment in the Zinoviev trial rested upon meetings of the accused in Copenhagen. Now it had been easy to prove that Lev Sedov had not gone to Copenhagen, and that the hotel where he had supposedly given instructions to his accomplices no longer existed. This time, to prevent any verification, a clandestine aircraft journey by Piatakov to Trotsky was envisaged, where Trotsky, after giving him the order to extend the terrorist and sabotage activity, had 'informed him of his negotiations with Rudolf Hess, the second person in the Hitlerite hierarchy, with a view to the next war against the USSR'. The assertion was soon refuted by corroboratory witnesses, among them that of the director of the Kyeller airport near Oslo, where the aircraft would have had to land. (Ten years later, at the Nuremberg War Crimes Tribunal, Hess was in the dock; it would have been easy to question him about these 'negotiations'. Some American and British writers and journalists addressed a request to the presiding judge, the members of the court and the prosecutors, asking for Hess to be questioned on this particular point. This was a challenge to the Russians; they protected themselves by refusing to take it up. Repeating the celebrated formula of Judge Delegorgue in the Zola trial, during the Dreyfus affair,[115] they insisted that the questions, which would have forced them to confess, to admit their lies publicly, were not posed – both these and also those connected to the Stalin-Hitler Pact of 1939, among others.)[116]

After this second trial, which repeated and extended the intrigues of the first, the American Committee decided to convene a giant meeting in New York to bring the affair to public attention. On 9 February, 6,500 people took their places in the vast hall of the Hippodrome. It had been announced that Trotsky would speak from the podium by telephone. The Stalinists did not dare to interfere with the meeting (any more than they could provide any 'proof') but they resorted to sabotage, real this time. When the chairman called on Trotsky, the radio remained silent. Several unsuccessful attempts to fix it revealed that the transmission apparatus had been put out of order. But this sabotage did not put the organisers at a loss. They had taken the precaution of providing themselves in advance with the text of the speech, and if those present could not hear the voice of Trotsky, they did hear his explanations, his arguments, and his decisive refutations of the absurd accusations levelled against him. 'I will appeal,' he said to begin with, 'only to reason.' But the Moscow trials were 'based on absurdity'. There were unbelievable contradictions. Yesterday the accused were dreaming only of killing Stalin, and now suddenly they were singing his praises; Trotsky was always the instigator of murder attempts that never took place, and gave orders by means of letters that were never produced:

> The pseudo-plot, and the confessions, the theatrical judgement and the entirely real executions, all were arranged by one and the same hand. Whose? *Cui prodest*? Who benefits? The hand of Stalin! The rest is deceit, falsehood and idle babbling about the 'Russian soul'. In the trials there did not figure fighters, nor conspirators, but puppets in the hands of the GPU. They play assigned rôles. The aim of the disgraceful performance: to eliminate the whole Opposition, to poison the very source of critical thought, to definitively ensconce the totalitarian regime of Stalin.[117]

No man of good faith could be found to deny that these trials were disturbing and disquieting conscious public opinion. Trotsky had twice declared himself ready to reply to a request for his extradition. Why was the Russian government avoiding it? It feared a public debate. But this debate must take place, and Trotsky asked for an international commission of enquiry into the trials to be set up, made up of men of unquestionable honesty and integrity. He was prepared to appear before such a public and impartial commission and submit documents and facts which would assist in discovering the truth. Then he made a declaration that profoundly moved the assembly: 'If this commission finds that I am guilty in the slightest degree of the crimes which Stalin imputes to me, I pledge in advance to place myself in the hands of the executioners of the GPU. That, I hope, is clear.

Have you all heard? I make this declaration before the entire world.'[118] This speech, printed and published immediately in a pamphlet under the title *I Stake My Life*, had an echo in America and beyond. How was it possible to reject a request formulated in this way? Commissions of this type had been set up in the past, and their decisions had always been considered valid – obviously, except by those who had suffered their consequences.

The philosopher and educationalist John Dewey enjoyed an exceptional authority, not only in America, but throughout the world; he was universally revered and respected for his integrity and his long working life.[119] He agreed to become part of the commission and to preside over it. Suzanne La Follette took charge of the secretariat. The other members were John Chamberlain, a journalist, EA Ross, a professor of sociology and the author of two books on the origins of the Russian Revolution, the result of enquiries made on the spot, Benjamin Stolberg, an author and journalist, Otto Rühle, a member of the Reichstag in 1914, and one of the first to oppose the war along with Liebknecht, Wendelin Thomas, the leader of the Wilhelmshaven Revolt of 7 November 1918, Carlo Tresca, an anarcho-syndicalist militant, the editor of *Il Martello*, an anti-fascist and anti-Stalinist organ, and Francisco Zamora, a journalist and formerly a member of the national committee of the Mexican Workers Federation.[120] The French committee chose me to go to America to take part in the work of the commission.

As soon as it was set up, the commission decided to question Trotsky. As he could not come to New York, since the America of Roosevelt had also refused him even a temporary authorisation to stay, a preliminary or investigatory commission was formed to send to Mexico. Along with John Dewey and Suzanne La Follette, it included Ben Stolberg, and Carleton Beals, a journalist then stationed in Mexico,[121] took the place of Otto Rühle.

The Commission held its sessions in Coyoacan, in the house the painter Diego Rivera had put at Trotsky's disposal. Letters had been sent to the Russian ambassador in Washington, the American and Mexican Communist Parties, the League of Nations, and the trade union organisations, asking them to send a representative who would have complete freedom to produce any document and to ask any question. The Stalinists alone refused, even though it was an ideal opportunity to produce their proofs. The first session took place on 10 April 1937 at 10 o'clock in the morning in a room, generally Trotsky's office, large enough to receive the representatives of the invited organisations, the journalists and the photographers. In opening the session, John Dewey declared:

> The fact that hearings are being held in which a foreigner will defend himself before foreigners on Mexican soil is an honour to Mexico, and a reproach to those countries whose political system or current policy bars the holdings of our meetings on their soil ... This Commission, like many millions of workers of city and country, of hand and brain, believes that no man should be condemned without a chance to defend himself ... In the United States, it has long been customary for public-spirited citizens to organise committees for the purposes of securing fair trials where there was suspicion concerning the impartiality of the courts ... I cite just two instances in this connection: The Tom Mooney Defense Committee and the Sacco-Vanzetti Defense Committee, with which many members of the American Committee for the Defense of Leon Trotsky cooperated ... The present case differs from those I have cited in one important point. In this case there exists no legally constituted court before which the accused may plead his case. Twice, in their absence, both Leon Trotsky and his son, Leon Sedov, whose guilt or innocence hangs upon that of his father, have been declared guilty by the highest tribunal of the Soviet Union. And Trotsky's repeated demands that the Soviet government ask for his extradition, which would automatically have brought him before either a Norwegian or a Mexican court, have been ignored. Therefore, it became part of the function of his defence committee to initiate the formation of an impartial body before which his side of the case could be heard.[122]

The commission held 13 sessions during 10–17 April. All the

counts of the indictment, even the most peculiar or the most absurd, were minutely examined. There was only one incident when one of its members, Carleton Beals, became provocative to cover up his withdrawal. Being pro-Stalinist at the time, and not being able to accept the evidence, it only remained for him to withdraw. Upon its return to New York, the commission organised a meeting to keep the public posted on its investigations; it took place on 9 May at the Mecca Temple. John Dewey took as the theme of his speech that truth was on the march, and so close was the resemblance with the Dreyfus affair that it had to be a crime for political reasons. The men who had constantly done their utmost to prevent the formation of the committee redoubled their efforts when they understood the way the enquiry was going, unmasking their lies. Dewey condemned their attitude without needing to raise his voice: 'To hold Trotsky guilty of the specific charges of which he was convicted,' he said, 'because of his well-known opposition to the present rulers of the USSR is not fair or square.' He blamed the liberals for evasion very close to intellectual dishonesty, 'for if liberalism means anything, it means complete and courageous devotion to freedom of inquiry'.[123] The transcript of this patient investigation was then published by Harper in New York under the title of *The Case of Leon Trotsky*. The size of the volume – 620 pages in octavo – shows the extent of the enquiry. Since Vyshinsky had invoked 'the historical connection which confirms the theses of the indictment on the basis of the Trotskyites' past activity',[124] the commission became immersed in the history of Bolshevism from its origins.

The work was finished at the beginning of December, and in the course of a meeting held in New York on the 12th Dewey was able to announce the verdict of the commission: Trotsky and Sedov were pronounced not guilty. He said:

> The implications of this finding are profoundly disturbing ... The present regime is seeking to identify political opposition to itself with criminal activity against the Soviet Union and people ... Shocking is the systematic use by the Communist parties throughout the world of the vicious 'Trotskyist-terrorist-Fascist' amalgam as a means of destroying political opposition and even of justifying gross frame-ups and assassination. Even in

> this country the Communist Party and its labor and liberal sympathisers have used this strictly amoral tactic, indistinguishable from the tactic of fascism, to slander and persecute opposition.

He described this attitude as 'an extraordinary corruption of the idealistic heritage of the Russian Revolution', revealing 'a danger against which our own people must defend themselves without illusion and without compromise'.

❖ ❖ ❖ ❖

The telegrams from New York brought a rare happiness to the house in Coyoacan. It was the first cheering news since their hard exile. The deception had been definitively exposed; the work of the commission and its decision came as a great relief to Trotsky; the Stalinist press, obedient to its instructions, repeating its lies and falsifications, could from now on only deceive those who wanted to be deceived, and about whom nothing more could be done. The report of the commission was for today and forever. Harper issued it at the beginning of 1938 under the title of *Not Guilty*. John Dewey had made sure that each of the prosecutor's allegations had been examined and dealt with according to the usual courtroom procedures; the accumulated evidence was grouped around each accusation; the gross manipulative tricks were uncovered one after the other. Bit by bit the indictment broke down; and even if the results of this work were limited for the moment, the report remained, as the writer James T Farrell noted, 'a model for any future efforts of this kind ... a monument to all who worked in this enterprise. It is an example of democratic thinking, reasoning, procedure and of Dewey's own conception of methods of free inquiry.'[125]

Their happiness was to be of short duration. Beginning in the first weeks of 1938, Trotsky and his faithful companion were dealt two terrible blows. Their eldest son, who had become their constant collaborator since their deportation to Asia, and had been known since then as Leon Sedov, died in Paris on 16 February. He had entered a clinic a few days earlier to undergo an operation without risk – for appendicitis – and there had been no complications at all; he was about to come out, and suddenly, that was the end. Was it carelessness, negligence in nursing, or a crime of the NKVD? The means at the disposal of his friends did not allow any reply to these questions, and the judicial authorities were hardly predisposed in favour of a serious investigation that could help discover the truth. It was Diego Rivera who took upon himself the unhappy duty of informing the parents. Completely taken aback, Trotsky made him repeat his words, and then pushed him rudely out of the room. He wanted to be alone, and for several days he saw no one. When he was able to accept the inevitable, he wrote in memory of his son these unique pages, in which he gave full flow to his grief:

> As I write these lines, with Leon Sedov's mother by my side, telegrams of condolence keep coming from different countries. And for us each telegram evokes the same appalling question: 'Can it really be that our friends in France, Holland, England, the United States, Canada, South Africa and here in Mexico accept it as definitely established that Leon Sedov is no more?' Each telegram is a new token of his death, but we are unable to believe it as yet ...
>
> Of that older generation whose ranks we joined at the end of the last century on the road to revolution, all, without exception, have been swept from the scene. That which Tsarist hard-labour prisons and harsh exile, the hardships of emigration, the civil war, and disease has failed to accomplish has in recent years been achieved by Stalin, the worst scourge of the revolution. Following the destruction of the older generation, the best section of the next, that is, the generation which awakened in 1917 and which received its training in the 24 armies of the revolutionary front, was likewise destroyed ... He himself survived only by a miracle, owing to the fact that he accompanied us into exile and then to Turkey. During the years of our last emigration we made many new friends, some of whom have entered intimately into our lives, becoming, as it were, members of our family. But we met all of them for the first time in these last few years when we had already neared old age. Leon was the only one who knew us when we were young; he became part of our lives from

the very first moment of his self-awakening. While young in years, he still seemed our contemporary. Together with us, he went through our second emigration: Vienna, Zurich, Paris, Barcelona, New York, Amherst (concentration camp in Canada), and finally Petrograd ...

Of his own volition Leon left the Kremlin for a proletarian student dormitory, in order not to be any different from the others. He would not ride with us in an automobile, refusing to make use of this privilege of the bureaucrats. But he did participate ardently in all Red Saturdays and other 'labour mobilisations', cleaning snow from the Moscow streets, 'liquidating' illiteracy, unloading bread and firewood from freight cars, and later, as a polytechnic student, repairing locomotives. If he did not get to the war front, it was only because even adding two or as much as three years to his age could not have helped him; for he was not yet 15 when the civil war ended. However, he did accompany me several times to the front, absorbing its stark impressions, and firmly understanding why this bloody struggle was being waged ... In this child, growing to boyhood and adolescence, a sense of duty and achievement awakened early.

In 1923, Leon threw himself headlong into the work of the Opposition. It would be entirely wrong to see in this nothing more than parental influence. After all, when he left a comfortable apartment in the Kremlin for his hungry, cold and dirty dormitory, he did so against our will, even though we did not resist this move on his part. His political orientation was determined by the same instinct which impelled him to choose crowded streetcars rather than Kremlin limousines. *The Platform of the Opposition* simply gave political expression to traits inherent in his nature. Leon broke uncompromisingly with those of his student friends who were violently torn from 'Trotskyism' by their bureaucratic fathers and found a way to his baker friends. Thus, at 17 he began the life of a fully conscious revolutionist. He quickly grasped the art of conspiratorial work, illegal meetings, and the secret issuing and distribution of Opposition documents ... Leon had exceptional mathematical ability. He never tired of assisting worker-students who had not gone through grammar school. He engaged in this work with all his energy; encouraging, leading, chiding the lazy ones – the youthful teacher saw in his work a service to his class ...

In the winter of 1927, when the police massacre of the Opposition began, Leon had passed his twenty-second year. By that time a child was born to him and he would proudly bring his son to the Kremlin to show him to us. Without a moment's hesitation, however, Leon decided to tear himself away from his school and his young family in order to share our fate in central Asia. In this he acted not only as a son but above all as a co-thinker. It was essential, whatever the cost, to guarantee our connection with Moscow ...

In the chaos of the Alma Ata public library he had already studied the files of *Pravda* for the Soviet years and gathered the necessary quotations and references with unfailing resourcefulness. Lacking this precious material and without Leon's subsequent researches in archives and libraries, first in Turkey, later in Berlin, and finally in Paris, not one of my works during the past 10 years would have been possible ... My son's name should rightfully be placed next to mine on almost all my books written since 1928 ...

So intimate a collaboration did not, however, mean that no disputes or occasionally even very sharp clashes arose between us. Neither at that time, nor later in emigration – and this must be said candidly – were my relations with Leon by any means of an even and placid character. To his categorical judgements, which were often disrespectful to some of the 'old men' of the Opposition, I not only counterposed equally categoric corrections and reservations, but I also displayed toward him the pedantic and exacting attitude which I had acquired in practical questions. Because of these traits, which are perhaps useful and even indispensable for work on a large scale but quite insufferable in personal relationships, people closest to me often had a very hard time. And inasmuch as the closest to me of all the youth was my son, he usually had the hardest time of all. To a superficial eye it might even have seemed that our relationship was permeated with severity and aloofness. But beneath the surface there glowed a deep mutual attachment based on something immeasurably greater than bonds of blood – a solidarity of views and appraisals, of sympathies and antipathies, of joys and sorrows experienced together, of great hopes we had in common ...[126]

But the Russian question continued to occupy the centre of his attention. While in Prinkipo he became the actual editor of the *Biulleten Oppozitsii* from its inception (the middle of 1929), and took complete charge of this work upon his arrival in Berlin (the beginning of 1931), to where the *Biulleten* was immediately transferred from Paris. The last letter we received from Leon, written on 4 February 1938, 12 days before his death, begins with the following words: 'I am sending you page-proofs of the *Biulleten*, for the next ship will not leave for some time, while the *Biulleten* will come off the press only tomorrow morning ...' On 16 February, the Mexican evening papers carried a brief dispatch on the death of Leon Sedov following a surgical operation. Absorbed in urgent work I did not see these papers. Diego Rivera on his own initiative checked this dispatch by radio and came to me with the terrible news. An hour later I told Natalia of the death of our son – in the same month of February in which 32 years ago she brought me in jail the news of his birth. Thus ended for us the day of 16 February, the blackest day in our personal lives.[127]

❖ ❖ ❖ ❖

After the death of his son came the end of a friend. This was no less of a blow, and in a sense, even harder. Christian Rakovsky[128] was his oldest, closest and dearest friend. Trotsky met him for the first time in 1903, and met him again during the Balkan wars; he had stayed with him in his native Romania where he carried on the harsh struggle of the socialist pioneers. He met him once more during the World War at the Zimmerwald internationalist conference, and later in Russia after the revolution. He was one of the first opponents of Stalinism and the first to be struck at. Stalin sent him to the Ukraine where he succeeded in enormous tasks and then sent him as ambassador to London where there was then nothing to do. Trotsky could not fail to understand that it was through Rakovsky and the Opposition that they wanted to strike at him; he was annoyed by it: why not go at him openly? And that this Christian, this lifelong friend, had put his signature to a declaration that read: 'I have known since 1926 that Trotsky was an agent of the intelligence service; he told me himself.' The fact that he had not written it himself, and had only signed it, did not lessen the pain, any more than the fact that he was among other men who had also signed similar declarations, all of them directed against the man who was absent from the court, but always present in the indictment. The Zinovievs, the Piatakovs and the Radeks conducted themselves in this way. But they had been comrades in the struggle. Christian Rakovsky had been a friend.

On 2 March 1938, a fresh batch of old Bolsheviks was led before the same 'supreme' court. They were the ones who had been the most faithful and staunchest allies of Stalin in the struggle against Trotskyism. They had occupied the highest positions: Rykov was Lenin's successor as Chairman of the Council of Peoples' Commissars. Bukharin had directed the Communist International and the party journal, *Pravda*; Tomsky was the head of the trade union organisation. They had understood too late when Stalin had cut off all retreat; it was now as beaten men that they came before the court (Tomsky committed suicide to avoid the shame of 'confessing'). The sessions went on until 13 March. The prosecutor had fabricated an 'anti-Soviet bloc of Rights and Trotskyites', but he was no longer Yagoda; he had changed places and was now in the dock. During the opening interrogation one of the accused, Krestinsky,[129] indirectly revealed the mechanism behind the confessions. During a full session, he stood up to Vyshinsky: 'Yes, I signed these declarations as I was told, but they are only lies!' He had to withdraw his statement the next day. When he came back before the court, he confessed all Vyshinsky required.

Thus Stalin could get away with everything. He exploited to the full an international situation that would allow him to rid himself, one after the other, of the men of the revolution and install his personal power by such contemptible means that the over sensitive 'anti-fascists' pretended to ignore them; others invoked 'the Russian soul' and Dostoyevsky,[130] and some were found who claimed that this was true democratic justice. However, the public trials were becoming further apart: there were only five months between the first and the second, but 14 months intervened between the second and the third. The work of the Commission of Inquiry perhaps had some effect. But the executions did not end. From time to time, the newspapers announced the discovery of 'centres of Trotskyism, sabotage and espionage' – the hallowed formula; if there were trials, the press said nothing about them; it only announced that between May and June 83 executions had taken place in the Far East.

Of all these executions without a public trial, or indeed without a trial of any sort, there were some, however much one had begun to get used to what was happening, that created real bewilderment: those of Tukhachevsky and the top leaders of the army. 'Stalin, having beheaded the party and Soviet apparatus, has proceeded to decapitation of the army,' stated Trotsky;[131] but recalling the facts that Tukhachevsky had been relieved of his command on 11 May and sent to the provinces, and that these were men whom he knew well, he was nonetheless obliged to fall back on hypotheses for the causes of this massacre, so well kept was the secret:

> If the past of those who were shot and the particular features of each are weighed accurately, it is hard to conclude that they were connected by any common political programme ... Given the danger of approaching war, the most responsible commanders could not help becoming alarmed by the fact that Voroshilov stood at the head of the armed forces. There need be no doubt that in these circles the candidacy of Tukhachevsky was put for-

> ward to replace Voroshilov. In its first stage, the generals no doubt tried to base their 'plot' on Stalin, who had been playing his usual ambiguous game for a long time, exploiting the antagonism between Voroshilov and Tukhachevsky. Tukhachevsky and his adherents apparently overestimated their forces. Placed in a situation where he had to choose at the last moment, Stalin preferred Voroshilov, who until then had remained his submissive instrument, and surrendered Tukhachevsky to the executioners as one who could become a dangerous adversary.[132]

Stalin did not deign to enlighten public opinion, any more than the sections of the Communist International. He contented himself with allowing 'well informed' 'anti-fascists' to say that Tukhachevsky and the generals were allied with Hitler.

> Let us not forget that after Hitler's rise to power ... Soviet diplomats did not stint in making obliging declarations in regard to fascism that today have a scandalous ring. The philosophy for this policy was provided by Stalin: 'Above all we must protect the construction of Socialism in our country. Fascism and democracy are twins, not opposites. France will not attack us and the threat from Germany can be neutralised simply by collaboration with her.[133]

❖ ❖ ❖ ❖

Seeking to disentangle the causes of these trials and executions, and of the situation that permitted them, Trotsky wrote that:

> A revolutionary epoch brings the popular masses close together. On the other hand, a period of reaction signifies the triumph of centrifugal forces. During the last 14 years not one single breach in the Bolshevik party has been closed up again, not one wound has healed, not one conflict has ended in reconciliation. Capitulations and

> acts of self-abasement have not helped. The centrifugal forces have acted to enlarge the slightest opening until it is transformed into an unbridgeable chasm. Anyone drawn into this opening, even by his little toe, has been lost irredeemably.[134] [Stalin] ... seeks to strike not at the ideas of his opponent, but at his skull.[135]

Accused and condemned by his court, Trotsky escaped him and remained free to denounce the fraud. With a cruelty of which history offers few examples, Stalin revenged himself upon him by taking his children, his friends, and his secretaries: his two daughters, Nina and Zinaida;[136] his two sons, the eldest dying in the suspicious circumstances we have described, whereas the younger, Sergei, imprisoned under the monstrous accusation of poisoning the workers in the factory where he worked, disappeared into the concentration camps and deportation;[137] his secretaries: the Russians Glazman, Sermuks, Poznansky and Butov,[138] for whom the generally conventional expression of faithfulness and devotion even unto death was to become literally true; the German Rudolf Klement,[139] kidnapped in France; the Czech Erwin Wolf, taken in Barcelona;[140] Walter Held, a refugee from Germany and a naturalised Norwegian, who in his haste to join Trotsky in Mexico was arrested while crossing Russian territory, and his wife and child along with him;[141] Ignace Reiss, marked out for death when the shame of the first Moscow trial made him break publicly with the party, who was lured into a trap in the Lausanne suburbs;[142] Andrès Nin and Kurt Landau, picked up by the GPU in Spain during the civil war (political differences separated them from Trotsky, but they were irreconcilable oppositionists).[143] It is a long list. It was to become even longer after Trotsky's death. Walter Krivitsky, a friend of Ignace Reiss, disgusted as he was by the Moscow trials, was found dead in a Washington hotel room;[144] a member of the International Commission of Inquiry, Carlo Tresca, was killed in New York in broad daylight without anyone even being able to ascertain whether it was a Stalinist crime, for Tresca had equally opposed Stalin and Mussolini in his newspaper.

Some, incapable of living outside the party or outside Russia, or depressed by illness, committed suicide: Joffe, an old friend;[145] Glazman, his secretary; and his eldest daughter

Zinaida. One grandson alone remained to Trotsky, Sieva, the son of Zinaida. He had lived with Leon Sedov after the death of his mother. He was still in France, and Trotsky wanted to have him with him. Some friends arranged the voyage and went to Mexico with the child a short time before war broke out, at the beginning of July 1939.[146]

❖ ❖ ❖ ❖

Trotsky greatly needed a rest at this time. Resilient and courageous though he was, the trials and the blows that Stalin had inflicted upon him had worsened the ailment against which the doctors had shown themselves impotent, and the unceasing work wore him out. As soon as it was possible to go away the entire household went to stay in Taxco beyond the mountains that loomed over Mexico in the west, and where the climate was less harsh, in a villa where an American professor gave a hearty welcome to the refugees. He was an expert in Mexican studies, and during the university holidays he organised a sort of seminar in Mexico, and at the end of the courses he came with his students to Coyoacan for a long general conversation. Both professor and students, profiting from this unique opportunity, questioned Trotsky on all sorts of subjects relating to the great issues of the day.[147] In exchange, he put his house at Trotsky's disposal, and he went to stay there as circumstances allowed. In the morning they went for a long walk in the neighbourhood; in the afternoon the terrace, shaded from the sun, allowed a welcome rest; Trotsky played long games of draughts and chess with his grandson, or immersed himself in the French books that visitors brought him. They were days of relaxation and real rest; there was only a cursory glance at the newspapers; France and the European disturbances seemed far away.

But what was happening at the end of this month of August? Every night I went down to town to look at the headlines of the newspaper that was printed there in the afternoon. One night, no busier than the others, one headline took up the whole of the front page: 'Ribbentrop has gone to Moscow'. I hurried back to the house, and I had barely passed on the information than Trotsky cried: 'It means war!' There can be no doubt that he had written and explained on many occasions that at a critical point Stalin would make a deal with Hitler; but we did not want to believe it.

The rest cure was over. Telegrams and cables came one after the other, and the telephone rang. What does Trotsky think about the Stalin-Hitler Pact? What are going to be the consequences? For war? For communism? Stalinist realism provoked momentary disgust, but Mexicans judged the new situation with a certain amount of detachment; he had grievances against all the belligerents, and did not want to take sides with any of them. To the astonished journalists who questioned him, Trotsky replied, 'You are discovering Stalinist duplicity, lying and crimes a little too late. You were, however, able to see it at work during the Moscow trials and the "purges"; but you looked at all that from the point of view of observers whom these machinations did not touch directly, and occasionally with some satisfaction you thought that this was the revolution devouring itself.'

❖ ❖ ❖ ❖

Frida Kahlo's house that Diego Rivera had put at Trotsky's disposal could only have been a temporary residence. It was not easy to find another, for it had to be large, with an affordable rent, and above all it had to be possible to arrange it to assure the maximum possible security: the Stalinists were launching incessant attacks with unheard-of violence. They finally decided upon a neighbouring house at the end of the Avenida Viena, unfortunately quite distant from the main road linking Mexico City and Coyoacan, incompletely and dangerously isolated where the avenue ran alongside some waste land. The living quarters were a ground floor building made up of three rooms in a row, at right angles to two other rooms converted into a library and a dining room; the corridor that continued led to a sort of two-storied square tower, and opposite, at the end of a wall, was a flimsy construction made up of four cubicles set aside for the secretaries. The garden stretched as far as the next property, separated from it only by an ordinary partition wall.

A surprise awaited the visitor who came here for the first time. As soon as he emerged from the garage, he found an unexpected sight in front of him: a row of hutches filled only with white rabbits; Trotsky took great care of them, fed them, watched over them, and followed their litters; this collection of whiteness enchanted him. Occasionally leaving his office he enjoyed coming to see them. More usefully, hen-coops had been installed behind and set back from the hutches for the three groups: White Leghorns, Cochin-Chinese and a variety of Houdan, which supplied the household with eggs for breakfast: most of the guardian-secretaries were Americans.

After the return from Taxco the house resumed its life, and, if possible, at an accelerated rhythm. An electrician came to fix an antenna on the roof; they had to think in terms of collecting the maximum information on political and diplomatic moves, and on the military operations. However, this magnificent installation produced nothing from anywhere; they remained dependent on the Mexican radio stations, but during the first months there was nothing to pick up apart from the grumbling of the war correspondents who had set out fully equipped for a campaign that did not happen – they were to be well rewarded much later. Up at seven o'clock as usual, Trotsky had already read the two main Mexican dailies by the time he came to the table for his breakfast. He had a welcoming word for his secretaries, and then summarised the news he had gleaned from the papers, and commented on them. His prophecies, which often seemed pessimistic in the eyes of those disquieted by the successes of Hitler – how could Poland stand up to the German onslaught when nothing was moving in the west? – were regularly confirmed. Hitler's hysteria had masked the reality of German power – and at length it would lead Germany yet again to disaster, but only in the long run. To his American secretaries, all too inclined to mock too quickly the adversaries smashed by the German army, and above all not being able to foresee the entry of America into the war, he said: 'Your turn will come, and quicker than during the First World War.' He wrote articles for press agencies, newspapers, always making sure that they were published in their entirety, without omissions or alterations. The great American newspapers were not afraid to put to their readers ideas that were different and even opposed to their political line, leaving it to the editorial page to reply. One journal, the *St Louis Post Dispatch*, which enjoyed a well-deserved reputation for integrity, published in full Trotsky's replies to the questions put to him, and took up a whole page of its Sunday edition.[148] Thus Trotsky earned his daily bread from his writing, as he had done all his life.

❖ ❖ ❖ ❖

One day a telegram arrived from New York that gave rise to a lively ferment in the Avenida Viena beehive. The secretariat of the Dies Committee asked Trotsky to get ready to appear before an inquiry. This committee had been formed by the House of Representatives to inquire into communism in particular.[149] The tortuous policy of Stalin and his pact with Hitler following the tactic of the anti-fascist Popular Front had posed all sorts of questions for the Americans, who were ill-equipped to orient themselves in the developments of policies of whose first principles they were ignorant, in new complex situations which could end with America's participation in the war. Such investigations are one of the peculiarities of American politics. The Senate or the House of Representatives decides to undertake them when a problem of national or international importance is put before the country. Depending on the times and the situations that exist, these committees can be of the McCarthy type – which is going on at the time these lines are being written – or, for example, of the LaFollette Committee type, which inquired into the violation of trade union rights, and brought to light, through the very depositions of the interested parties, their illegal practices of sneaking and spying on the workers, their organisations of auxiliary police and strike breakers, and by making them public, contributed to their disappearance. These committees were invested with full powers, and any person cited before them was compelled to appear and reply to the questions put to him. As far as Trotsky was concerned, his appearance before the Dies Committee would bring precious advantages. To start off with, there was leaving Mexico and breathing the air of a great industrial nation as yet outside the war, but which would not remain so for long. He would thereby have the use of a commanding platform to expound his ideas, and he would be able to use it without even having the need to moderate his speech, as he did for the articles he wrote for newspapers and agencies. His attitude as regards the USSR confused his enemies and some of his supporters at one and the same time; the inflexible firmness with which he always brought to the fore the unconditional defence of the USSR naturally appeared to justify those who claimed that he was basically in agreement with Stalin, and that their public quarrels were only a camouflage intended to fool public opinion outside Russia. His wardrobe being somewhat limited, he ordered a suit to present himself decently before the committee. But the tailor had not completed his work when a fresh telegram dashed these hopes: the American government was in no way disposed to give permission for the necessary stay, any more than it had been when it was a matter of the inquiry about the Moscow trials. The Stalinists who found in this invitation a pretext for fresh attacks found themselves on the side of Yankee imperialism.

❖ ❖ ❖ ❖

A split that became inevitable separated Diego Rivera from the Avenida Viena. Trotsky was so grateful to him that he did everything to avoid it. To begin with and for a time relations had been excellent. When André Breton stayed in Mexico, the three men had examined at length the position of revolutionary artists and had drawn up a declaration in common. But the great painter Diego Rivera was politically unstable. It was as an artist, and on account of the things done to the artists in Russia during the Stalin period which he had witnessed during a long stay in Moscow, that he had come over to the Opposition. When the electoral campaign began to chose a new president to succeed General Cardenas, Diego Rivera, to the great astonishment of his friends, took a public and active part on behalf of the man who was the candidate of reaction, General Amazan, against the party of the Mexican Revolution, Cardenas' party. Trotsky naturally had no intention of becoming involved with this electoral campaign, and above all of supporting Amazan; and he tried on several occasions to convince Diego Rivera that he was taking a wrong path. But the painter was obstinate, and he had to break with him.[150]

Trotsky would have loved to mingle freely in the life of Mexico, to go to the cinema when there was an interesting film, to go to the various exhibitions put on by artists passing through, or to the symphony concerts conducted by Carlos Chavez, whom he had the opportunity of getting to know. But all these simple distractions were forbidden him. On the orders of the NKVD, the Stalinists carried on a constant surveillance around the house; they were always ready to provoke public incidents in order to write that the presence of Trotsky was a permanent cause of trouble, and that he ought to be expelled. Excursions had to be prepared and organised like veritable expeditions to a specific part of the country. They generally profited from the presence of American workers who had come over for a few days by automobile, since three cars were necessary for security. They set out early in the morning with provisions for a picnic. While the secretaries were sent off looking for wood, lighting a fire, and preparing hot dogs, Trotsky went off looking for cacti, happy to be able to find new types and bring them back to the house. These days out in the fresh air in the desert regions burning with the sun were days of complete freedom, a break with the daily labour carried out in very difficult conditions; work and discussions were at a standstill. The days were too rare, one a month, and they were often cancelled due to circumstances.

Many of the Spanish revolutionaries found refuge in Mexico: there were socialists, anarcho-syndicalists and members of the POUM (the Workers Party of Marxist Unity, that of Andrès Nin). Some of them came as individuals to Coyoacan to discuss and study with Trotsky the causes of the defeat, and draw lessons from it. One afternoon there was a whole group of 30 militants of various opinions. Trotsky now spoke a precise and correct Spanish, which astonished his visitors: 'It is greatly needed, since Mexico requires it of me.' But he was too much of a perfectionist to exceed the limits of his knowledge of the language. What emerged in his analyses and discussions was the clarity of his thought, and the ease with which he organised his proof. A young Socialist objected to a severe judgement on the policy of Largo Caballero; 'He ought not to forget,' he said, 'that he attempted to resist the demands of the Stalinist envoys and preferred to retire from office rather than carry out their orders.' 'I have not forgotten it,' replied Trotsky, 'and if I had to write a biography of Caballero I would certainly mention this fact, which is to his credit. But we are now discussing the policy in general of the leaders of the Spanish Republic as a whole, and we cannot close our eyes to the serious mistakes that they made.'[151]

Such visits were particularly welcome to him; they were also a useful interruption to work that began early in the morning, and did not finish until 10 o'clock at night. His methods of work were the same as in Russia. He could dictate letters in English, French, German and Spanish, but he was only completely at ease with Russian, and then he had to have recourse to a dictaphone; a Russian secretary had the job of transcribing the articles recorded on the cylinders. This was the first draft that he took up again, altered, corrected and lengthened the proofs, which in their length occasionally assumed the appearance of the love letters on Japanese prints.

Chapter Five: In Mexico (Part Two)

A great and serious discussion that began after the outbreak of war was going to cause him a great deal of concern. Because of the Stalin-Hitler Pact and the outbreak of war that it entailed, an important faction in the American section of the Fourth International came out in favour of dropping the slogan of the 'defence of the USSR'. Trotsky opposed this; according to him it would be an unjustifiable retreat, a serious mistake. The debate went on in letters, articles and oral discussions for several months, and ended with a split within the American section, which had repercussions inside the parties and groups of the Fourth International. This collection of letters, articles and long discussions (published under the title of *In Defence of Marxism*) is an important one. They were Trotsky's last writings, and the debate and polemic, often quite sharp, that they provoked with a faction of the American Trotskyists, led him to refine his thinking about the fresh problems posed by the outbreak of the war.

The slogan of the 'defence of the USSR' had already stirred up controversies within the groups and parties of the Fourth International; and every time a fresh 'turn' accentuated and emphasised the degeneration of the Soviet Union, voices were raised to demand that it be abandoned; it is impossible from now on, they said, to consider the Stalinist state as a workers' state, and above all impossible to talk about defending the USSR, for the workers would no longer understand. Trotsky replied patiently; he was not always convincing, but divergence on this point remained tolerated. But the pact that Stalin had concluded with Hitler after having mobilised the anti-fascist forces against him, and the new world war that immediately followed its signing, the partition of Poland and the seizure of the Baltic states put new life into the criticisms, and it was no longer a question of individual positions, but of an important faction of the American party. And Trotsky himself severely criticised Stalinist policy in his articles and public declarations.

However, he remained intransigent on the position that he had not ceased defending. It was not that he considered it immutable, valid both for today and forever. Events were too much in flux, and the general situation, and that of the USSR in particular, were so unstable and changing so constantly for his evaluation to be unchangeable. On the question of the creation of a Fourth International, for example, he had shown that he knew how to draw lessons from the facts and adapt his thought to them; when he arrived in Prinkipo in 1929 he protested against those who accused him of wanting to create a new International; but four years later, when the German Communist Party went down without a struggle, he very quickly proclaimed the death of the Communist International and the necessity for preparing for the formation of a new international grouping. But the Communist International was not the Soviet regime, and however harsh and however violent it was, his critique of Stalinism always stopped short of the regime itself. At the beginning of his exile, he was careful to warn his supporters in the rest of the world against any confusion between Stalinism and the USSR. The former must be mercilessly opposed, but it was necessary to defend the USSR. A new pamphlet published in New York collected together texts stretching over 10 years. The theme did not vary: 'To defend the USSR, as the main fortress of the world proletariat, against all the assaults of world imperialism and of internal counter-revolution, is the most important duty of every class-conscious worker.'[152]

But it should not be thought that this defence of the USSR that he urged on his supporters be confused with that of the 'professional' – often paid – defenders of the USSR. It was always aimed against two threats – from inside, which was the Soviet bureaucracy; and from outside, which was world imperialism, and it required a tactic appropriate to the needs of the time. At the beginning of 1932, when the rise of Hitler showed that Germany was from then on 'the key to the international situation', he wrote:

> The conquest of power by the German and

> European proletariat is a task infinitely more real and immediate than the building of a closed and self-sufficient society within the boundaries of the USSR.
>
> Unconditional defence of the USSR, the first workers' state, against the inside and outside foes of the proletarian dictatorship.
>
> But the defence of the USSR cannot be carried on with the eyes blindfolded. International proletarian control over the Soviet bureaucracy. Merciless exposure of its national-reformist and Thermidorean tendencies that find their generalisation in the theory of socialism in one country.[153]

And he called for 'a general plan for the joint socialist construction of the USSR and Germany'.[154]

But his warnings were in vain. Hitler was in power. It was now a difficult situation, more difficult for the workers, but it in no way altered the tactic. On 1 October 1933, he wrote:

> Every day, the foreign policies of the Kremlin deal new blows to the world proletariat. Adrift from the masses, the diplomatic functionaries under the leadership of Stalin trample over the most elementary revolutionary feelings of the workers of all countries, first of all, to the great detriment of the Soviet Union itself. But in this, there is nothing unexpected. The foreign policies of the bureaucracy supplement the domestic. We fight as much against the one as the other. But we wage our struggle from the standpoint of defending the workers' state.[155]

With the conclusion of the 'Stalinazi' pact and what followed it these 'blows' of Stalinist diplomacy became so intolerable that more or less numerous factions within the sections of the Fourth International considered that a change in attitude with regard to the USSR was now indispensable. This was mainly the case with the American section with which, on account of the circumstances, Trotsky was in permanent and direct contact. A great debate took place between New York and Coyoacan which lasted several months, and ended in a split.

Trotsky well understood the indignation that the pact provoked, and the agreements concluded between the Russians and the Germans, and then the aid Stalin provided for Hitler, but one must not allow oneself to be carried away by sentimental feelings, and lose the detachment necessary for making an exact appraisal of what was obviously a difficult situation. He wrote:

> The comrades are very indignant about the Stalin-Hitler pact. It is comprehensible. They wish to get revenge on Stalin. Very good. But today we are weak, and we cannot immediately overthrow the Kremlin. Some comrades try then to find a purely verbalistic satisfaction; they strike out from the USSR the title, workers' state, as Stalin deprives a disgraced functionary of the order of Lenin. I find it, my dear friend, a bit childish.[156]

And he put forward some precise, and according to him, indispensable rules:

> 1. Our definition of the USSR can be right or wrong, but I do not see any reason to make this definition dependent on the German-Soviet pact.
>
> 2. The social character of the USSR is not determined by her friendship with democracy or Fascism. Who adopts such a point of view becomes a prisoner of the Stalinist conception of the People's Front epoch ...[157] We do not say: 'Everything is lost, we must begin all over again.' We clearly indicate those elements of the workers' state which at the given stage can be salvaged, preserved, and further developed ... A totalitarian regime, whether of Stalinist or fascist type, by its very essence can be only a temporary transitional regime ... 'Defence of the USSR', as interpreted by the Comintern ... is based on renunciation of independent class politics. The proletariat is transformed – for various reasons in varying circumstances, but always and invariably – into an auxiliary force of one bourgeois camp against

> another ... We are not a government party; we are the party of irreconcilable opposition, not only in capitalist countries but also in the USSR. Our tasks, among them the 'defence of the USSR', we realise not through the medium of bourgeois governments and not even through the government of the USSR, but exclusively through the education of the masses through agitation, through explaining to the workers what they should defend and what they should overthrow. Such a 'defence' cannot give immediate miraculous results. But we do not even pretend to be miracle workers ... The defence of the USSR coincides for us with the preparation of world revolution ...[158]

On the question of the territories occupied by the Russian army, the information then available was insufficient and contradictory. The most reasonable hypothesis, according to Trotsky, was that in the territories intended to be incorporated into Russia, Moscow would move to the confiscation of the large landed estates, and would nationalise the means of production. This would take place 'not because the bureaucracy remains true to the socialist programme but because it is neither desirous nor capable of sharing the power, and the privileges the latter entails, with the old ruling classes in the occupied territories ... The statification of the means of production is ... a progressive measure. But its progressiveness is relative; its specific weight depends on the sum-total of all the other factors.'[159]

The progress of the war constantly posed new problems. These were, to begin with, the partition of Poland; then there was the occupation of Norway – successfully accomplished – and that of Finland – messed up in part. Trotsky was occasionally mistaken in the predictions he made – he was not always in possession of accurate information at the time, but these were minor errors which changed nothing in the essentials. What was important was to extract the essence in order to form an accurate picture of the whole. Linking together these two fresh problems he wrote:

> Because of the degeneration of the workers' state, the Soviet Union turned out at the threshold of the second imperialist war to be far weaker than it

> need have been. Stalin's agreement with Hitler had as its objective the securing of the USSR from a German assault and, generally, securing the USSR from being drawn into a major war. While seizing Poland, Hitler had to protect himself on the east. Stalin was compelled, with Hitler's permission, to invade eastern Poland in order to avail himself of some supplementary guarantees against Hitler on the western boundary of the USSR. As a result of these events, however, the USSR acquired a common frontier with Germany, and by virtue of this very fact the danger from a victorious Germany became much more direct, while Stalin's dependence on Hitler was greatly increased.
>
> The episode of the partitioning of Poland had its development and sequel in the Scandinavian area. Hitler could not have failed to give some intimation to his 'friend' Stalin that he planned to seize the Scandinavian countries. Stalin could not have failed to break into a cold sweat. After all, this signified complete German domination of the Baltic Sea, of Finland, and hence constituted a direct threat to Leningrad. One again Stalin had to seek supplementary guarantees against his ally, this time in Finland. However, he met with serious resistance there. The 'military excursion' dragged on. Meanwhile Scandinavia threatened to become the arena of major warfare. Hitler, who had completed his preparations for the blow against Denmark and Norway, demanded that Stalin conclude an early peace. Stalin had to cut his plans short, and renounce sovietising Finland. These are the salient features of the course of events in the European north-west.[160]

The resistance of the Finnish people, which occasioned general surprise, verified a thesis of the Fourth International, in which it emphasised (in 1934) 'the monstrous development of Soviet bureaucratism and the wretched living conditions of the toilers have drastically reduced the attractive power of the USSR for the world working class'. The Soviet-Finnish war 'revealed graphically and completely that within gunshot of

Leningrad, the cradle of the October Revolution, the present regime of the USSR is incapable of exercising an attractive force'.[161]

It was a difficult debate, since it failed to convince some devoted elements from whom he had to split. But it was a discussion of ideas which Trotsky in the end regarded as fruitful, because according to him it contributed to clarifying and refining the concepts upon which the Fourth International was based. But he had simultaneously to carry on another more irritating and sickening debate, where his antagonists were the Mexican Stalinists, led and incited by the agents of the NKVD installed in New York and Mexico. They controlled a daily paper, *El Popular*, the supposed organ of the Mexican Workers Federation, and a monthly magazine, *Futuro*, the organ of the anti-fascist intellectuals, and a workers' university, where they corrupted the minds of young studious workers, not to mention the Communist Party's own periodical, which had very few readers. Their tactic, which was to repeat the same lies unceasingly, never varied: Trotsky is a danger to Mexico, he is disturbing its internal tranquillity, he is joining with the leaders of the counter-revolution in preparing blows against the Mexican republic, attempting to compromise its international relations and pull it into the camp of the imperialists, whose agent he was. Their 'directed' campaign only ceased for a while when Trotsky, putting them on the spot, publicly challenged them to bring their accusations before an impartial commission. To the written propaganda was added a more odious oral propaganda, because its agents expressed themselves without disguising their aims; the speakers were more explicit than the journalists: it was a permanent incitement to murder. Shouts broke out from time to time in the meetings that they organised, and accomplices dotted about in the hall cried out: '*Muerte a Trotsky!*' A conference of members of the teaching profession ended with shouts of 'Death to Trotsky!', as one newspaper announced in huge letters. That was the tone. The incitement took on so deliberate a character, and became so threatening that the Mexican authorities decided to set up a special police post along one of the walls of the house. It was a vain protection, for the agents of the NKVD had ample means at their disposal, and Stalin was no doubt becoming very impatient in Moscow. After the threats, they went over to action. At dawn on 24 May 1940, following a well-worked-out plan, an armed band led by the painter Siqueiros[162] attacked the house: some of them were dressed in policemen's uniforms; this stratagem easily allowed them to neutralise the special police post set up outside; and by some means that still remains unexplained they succeeded in getting the garage door open. The way in which they spread out inside showed a perfect knowledge of the layout. Some, posted behind trees in the garden, commanded the different exits, firing off their machine guns at rapid intervals, using the windows to adjust their aim. Trotsky and his guards were thus completely isolated and cut off. There were minutes of anguish that seemed interminable. Then suddenly absolute silence, and a cry from his grandson, Sieva, wounded by the attackers when they retreated. Trotsky and Natalia had escaped the bullets fired from outside; at the first shots they had thrown themselves into a corner of the room where the attackers, even though they were firing from various directions, could not reach them. The walls of their room were scored with bullet holes, along with the bedstead and the pillows.

Policemen and journalists arrived when the news of the attempted assassination got round, but the gang was able to get away unscathed just as it had come, even though its approach must have aroused suspicions in the night. Newspapers published photographs and accounts. The NKVD agents had messed up their assassination attempt; what were they going to say about it? To begin with they tried mockery – what, so many bullets fired, and no casualties? Then, since mockery was not enough, they wrote that there had been an assassination attempt all right, but it was a simulated one; the whole thing was a put-up job by Trotsky. This grotesque fabrication even got as far as New York, for they had accomplices or compliant people everywhere; a weekly magazine once renowned as an honest mouthpiece of American liberalism, *The Nation*, welcomed correspondence from Mexico taking up the theme of the simulated assassination.[163] But that was nothing yet. In spite of the evidence, and to everyone's amazement, the judicial and police authorities who came to investigate adopted as their own the untenable theory of a simulated attempt. And instead of applying themselves without delay to searching for the perpetrators of the attempted killing, they arrested and imprisoned two of the secretaries. The Stalinists had not been able to kill them; were they then going to succeed in blaming Trotsky and his people, forcing their expulsion, and perhaps allowing them to be handed over to the NKVD? The situation became so serious that on 27 May Trotsky decided to write to the public prosecutor, the chief of the police, and the minister of the interior. In a long letter he set out a number of facts typical of the usual practices of the NKVD outside Russia; they were of decisive importance, he insisted, for the 'general handling of the judicial investigation', for what must be emphasised above all is that 'the attempted assassination could only have been instigated by the Kremlin'.[164] This is not to say that Lombardo Toledano and the Mexican communist leaders had taken a direct part in preparing and carrying out the assassination attempt: 'The GPU has a strict division of labour. Known persons are assigned the task of propagating the slanders against me. Lesser known but more serious agents are assigned the task of assassination.'[165] Finally, he demanded that the Stalinist militant David Alfaro Siqueiros be questioned – he was the leader of the gang, as was soon proved, and admitted by him. (Benefiting from a personal amnesty, he returned to Mexico, and on 23 April 1947, in a statement printed in the newspaper *Excelsior*, he explained it thus: 'I have not denied, nor will I ever deny, my responsibility in the affair, but I stress that I was acting as an independent agent. I feel obliged to say that I consider my part [in the attack at Coyoacan] as one of the most honourable acts of my life.')[166] It became impossible for the judicial investigation to go on in the way it had done. Giving up the theory of a simulated murder attempt, it was easy for it to discover who was guilty. Natalia Trotsky wrote:

> The inquiry showed that two women, Anita Marinez and Julia Barradas de Serrana, who had been living in our neighbourhood for a short time, had established amorous relations with several of the policemen detailed to guard our house. They had subsequently disappeared, but were traced and arrested; they admitted that they had been instructed to watch Trotsky and to seduce the policemen. They had been hired and paid by Antonio Pujol, secretary to the communist painter David Siqueiros. One of the women was the wife,

> or, more accurately, one of the wives, of a former member of the Spanish International Brigade, Serrano.[167] Several hours before the attack they had been advised to disappear from the scene ... Another of the arrested was Nestor Sanchez Hernandez, a communist and a 'captain' in the International Brigade.[168] He gave a detailed account of the preparations for the crime in which he had taken part. He spoke of ... David Alfaro Siqueiros ... Twenty-seven people in all were arrested and their statements made clear what had actually happened ...[169]

When the editors of *El Popular* and *Futuro*, who had been accused by Trotsky of preparing the moral ground for the attempt, had the impudence to announce their attention of suing him for deformation of character, Trotsky replied with a simple list of the articles and cartoons directed against him by the perpetrators of the attempt in each magazine number, even before he had landed at Tampico;[170] the one preceding the actual attempt was very revealing. Since they were at that time – 25 March 1940 – in the period of the Stalin-Hitler Pact, the author had then written that 'the Gestapo expelled from its own bosom Trotsky's spies';[171] 'today it is completely evident that Trotskyism in Latin America is no more than an agency of penetration, confusion, provocation and espionage in the service of the Wall Street imperialists'.[172] Trotsky's conclusion was, 'some of them ... attacked me directly with the pen or pencil, before attacking me with the machine gun and the revolver'.[173]

David Siqueiros and Antonio Pujol were arrested on 4 October at Hostotipaquilla, a straggling village in the state of Jalisco, where until then they had enjoyed the protection of the local authorities. Before they appeared before the court 'anti-fascist' intellectuals happened to address the President of the Republic in these words: 'We warmly express,' they declared, 'our moral support of the great Mexican artist ... We appeal to the court to take into account the transcendental qualities of this artist's work which – we are convinced – must be considered one of the most authentic expressions of our culture.'[174] But when he had been set at provisional liberty, Siqueiros soon disappeared, going first to Cuba and then to Chile. When he returned to Mexico, his dossier had disappeared, and he could no longer be called before a court.

Even if the perpetrators of this assassination attempt had killed nobody in the house on the Avenida Viena, they did however take one victim. The secretary who was on guard on the night of the attempt and who had allowed them to enter, taken in by one of their ruses, was kidnapped. For a month it was impossible to find any trace of him. His corpse was discovered on 25 June, covered up with quicklime, in a shack in the Desierto de los Leones.[175]

❖ ❖ ❖ ❖

'All well and good, they are going to leave you alone now!' the Mexican friends who came to congratulate Trotsky on escaping the assassination attempt invariably said, a natural reaction of simple souls at such a heinous crime. Articles in newspapers were one thing; they could be scorned. But the means employed in this machine-gun assault provoked indignation and revulsion. Trotsky had to contradict them every time: 'You are mistaken,' he would reply, 'on the contrary, after this hold-up they are going to redouble their efforts, and resort to fresh deceptions.'

But how do you defend yourself against an all too certain recurrence? Some American Trotskyists who quickly came over elaborated a series of measures and carried them out as far as their means allowed: doors and closed windows must be protected from machine guns; there must be a net for protection against grenades, which it would be easy to throw in from outside; a shield was set up; masons raised the walls; a system of automatic electric alarms was put in place; the guards were reinforced and more heavily armed. Trotsky was grateful for this evidence of loyalty and support; these were obviously necessary measures; however, they kept the memory of the attempt in his mind. He had more and more the feeling of being a prisoner in a prison that did not assure his safety. He was alone, with no other weapon than his pen, his intelligence and his revolutionary passion, struggling against a devilish, patient, Asiatic plot, with immense means at its disposal and accomplices everywhere. It was hard to hold on at times; his insomnia got worse; hypertension gripped him. And he did not even get from his work the enjoyment he normally experienced when he was at his desk, in front of his papers; he had to give up his time to a biography of Stalin, when there were so many other books, such as the *Lenin*, of which only the first volume completed appeared in Paris in 1938,[176] or again, an essay on Marx and Engels, the supreme example of two revolutionaries closely linked by a whole life of work together.[177] But he was not able to honour the agreements he had made with his American publisher, and if the editor did agree to grant him the necessary delays, he asked in exchange for a biography of Stalin, which he thought could be rapidly written, and was now more topical than that of Lenin. The assassin did not allow it to be finished; only the first chapters had been completely drafted, and the others were only partly so. The book, unfinished as it was, was published by Harper, and was going to be put on sale when Hitler turned against his partner. For reasons no doubt not merely his own, the publisher judged that it was an inopportune time to bring out the book; he asked the reviewers who had already received their copies to return them to him, and the book was only published after the fall of Hitler.[178]

Trotsky was all too right in thinking that the Stalinist agents had not given up their plans. Evidence and later revelations allow us to reconstruct the preparations for the murder step by step; it was systematically prepared without let-up for three years. Alongside the public preparations by means of newspapers and meetings launched in Mexico when Trotsky was still at sea on the Norwegian cargo boat, another, secret preparation was being carried on in New York by a special squad that thought up and carried out a plan that allowed them to get a 'killer' into America and introduce him into Trotskyist circles. The main editor of the communist daily, Louis Budenz,[179] was put in charge of the link between the party and the secret service agents. These above all wanted to obtain information on the Trotskyist organisation and its members, and this is how they learned that a young New York Trotskyist, Sylvia, whose sister was at one time in Trotsky's secretariat in Coyoacan, was going to France in 1938. At the time she set off they put next to her a travelling companion who arranged for her to be introduced on her arrival in France to a man who was not a member of a Trotskyist party, but sympathetic and who wanted to help; he was called Jacson. Intimate relations were established between him and Sylvia which took a whole year to consolidate in France. The approach of war hastened the return of Sylvia to America, where Jacson joined her. He was going there to work, so he said, for a businessman, a friend of the family, who had set himself up in Mexico, a recognised centre for trade in wartime. Sylvia was attached to an institution in New York; she arranged leave and went off to Mexico. She had taken part in the discussions in New York that were going on inside the party, above all over internal matters, and then over 'the defence of the USSR'; she counted herself among the 'revisionists'. She naturally came to Coyoacan, where she was subjected to Trotsky's friendly criticisms, and the more caustic ones of his secretaries. She came and went, often alone. Jacson was in no hurry to approach the house. He had put up Sylvia in a comfortable apartment, owned a Buick, and spent generously: the affairs of his businessman were going well. He played his rôle well.

It was the first murder attempt that allowed him to introduce himself into the house. The attackers had taken one of the two cars from the garage and had damaged the other. Jacson offered the use of his own and showed himself anxious to take on all the errands and tasks that could be entrusted to him; when he went to New York for a few weeks, he left his car completely at the disposal of the secretaries, with whom he was now in frequent contact. When he visited, to begin with he was happy to meet Trotsky in the courtyard, but then he asked to submit to him the draft of an article he wanted to write, allowing him to understand that he was in disagreement with Sylvia over 'the defence of the USSR'. Upon his return from New York, he came to Coyoacan at the end of July, and then on 8, 10 and 17 August. That day he was able to go through a rehearsal of his plan. Joseph Hansen, the American Trotskyist who was in charge of security, has provided the following account of this visit, and the one after it, three days later:

> On 17 August, Jacson showed Trotsky a draft of an article he intended to write on the recent dispute in the Fourth International over the Russian question. Trotsky invited Jacson to come into his study while he read the draft. This was the first time Jacson was alone there with Trotsky ... Trotsky offered a few suggestions to the author, but told Natalia that the draft showed confusion and was

without particular interest ... On 20 August, Jacson came to the house with the finished article ... It was Jacson's plan, apparently, to kill Trotsky with one blow, silently, and then to leave the house as he had come, without arousing attention – with his revolver gripped in his pocket in case it was necessary to shoot his way out. He carried a large sum of money in his pocket – $890 – indicating that he hoped to escape. Besides this, he carried a letter of 'confession', obviously dictated by the GPU – planted on him for discovery by the police in the event he was shot by the guards ... Jacson met Trotsky near the rabbit hutches, told him that he had brought the finished article, and he and Sylvia were leaving for New York the following day. Trotsky responded with his typical cordiality, but continued placing dried alfalfa in the feed troughs ... Catching sight of Natalia on the balcony between the kitchen and the dining room, Jacson left Trotsky. He wore his hat, kept his raincoat pressed to his body as he advanced to make his greeting. To Natalia he appeared nervous and absent-minded, as if he were in deep distraction. Jacson asked her for a glass of water; he was very 'thirsty' he explained. Natalia offered him tea ... Jacson refused, however ... He returned with Natalia to Trotsky's side at the rabbit hutches. 'You know that Jacson and Sylvia are returning to New York tomorrow?' asked Trotsky. 'They have come to say goodbye.' Then in Russian: 'We should prepare something for them.' A few minutes' conversation passed before Trotsky without enthusiasm asked, 'You wish me to read your article?' 'Yes.' 'Good, we can go into the study.'... Trotsky seated himself at the wide table, scattered with books, newspapers, and manuscripts. Near an ink-well a few inches from his hand lay his .25 calibre automatic – it had been oiled and reloaded just a few days before. He began reading Jacson's article. Jacson sat behind and to the left of Trotsky, near the switch that would set off the alarm system. 'The opportunity was too good to be lost,'

> Jacson told the police afterward. 'I took the piolet. I raised it up high. I shut my eyes and struck with all my strength ... As long as I live I can never forget his cry ...' Blood spattered over the desk ... on the last pages of the manuscript of Trotsky's biography of Stalin.
>
> But Trotsky still had enough strength to turn round at a bound and attack the murderer ... The secretaries ran in and got control of the assassin, and in their anger would doubtless have finished him off if Trotsky had not said to them, 'Tell the boys not to kill him ... he must talk ...'[180]

As Jacson regained consciousness, he moaned: 'They made me do it ... They've got my mother ... They have put my mother in prison.'[181]

The x-ray examination showed a wound so deep that the case was regarded as absolutely hopeless by several of the doctors; however, others did not give up; a brain specialist was going to come by plane from the University of Johns Hopkins ... But Trotsky was 60 years old: his body, gravely weakened by years of exile so full of Stalinist crimes, could not win. During the night of 21 August, at 7.25pm, his heart ceased to beat.

From 22 to 27 August, the body was exposed in a chapel of rest, surrounded by a guard of honour made up of Mexican workers and his secretaries. Outside long queues formed constantly, made up almost exclusively of the poorest people, many of them barefoot. An enormous procession assembled for the funeral. In the cemetery, American, Mexican and Spanish orators rendered homage to the great revolutionary; one of them translated into Spanish Trotsky's last words: 'I am sure of the victory of the Fourth International. Go forward!'[182] His American friends wanted the funeral to take place in New York to allow the American workers to show their disapproval of this Stalinist crime. But Roosevelt's government refused to allow it. There had not been a visa for the living; nor was there one for the dead.

Condemned to 20 years' imprisonment, and jailed for 13, the assassin never 'talked'. In the course of the investigation and trial, he limited himself to providing often different and always false versions of motives for his actions, simply refusing to reply when pointed questions became too embarrassing. He even succeeded in hiding his identity, and the various identities he used – Frank Jacson, a Canadian, and Jacques Mornard Van-dendreschd, born to Belgian parents in Teheran, did not stand up to verification. However, thanks to patient researches carried on in different countries, Julián Gorkin[183] succeeded in discovering his real identity. His name was Ramon Mercader; he was born in 1904, the third son of Pablo Mercader, born in Barcelona on 20 August 1884 and of Eustasia Maria Caridad del Rio Hernández, born in Santiago de Cuba on 29 March 1882. This discovery was confirmed by an investigation carried out completely independently by a Mexican criminologist, Doctor Alfonso Quiroz. In the course of a journey to Spain, Doctor Quiroz had the opportunity to examine a police file which was able to remove all doubt: the finger print he found exactly coincided with that taken in Mexico. Ramon Mercader del Rio figured in the Madrid police files for having taken part in a clandestine meeting of the committee of the Communist Youth in a Barcelona café on 12 June 1935. The question of his identity was therefore definitively confirmed. We should, however, mention the statements a Mexican lawyer has just made. In a letter published in Mexico's most important daily newspaper, *El Universal*, this lawyer, Felipe Alvahuante, affirms that the assassin is a Russian, that he is an ex-pupil of the Moscow Military Academy, and that he was chosen by Stalin himself to follow Trotsky across the world with the mission of doing away with him when Stalin judged that the moment had arrived. He accused in a categorical manner the then leaders of the Mexican Workers Federation of being responsible for the assassination. He specifically named Lombardo Toledano,[184] Fidel Velázquez and Narciso Bassols, the former Mexican ambassador in Moscow and then in Paris;[185] they had, he wrote, 'prepared the assassination materially and morally'. It is only a matter of allegations, but some of them are already incontestable, and the whole is so reasonable and coherent that this new direction of investigation cannot be set aside. In the course of his investigation, Doctor Quiroz came to the conclusion that the assassin was acquainted with the Russian language – which he always denied – and as for the moral responsibility of the individuals specifically identified in the assassination attempts, no one can be in any doubt today.[186]

Notes

1. See LD Trotsky, *The First Five Years of the Communist International*, London, 1973, Volume 1, pp88–122, 165–73, 190–2, and 211–22; Volume 2, pp44–58, 91–118, 124–82, 275–94, and 334–40.
2. For Thorez's support for Trotsky in 1924, see Chapter Two above, p52. *The New Course*, originally written in 1923, was reprinted in English in 1965 by the University of Michigan Press with an introduction by Max Shachtman.
3. LD Trotsky, 'C'est La Marche des Evenements', 25 February 1929, *Writings of Leon Trotsky, 1929*, New York, 1975, p21.
4. LD Trotsky, 'Where is the Soviet Republic Going?', 25 February 1929, *Writings of Leon Trotsky, 1929*, op cit, p45.
5. LD Trotsky, 'Stalin's Victory', 25 February 1929, *Writings of Leon Trotsky, 1929*, op cit, pp42–3.
6. LD Trotsky, 'Is Parliamentary Democracy Likely to Replace the Soviets?', 25 February 1929, *Writings of Leon Trotsky, 1929*, op cit, p56.
7. These were the 'Big Three' politicians representing the main victorious powers at the Versailles settlement. The American President Woodrow Wilson (1856–1924) had included the evacuation of Russia in one of his Fourteen Points, but both the British Prime Minister, David Lloyd George (1863–1945) and the French leader, Georges Clemenceau (1841–1929), were supporting various White armies in attempting to overthrow the Bolshevik state.
8. On the work of Trotsky's son, Leon Sedov (1906–1938), see below, pp198–202, John G Wright, 'Leon Sedov', *Fourth International*, Volume 5, no 2, February 1944, pp54–5, and Pierre Broué, *Léon Sedov: Fils de Trotsky, Cahiers Léon Trotsky*, nos 13–14, March 1983, and *Léon Sedov, fils de Trotsky, victime de Staline*, Paris, 1993.
9. Fischer Verlag published *My Life* in 1929; English editions were brought out New York in 1930 and 1960. These additional chapters bringing the account up to Trotsky's death in 1940 were written by Rosmer for the French edition published in 1953.
10. Nikolai Bukharin (1888–1938), Stalin's chief theorist up to 1929 and leader of the Comintern, Alexei Rykov (1881–1938), Chairman of the Council of People's Commissars, and Mikhail Tomsky (1886–1936), head of the soviet trade unions, were all leaders of the Right Opposition. The two former were defendants in the Trial of the Twenty-One in 1938, but Tomsky committed suicide before he could be brought to trial.
11. Gregory Yevseyevich Radomysslsky, generally known as Zinoviev (1883–1936), the head of the Comintern, and Lev Borisovich Rosenfeld (1883–1936), called Kamenev, were inseparable allies, and formed the 'Troika', or Triumvirate, alliance with Stalin against Trotsky in 1923. They later joined the Left Opposition, but soon recanted. They were executed after the Trial of the Sixteen.
12. LD Trotsky, *The Stalin School of Falsification*, London, 1974, pp xv, xvii.
13. LD Trotsky, 'Letter to the Bureau of Party History', 21 October 1927, and 'Two Speeches at the Session of the Central Control Commission, *The Stalin School of Falsification*, op cit, pp1–70, 99–126; the speech to the Central Committee referred to may be 'The Fear of Our Platform', 23 October 1927, *The Challenge of the Left Opposition, 1926–27*, New York, 1980, pp437–48.
14. LD Trotsky, *The Third International After Lenin*, New York, 1970, p xxxvi.
15. Hagia Sophia was the Cathedral of the Holy Wisdom, the high point of Byzantine architecture built in Constantinople by Anthemius of Tralles for the Emperor Justinian in 532–537AD. Converted into a mosque by the Ottomans,

it is now a museum and a noted tourist attraction.

16. For the 'Third Period', see above, p63 n8. It was marked by masses of ultra-left rhetoric and attacks on all other tendencies in the workers' movement as 'fascist'.
17. LD Trotsky, 'The Third Period of the Comintern's Errors', 8 January 1930, *Writings of Leon Trotsky, 1930*, New York, 1975, p34. Wilhelm Christian Weitling (1808–1871) was an early German working-class leader, and a utopian thinker.
18. LD Trotsky, 'Defence of the Soviet Republic and the Opposition', 7 September 1929, *Writings of Leon Trotsky, 1929*, op cit, pp262–303.
19. The ILP was about to move leftwards towards its ultimate break with the Labour Party. This was a result of the actions of the second Labour government of James Ramsay MacDonald (1866–1937), which cut the dole in the middle of the slump. On his refusal to admit Trotsky, see S Bornstein and A Richardson, *Against the Stream*, London, 1986, pp37–8, 127ff; J Paton, *Left Turn*, London, 1936; LD Trotsky, *My Life*, New York, 1960, pp574–8; R Gott, 'How Trotsky was Kept Out of England', *Guardian*, 15 August 1970; C Holmes, 'Trotsky and Britain: The Closed File', *Bulletin of the Society for the Study of Labour History*, no 39, Autumn 1979, p36; Vladimir Katine, 'Pour complaire à Staline, les Britanniques ont refusé le visa à Trotsky', *Cahiers Léon Trotsky*, no 71, September 2000, pp79–81.
20. The ministry of Hermann Müller (1876–1931), which included Gustav Stresemann (1878–1929) as Foreign Secretary, known as 'the Grand Coalition' because it included the Liberal and Centre parties as well as the SPD, was the last democratic government in Germany before the rise of Hitler. On its refusal to grant Trotsky asylum, cf LD Trotsky, 'A Lesson in Democracy I Did Not Receive', 22 April 1929, *Writings of Leon Trotsky, 1929*, op cit, pp100–7.
21. Victor Serge and Natalia Sedova Trotsky, *The Life and Death of Leon Trotsky*, London, 1975, p188; LD Trotsky, 'In Defence of the Russian Revolution', 27 November 1932, *Leon Trotsky Speaks*, New York, 1972, p269.
22. Alexandra Mikhailovna Demontovich Kollontai (1872–1952), a feminist icon, had been a Menshevik before 1915, and a leader of the Workers' Opposition in 1921. Her early submission to Stalin gave her the rare distinction of being one of the few members of Lenin's Central Committee to survive the purges.
23. Serge and Sedova, op cit, pp188–9. Thorvald Stauning (1873–1942) was the Social Democrat prime minister in a coalition with the Liberals. On Trotsky's speech and the so-called conference, see also the eyewitness report of Harry Wicks, *Keeping My Head*, London, 1992, pp149–57.
24. Mustafa Kemal Pasha, known as Atatürk (1880–1938) led the Turkish Revolution that overthrew the Sultan, and went on to modernise his country, ruling as an authoritarian president until his death.
25. Edouard Daladier (1884–1970), a Radical, was Prime Minister of France on several occasions during the 1930s. He is famous for his part in signing the Munich agreement.
26. Serge and Sedova, op cit, p192.
27. Taking office in the aftermath of the Wall Street Crash of 1929, President Franklin Delano Roosevelt (1882–1945) began his 'New Deal' to restore the US economy in 1933. Massive government spending to reflate the economy involved coming off the gold standard, while some countries, such as Britain, had worsened the deflation by mistakenly returning to it shortly before.
28. Edouard Beneš (1884–1948) succeeded Masaryk as President of Czechoslovakia, and was one of the main architects of the Little Entente between the Eastern European countries. The Anschluss was the annexation of

Austria by Germany in 1938. Any form of union between them had been forbidden by the Treaty of Versaillles.

29. LD Trotsky, 'Against National Communism! Lessons of the Red Referendum', 25 August 1931, *The Struggle Against Fascism in Germany*, New York, 1972, p93. We have slightly amended the English translation here in line with the French, since it contains a significant political difference. The 'Red Referendum' was a joint campaign carried on by the Nazis and the Communists to collect signatures to bring down the Social Democratic Prussian regional government in 1931.
30. LD Trotsky, 'The Austrian Crisis and Communism', 13 November 1929, *Writings of Leon Trotsky*, 1929, op cit, pp392–5.
31. LD Trotsky, 'Against National Communism! Lessons of the Red Referendum', 25 August 1931, *The Struggle Against Fascism in Germany*, op cit, pp94, 104. Richard Scheringer was an officer who had been tried for Nazi sympathies whilst in the army. He later went over to the Communists and became one of their main publicists. See Lieutenant D Scheringer, 'From Fascism to Communism', *Labour Monthly*, Volume 8, no 5, May 1931, pp300–2.
32. LD Trotsky, 'The Turn in the Communist International and the Situation in Germany', 26 September 1930, *The Struggle Against Fascism in Germany*, op cit, p74.
33. LD Trotsky, 'Workers' Control of Production', 20 August 1931, *The Struggle Against Fascism in Germany*, op cit, pp77, 78, 80.
34. The slump led to the overthrow of the military dictatorship of Don Miguel Primo de Rivera y Orbaneja (1870–1930) in Spain, who left office and drank himself to death in Paris. This was the beginning of a period of instability that led to the fall of the king and the proclamation of a republic.
35. LD Trotsky, 'The Creation of Soviets', 12 December 1930, *The Spanish Revolution, 1931–39*, New York, 1973, p65.
36. LD Trotsky, 'Unify the Communist Ranks', 24 April 1931, *The Spanish Revolution, 1931–39*, op cit, p108.
37. Maxim Litvinov (1876–1951) was Stalin's Commissar for Foreign Affairs during the period of the Popular Front. He was very quickly removed when Stalin began negotiations with Hitler in 1939.
38. Pierre Laval (1883–1945) was the French foreign minister who negotiated the Franco-Russian pact of 1935. He later collaborated with the Germans in running the Vichy regime during the Second World War, and was executed as a traitor at the end of it.
39. LD Trotsky, 'Whither France?', October 1936, *Leon Trotsky on France*, New York, 1979, pp47–8.
40. The French had been allowed to exploit the coal of the Saar basin under the control of the League of Nations at the Treaty of Versailles. After 15 years a plebiscite was to decide upon its future, becoming due in 1935.
41. LD Trotsky, 'Whither France?', October 1936, *Leon Trotsky on France*, op cit, p44.
42. The 'Neos' or Neo-Socialists were the right wing of the SFIO expelled in 1933 for voting to cut the salaries of public employees.
43. The left wing of the SFIO was led by Marceau Pivert, and at times adopted Trotskyist positions. Upon expulsion from the SFIO in 1939 it formed the PSOP. See Jean-Paul Joubert, *Révolutionnaires de la SFIO*, Paris, 1977.
44. The right-wing organisations were known as Leagues. The most prominent was the Croix de Feu, led by Colonel Casimir de la Rocque. Profiting from the financial scandal of the Stavisky affair, in which government ministers were

implicated, they combined to attempt an attack upon the French parliament building in 1934.

45. Gaston Doumergue (1863–1937) had been president of France just after the First World War. He was recalled to head an authoritarian government set up in the aftermath of the League attacks, between February and November 1934. Pierre Flandin (1889–1958) followed him as prime minister between November 1934 and May 1935.
46. LD Trotsky, 'France at the Turning Point', 28 March 1936, *Leon Trotsky on France*, op cit, p140.
47. Albert Sarraut (1872–1962) headed several ministries (colonies, interior, and was even premier) in several French governments between 1934 and 1943.
48. Edouard Herriot (1872–1957) was a well-known leader of the Radicals and prime minister on several occasions in the 1920s and 1930s.
49. LD Trotsky, 'An Open Letter to the Workers of France', 10 June 1935, *Writings of Leon Trotsky, 1934–35*, New York, 1971, pp305–6, 313–4.
50. Konrad Knudsen (1890–1959), was a socialist journalist and MP who offered Trotsky hospitality whilst he was in Norway. The Storting was the Norwegian parliament. On Trotsky's stay in Norway, cf Nils Dahl, 'With Trotsky in Norway', *Revolutionary History*, Volume 2, no 2, Summer 1989, pp33-42.
51. Martin Tranmael (1879–1967) was secretary of the Norwegian Labour Party (1918) and editor of its main newspaper (1921–49).
52. Trygve Lie (1896–1968) was minister of justice in the Norwegian Labour government, and later General Secretary of UNO (1946–53). Trotsky's prophecy was confirmed when the Germans invaded in 1940 and the government had to go into exile in Britain.
53. Serge and Sedova, op cit, pp194–5.
54. The Matignon Agreement, signed in June 1936, granted these reforms as a way of defusing the French general strike. See Jacques Danos and Marcel Gibelin, *June '36: Class Struggle and the Popular Front in France*, London, 1986, Chapter 5, 'The Matignon Agreement', pp72–86; Daniel Guérin, *Front populaire, révolution manquée*, Paris, 1970, pp120–3.
55. LD Trotsky, 'The Decisive Stage', 5 June 1936, *Leon Trotsky on France*, op cit, pp155, 160.
56. LD Trotsky, 'The French Revolution Has Begun!', 9 June 1936, *Leon Trotsky on France*, op cit, p162.
57. LD Trotsky, 'Preface to Whither France?', 10 June 1936, *Leon Trotsky on France*, op cit, p28.
58. LD Trotsky, 'Deportation from the Soviet Union', 25 February 1929, *Writings of Leon Trotsky, 1929*, op cit, p29.
59. LD Trotsky, 'Foreword to 1929 French Edition', 15 April 1929, *The Third International After Lenin*, op cit, pp xxxv, xxxvi. FA Ridley was among those who were urging Trotsky to found a Fourth International at this time. See Bornstein and Richardson, op cit, pp55–6; FA Ridley, 'Marxism, History and a Fourth International', *Adelphi*, May 1932, reprinted in *Revolutionary History*, Volume 5, no 3, Autumn 1994, pp211–6.
60. 'The Declaration of Four', *Documents of the Fourth International*, New York, 1973, pp56–9. Trotsky drafted it out on 26 August 1933.
61. LD Trotsky, 'It is Impossible to Remain in the Same "International" as Stalin, Manuilsky, Lozovsky and Company', 20 July 1933, *Writings of Leon Trotsky, 1933–34*, New York, 1975, pp18, 20–22.
62. Rosmer is mistaken about the source of these quotations. They do not come from the preface to the French edition of *Terrorism and Communism* put out in

1936, but from *Whither France?* See LD Trotsky, 'Once Again, Whither France?', 28 March 1935, *Leon Trotsky on France*, op cit, pp115, 123–4.
63. The Fourth International was finally founded on 3 September 1938 in Rosmer's own cottage at Périgny.
64. LD Trotsky, 'France at the Turning Point', 28 March 1936 (the preface to the 1936 French edition of *Terrorism and Communism*), *Leon Trotsky on France*, op cit, p150.
65. Walter Duranty (1884–1957) was the *New York Times* correspondent in Russia, and a notorious defender of the Moscow trials (see SJ Taylor, *Stalin's Apologist: Walter Duranty, The New York Times Man in Moscow*, Oxford UP, 1990). Louis Fischer (1896–1970) reported in like manner for *The Nation*; Romain Rolland (1866–1944) had been a prominent pacifist during the First World War, but was a frequent fellow-traveller at Stalinist literary congresses during this period.
66. LD Trotsky, *The Revolution Betrayed*, London, 1973, p2. Beatrice Webb (1858–1943) and Sidney Webb (1859–1947), later Lord Passfield, were the main theorists of the Labour Party's right wing during the early part of the twentieth century. Their excessively boring book, *Soviet Communism, A New Civilisation*, was disseminated in thousands by the Stalinist-dominated Left Book Club. Its appendix includes the new Soviet constitution, drawn up by Bukharin and Radek, who were about to be shot.
67. LD Trotsky, *The Revolution Betrayed*, op cit, p3.
68. Ibid.
69. The Ninth of Thermidor 1794 was the date of the overthrow of Robespierre during the French Revolution. The word Thermidorean is generally used by Marxists to signify a period of reaction in the history of revolutions.
70. A muzhik was a Russian peasant.
71. LD Trotsky, *The Revolution Betrayed*, op cit, pp237–8.
72. Op cit, pp238–9.
73. Op cit, pp244–5.
74. Op cit, p248.
75. Op cit, p249.
76. Op cit, pp249–50.
77. Op cit, p252.
78. Op cit, pp253–4.
79. Op cit, pp255–6.
80. Op cit, p276.
81. Op cit, pp280–1.
82. Op cit, pp288–9.
83. Op cit, p290. The Spanish Civil War had broken out in July 1936, when the working class, inspired by anarchism and socialism, replied to an attempted military coup with a popular insurrection, later crushed largely due to the intrigues of the Stalinists behind the Republican lines. See LD Trotsky, *The Spanish Revolution, 1931–39*, op cit; Felix Morrow, *Revolution and Counter-Revolution in Spain*, New York, 1974; *Revolutionary History*, Volumes 1 no 2, Summer 1988, and 4, nos 1–2, Winter 1991–92.
84. LD Trotsky, *The Revolution Betrayed*, op cit, p231.
85. Op cit, p231. The Mikado was a popular term for the Japanese Emperor, at that time Hirohito. Japan had formally annexed Korea in 1910, set up the protectorate 'Empire of Manchukuo' over Manchuria in 1931–33, and gradually encroached upon China's north-eastern provinces during the following years. See Robert Louzon, *China: Three Thousand Years of History, Fifty Years of Revolution*, London, 1998, pp127, 130.

86. The Fabian Society, to which the Webbs belonged, was founded in 1884, and was one of the groups that played a part in the formation of the Labour Party. During this period it represented the most consciously reformist wing of the labour movement in Britain.
87. LD Trotsky, *The Revolution Betrayed*, op cit, pp302–5.
88. Léon Blum (1872–1950) was a leader of the French socialists and first premier of the Popular Front government of 1936. *Le Populaire* was the SFIO newspaper edited by him.
89. LD Trotsky, *The Revolution Betrayed*, op cit, p307. See Exodus, xxxiv, 20–3.
90. Carl Bernard Askvig (1885–194?) was the Norwegian chief of police, known to be sympathetic to Nazism.
91. Jean Van Heijenoort (1912–1986), Trotsky's secretary at the time, was arrested and deported from Norway. See Jean Van Heijenoort, *With Trotsky in Exile*, Harvard UP, 1978, pp89–90; Anita Burdman Feferman, *Politics, Logic and Love: The Life of Jean Van Heijenoort*, Wellesley, 1993, pp120–1; see the review in *Revolutionary History*, Volume 5, no 3, Autumn 1994, pp252–3.
92. LD Trotsky, 'In "Socialist" Norway', December 1936, *Writings of Leon Trotsky, 1936–37*, New York, 1978, pp25–30, 35.
93. LD Trotsky, 'In Closed Court', 11 December 1936, *Writings of Leon Trotsky*, 1935–36, New York, 1977, p471. Vidkun Quisling (1887–1945) founded the National Union Party, a semi-Fascist organisation, after previously being War Minister. He ran Norway under the German occupation during the Second World War, and was shot at the end of it. His name has been used ever after in the sense of collaborator.
95. Gustav Noske (1868–1946) was the right-wing Socialist Defence Minister who brought in the Freikorps to suppress the German Revolution in January 1919; Philipp Scheidemann (1865–1939) was SPD chancellor in the same government; they were responsible for the murders of Karl Liebknecht (1871–1919) and Rosa Luxemburg (1871–1919), the founders of the German Communist Party.
94. See LD Trotsky, 'Ibsen', 9 June 1901, in *Culture and Revolution in the Thought of Leon Trotsky*, *Revolutionary History*, Volume 7, no 2, 1999, pp4–15; see also 'Reading Ibsen Again', 17 and 22 October 1936, *Writings of Leon Trotsky, Supplement 1934–40*, New York, 1979, pp723–4. Ibsen's *An Enemy of the People*, in which Stockmann appears, was written in 1882.
96. LD Trotsky, 'On the Atlantic', 28 December 1936, *Writings of Leon Trotsky, 1936–37*, op cit, pp38–9.
97. Op cit, p40.
98. Ibid. Helge Krog (1889–1962) was a journalist and playwright. He translated Trotsky's *My Life* into Norwegian.
99. Jonas Lie (1899–1945) was joint chief of police, and a member of Quisling's party. He later ran the police force in Norway under the German occupation.
100. LD Trotsky, 'Zinoviev and Kamenev', 31 December 1936, *Writings of Leon Trotsky, 1936–37*, op cit, p49.
101. Op cit, p51.
102. Georges Danton (1759–1794) and Maximillien Robespierre (1758–1794) were Jacobin leaders overthrown and guillotined by the counter-revolution in France.
103. LD Trotsky, 'Zinoviev and Kamenev', *Writings of Leon Trotsky, 1936–37*, op cit, p50.
104. LD Trotsky, 'Why They Confessed Crimes They Had Not Committed', 1 January 1937, *Writings of Leon Trotsky, 1936–37*, op cit, p56. Hendrik Yagoda

(1891–1938) was the head of the GPU who organised the first Moscow trial, of the 16; he was himself a defendant in the third trial, of the 21. Andrei Vyshinsky (1883–1954) was an ex-Menshevik who was the prosecuting attorney during the Moscow trials. He had previously processed Kerensky's order to arrest Lenin during the Russian Revolution. See Arkady Vaksberg, *The Prosecutor and the Prey: Vyshinsky and the 1930s Moscow Show Trials*, London, 1990.

105. Sergei Kirov (1886–1934) was the head of the Leningrad Communist Party until his assassination by Nikolayev, an alleged supporter of Zinoviev, which was the pretext for the first Moscow trial. It has since been admitted that he was killed by the GPU.
106. LD Trotsky, 'Why They Confessed Crimes They Had Not Committed', *Writings of Leon Trotsky, 1936–37*, op cit, pp61–2. Ivan Smirnov (1881–1936) was a former Left Oppositionist who had capitulated to Stalin in 1929.
107. Diego Rivera (1886–1957) and his wife Frida Kahlo (1910–1954) were famous painters who put their house at Trotsky's disposal upon his arrival in Mexico. See *Revolutionary History*, Volume 7, no 2, 1999, pp203ff.
108. Serge and Sedova, op cit, pp210–1.
109. General Lazáro Cárdenas del Rio (1895–1970) was a reforming president of Mexico. He retired from office in 1940 to promote cooperative agriculture, and later to extend the electrification of the country.
110. Karl Bernhardovich Sobelsohn (Radek, 1885–1939) and Georgi Piatakov (1890–1937) were the main defendants in the second Moscow trial, the Trial of the Seventeen.
111. LD Trotsky, 'A New Moscow Amalgam', 21 January 1937, *Writings of Leon Trotsky, 1936–37*, op cit, p115.
112. Leon Sedov, *The Red Book on the Moscow Trial*, London, 1980.
113. LD Trotsky, 'A New Moscow Amalgam', *Writings of Leon Trotsky, 1936–37*, op cit, pp115–6.
114. Op cit, p123.
115. The conviction of the military officer Alfred Dreyfus (1859–1935) on a charge of espionage, was the most notorious miscarriage of justice in French history. A major part in the campaign to exonerate him was played by the famous novelist Emile Zola (1840–1902) in his *J'accuse!*
116. The Hotel Bristol, the supposed rendezvous in the first meeting, had been burned down 10 years before. Rudolf Hess (1894–1987) was the deputy leader of the Nazi Party. Finding himself reduced to a secondary rôle during the Second World War, he flew to Britain to attempt negotiations, and was one of the defendants at the postwar Nuremberg War Crimes Tribunal. Attempts by Natalia Trotsky, backed by several prominent figures such as HG Wells, George Orwell and Professor CEM Joad, and aided by the American and British Trotskyists, to question him on the allegations made against Trotsky during the Moscow trials were avoided by the tribunal ('Nuremberg Prosecution Asked: 1. To Give representation to Natalia Trotsky, 2. To Produce Evidence of Moscow Trials', *Socialist Appeal*, March 1946).
117. LD Trotsky, 'I Stake My Life!', 9 February 1937, *Leon Trotsky Speaks*, op cit, p285.
118. Op cit, p280.
119. John Dewey (1859–1952) was a noted American empiricist philosopher and theorist of education.
120. Suzanne La Follette (1893–1983) was a writer and journalist. John Chamberlain (1903– ?) was literary critic of the *New York Times*. Edward Alsworth Ross (1886–1951) was a liberal academic who had interviewed

Trotsky in 1918. See Al Richardson (ed), *In Defence of the Russian Revolution*, London, 1995, pp185–7. Benjamin Stolberg (1891–1951) was an author and labour journalist. Otto Rühle (1874–1943) was a former Reichstag deputy and a founder member of the German Communist Party, famous for his biography of Karl Marx (English translation, 1929). He later co-operated with Trotsky in compiling *The Living Thoughts of Karl Marx*, London, 1940. Wendelin Thomas (1884–?) was the leader of the Wilhelmshaven mutiny during the First World War. Carlo Tresca (1879–1943) was a prominent Italian Anarchist, later gunned down by unknown assailants in the streets of New York. Francisco Zamora Padilla (1890–1986) was a former member of the executive of the Mexican Workers' Federation and a professor of political economy.

121. Carleton Beals (1893–1979) was a journalist and author of books on Latin America, and a fellow-traveller of the American Communist Party (*Daily World*, 11 July 1979). He subsequently published an article denouncing the Dewey inquiry in the Mexican Stalinist magazine *Futuro*, to which Trotsky replied ('Mr Beals as a Witness', 18 May 1937, *Writings of Leon Trotsky, 1936–37*, New York, 1978, pp291–7). Beals had previously been a correspondent for Tass, and was later Chairman of the Fair Play for Cuba Committee ('Death of Carleton Beals: Paid Agent of Moscow', *The News Line*, 8 August 1979).

122. *The Case of Leon Trotsky*, New York, 1969, pp1–3. Tom Mooney (1882–1942) was a union organiser accused of setting off a bomb on a pro-war demonstration in 1916. Nicola Sacco (1891–1927) and Bartolomeo Vanzetti (1888–1927) were Italian Anarchists, falsely accused of robbery and murder. Broadly-based campaign committees agitated for their release. The two Italians were executed, but Mooney was finally pardoned in 1939.

123. John Dewey, *Truth is on the March, Report and Remarks on the Trotsky Hearings in Mexico*, American Committee for the Defense of Leon Trotsky, New York, 1937, p13.

124. *Not Guilty: Report of the Commission of Inquiry into the Charges Made Against Leon Trotsky in the Moscow Trials*, New York, 1972, p320.

125. James T Farrell, 'Dewey in Mexico', in Sidney Hook (ed), *John Dewey: Philosopher of Science and Freedom*, New York, 1950, pp375–6.

126. LD Trotsky, 'Leon Sedov – Friend, Son, Fighter', 20 February 1938, *Writings of Leon Trotsky, 1937–38*, New York, 1976, pp166–71. On the circumstances of his death, see Rob Sewell, 'How the GPU Infiltrated the Trotskyist Movement', *Socialist Appeal*, no 87, February 2001, pp8–10.

127. Op cit, pp171–2, 176-7.

128. Christian Georgievich Rakovsky (1873–1941), one of the pioneers of the Balkan socialist movement, was a defendant during the third Moscow trial, that of the 21. See Christian Rakovsky, *Roumania and Bessarabia*, WIL pamphlet, London, 1990; Gus Fagan (ed), *Christian Rakovsky: Selected Writings on Opposition in the USSR, 1923–30*, London, 1980.

129. Nikolai Krestinsky (1883–1938) was a former secretary of the Bolshevik Central Committee. He was the only victim before Traicho Kostov to expose the farce of the Stalinist purge trials in open court.

130. Fyodor Mikhailovich Dostoyevsky (1821–1881) was one of Russia's most noted novelists and short story writers, who often dealt with tragic themes.

131. LD Trotsky, 'The Decapitation of the Army', 17 June 1937, *Writings of Leon Trotsky, 1936–37*, op cit, p340. Mikhail Nikolayevich Tukhachevsky (1893–1937) was a Tsarist officer who had joined the Bolsheviks in 1918. He was a brilliant pioneer of tank warfare, and his removal had the effect of greatly disorganising the Russian armour during the Second World War. See his

speech, 'The Red Army and the Militia', 11 January 1921, in A Richardson (ed), *In Defence of the Russian Revolution*, op cit, pp163–74.

132. LD Trotsky, 'The Decapitation of the Army', *Writings of Leon Trotsky, 1936–37*, op cit, pp345–6. Kliment Voroshilov (1881–1969) was an old crony of Stalin's from the time of the Russian Civil War. He was removed as Defence Commissar on account of his incompetence during the Second World War.

133. Op cit, p346. Shortly after Hitler came to power, Molotov had remarked that fascism was a matter of taste.

134. Op cit, p338.

135. LD Trotsky, 'A Significant Episode', 30 December 1936, *Writings of Leon Trotsky, 1936–37*, op cit, p44.

136. Nina Lvovna Bronstein (1903–1928) was Trotsky's second daughter. She died of tuberculosis in Moscow. Zinaida Lvovna Bronstein (1901–1933) was her elder sister. She committed suicide in Berlin.

137. Sergei Sedov (1908–1938) was Trotsky's younger son. He took part in the hunger strike of the Trotskyists in Vorkuta, and was then taken off to be shot in Moscow. See LD Trotsky, 'The Arrest of Sergei Sedov', 27 January 1937, *Writings of Leon Trotsky, 1936–37*, op cit, pp158–9; P Richards, 'A Meeting with Trotsky's Son', *Fourth International*, no 10, Summer 1960, pp25–7; 'Kremlin Admits Shooting Trotsky's Son', *Militant*, 1 June 1990.

138. Mikhail S Glazman was Trotsky's secretary during the Russian Civil War, and committed suicide in 1924. See LD Trotsky, 'Mikhail Glazman', 6 September 1924, *Portraits, Political and Personal*, New York, 1977, pp64–8. NM Sermuks was the commander of Trotsky's armoured train, arrested in Alma Ata in 1928. IM Poznansky (1898–1938) was Trotsky's secretary from 1917 to 1927. He was shot in Vorkuta. Georgi Vassilievich Butov was Trotsky's Chief of Staff during the Civil War. He died on hunger strike in 1928.

139. Rudolf Klement (1910–38) was a German student who served as Trotsky's secretary in Turkey, and then as secretary of the international Trotskyist movement until he was murdered by the GPU in Paris on the eve of the foundation of the Fourth International. See Pierre Broué, 'Quelques collaborateurs de Trotsky', *Cahiers Léon Trotsky*, no 1, January 1979, pp73–5.

140. Erwin Wolf (1902–1937), was a Sudeten German Trotskyist sent to report on the Spanish Civil War. He was picked up by the GPU and disappeared in September 1937. Cf 'Quelques collaborateurs de Trotsky', *Cahiers Léon Trotsky*, no 1, January 1979, pp76–9.

141. Heinz Epe, known as Walter Held (1910–1942) was a Trotskyist who had fled Germany when Hitler came to power. He was taken from a train crossing the USSR with his family, and tortured and killed by Beria. Cf Pierre Broué, 'Walter Held', Nils Dahl, 'Some Memories of Walter Held', and Walter Held, 'Stalinism and the POUM in the Spanish Revolution', *Revolutionary History*, Volume 1, no 2, Summer 1988, pp7–17; 'The Walter Held File', *Revolutionary History*, Volume 1, no 4, Winter 1988–9, pp39–43; Nils Dahl, 'With Trotsky in Norway', *Revolutionary History*, Volume 2, no 2, Summer 1989, pp41–2.

142. Nathan Markovich Poretsky, known as Ignace Reiss (1899–1937) was a GPU officer who came over to Trotskyism. He was murdered by Russian agents in Switzerland. See Elizabeth Poretsky, *Our Own People*, Oxford, 1969.

143. Andreu Nin Pérez (1892–1937) was the leader of the POUM; Kurt Landau (1903–1937) was an Austrian revolutionary cooperating with the party. They were both picked up by the GPU, tortured and murdered during the Spanish Civil War. See *Revolutionary History*, Volume 1, no 2, Summer 1988, and 4, nos 1–2, Winter 1991–92.

144. Samuel Ginsburg, known as Walter Krivitsky (1899–1941) was a Russian intelligence officer who broke with the regime over the Moscow trials and Stalin's policy in Spain. He was found murdered in a hotel room. Cf WG Krivitsky, *I Was Stalin's Agent*, 1939; 'The Editors', 'The Murder of Krivitsky', *Fourth International*, Volume 2, no 2, February 1941, pp35–6.
145. Adolf Abramovich Joffe (1883–1927) was a Bolshevik diplomat and a friend of Trotsky. He committed suicide in protest at the Russian government's treatment of the Left Opposition, including its refusal to allow him to go abroad for an operation. His suicide note can be found in 'The Last Words of Adolf Joffe', *Leon Trotsky: The Man and His Work*, New York, 1969, and Trotsky's graveside speech, 'In Memory of AA Joffe', 19 November 1927, in LD Trotsky, *The Challenge of the Left Opposition, 1926–27*, op cit, pp470–2. See also Maria Joffe, *One Long Night*, London, 1978; Nadezhda A Joffe, *Back in Time*, Michigan, 1995.
146. These 'friends' were, of course, Alfred and Marguerite Rosmer.
147. Hubert Clinton Herring (1888–1967) was the author of *A History of Latin America*. The interview Trotsky granted to his Committee for Cultural relations with Latin America appears as 'On the Eve of World War 2', 23 July 1939, *Writings of Leon Trotsky, 1939–40*, New York, 1973, pp14–27.
148. LD Trotsky, 'The World Situation and Perspectives', 14 February 1940, *Writings of Leon Trotsky, 1939–40*, op cit, pp139–57. *The St Louis Post Dispatch* printed this interview on 10 and 17 March 1940.
149. Martin Dies (1901–1972) was a Texas Democrat who was the head of the House Un-American Activities Committee in 1939.
150. On Trotsky's split with Diego Rivera, see LD Trotsky, 'Difficulties with Diego', 6 December 1938, in *Culture and Revolution in the Thought of Leon Trotsky, Revolutionary History*, Volume 7, no 2, 1999, pp211–2. General Juan Andreu (1891–1965) was a right-wing candidate in the Mexican presidential elections of 1940.
151. Francisco Largo Caballero (1869–1946) was the leader of the UGT trade union and of the Socialist Party's left wing. He was removed from office as prime minister during the Spanish Civil War because he resisted the pressure of the Russians, and later testified on behalf of the POUM leaders at their show trial. See *Revolutionary History*, Volume 1, no 2, Summer 1988, and 4, nos 1–2, Winter 1991–92.
152. LD Trotsky, 'Problems of the Development of the USSR', 4 April 1931, *Writings of Leon Trotsky, 1930–31*, New York, 1973, p229.
153. LD Trotsky, 'What Next? Vital Questions for the German Proletariat', 27 January 1932, *The Struggle Against Fascism in Germany*, op cit, p255.
154. LD Trotsky, 'The Only Road', 14 September 1932, *The Struggle Against Fascism in Germany*, op cit, p320.
155. LD Trotsky, 'The Class Nature of the Soviet State', 1 October 1933, *Writings of Leon Trotsky, 1933–34*, op cit, p121.
156. LD Trotsky, 'The USSR in War', 25 September 1939, *In Defence of Marxism*, London, 1966, p28.
157. LD Trotsky, 'A Letter to James P Cannon', 12 September 1939, *In Defence of Marxism*, op cit, p1.
158. LD Trotsky, 'The USSR in War', 25 September 1939, *In Defence of Marxism*, op cit, pp3, 16, 20–1.
159. Op cit, pp22–3.
160. LD Trotsky, 'Balance Sheet of the Finnish Events', 25 April 1940, *In Defence of Marxism*, op cit, p213.

161. LD Trotsky, 'The USSR in War', *In Defence of Marxism*, op cit, p216; LD Trotsky, 'War and the Fourth International', 10 June 1934, *Writings of Leon Trotsky, 1933–34*, op cit, p303 (a slightly differing translation).
162. David Alfaro Siqueiros (1896–1974), a well-known Mexican artist and Stalinist who had served in the Spanish Civil War, masterminded the first attack upon Trotsky, and boasted openly about it afterwards (Norberto Valentini, 'Siqueiros Narra Atentado Contra Trotsky', *Ahora!* [Dominican Republic], 9 October 1972, an interview translated as 'Siqueiros Admits He Intended to Kill Trotsky in Raid', *InterContinental Press*, Volume 10, no 41, 13 November 1972, pp1238–40; Joseph Hansen, 'Siqueiros Finally Discloses Part of Truth', ibid; 'David Siqueiros Admits He Attempted to Kill Trotsky on Orders from Stalin: Artist's Confession Only Part of Truth', *The Militant* (USA), 24 November 1972). His speech to the tribunal is reproduced in DA Siqueiros, 'The Assault on the House of Leon Trotsky', *Revolutionary Democracy*, University Enclave, Delhi, Volume 6, no 1, April 2000, pp59–75. The only punishment history ever meted out to him was a kick up the backside from a French Trotskyist during some junketings in Havana.
163. See LD Trotsky, 'The Reptile Breed of The Nation', 18 June 1940, *Writings of Leon Trotsky, 1939–40*, op cit, p292.
164. LD Trotsky, 'Letter to the Mexican Attorney General', 27 May 1940, *Writings of Leon Trotsky*, 1939–40, op cit, p223.
165. Op cit, p227.
166. Serge and Sedova, op cit, p277.
167. David Serrano Andoneguí (1908—?) was a Stalinist agent who had served in the Spanish Civil War under the pseudonym of 'Julio Justo'. He was a notorious bigamist, with wives in both Spain and Mexico.
168. Nestor Sánchez Hernández (1917–?) had served with Siqueiros in the Spanish Civil War under the pseudonym of 'Captain Nestor'.
169. Serge and Sedova, op cit, pp259–60.
170. LD Trotsky, 'Supplementary and Indispensable Explanations of My 2 July Statements', 5 July 1940, *Writings of Leon Trotsky, 1939–40*, op cit, pp312–5.
171. Op cit, p306.
172. Op cit, p307.
173. Op cit, pp309–10.
174. Serge and Sedova, op cit, p277.
175. Robert Sheldon Harte (1917–1940), one of Trotsky's guards, had admitted the killers into the house during the first assassination attempt. He went off with them and was later found murdered. It was uncertain for a long time whether he was an accomplice, or simply careless, as Trotsky believed ('GPU Tried to Cover Murder with Slander', 25 June 1940, *Writings of Leon Trotsky, 1939–40*, op cit, pp293–4). The Mexican police investigator, Leandro A Sanchez Salazar (*Murder in Mexico*, London, 1950, pp87–96) was firmly of the opinion that Harte was a GPU agent, killed afterwards to shut his mouth. It was not until 1997 that the truth was finally established from the Russian archives, that Harte, who appears in them under the pseudonym of 'Amur', had indeed been recruited by their intelligence services in New York and sent to spy on Trotsky in Mexico (Rodrigo Fernández, 'Two Spaniards Tried to Kill Trotsky Before Mercader Did', *El País*, 16 November 1997; 'Extrait de l'histoire des services de renseignments soviétiques', in L'Assassinat de Trotsky: Documents, *Cahiers du CERMTRI*, no 99, December 2000, pp76–7; Pierre Broué, 'Du nouveau sur les crimes de Staline', *Cahiers Léon Trotsky*, no 72, December 2000, p106). For details of the controversy, cf Georges Vereeken, *The GPU in the Trotskyist*

Movement, London, 1976, pp319–27; *How the GPU Murdered Trotsky*, London, 1981, pp108–116, 238–9, 250, 299–303.

176. LD Trotsky, 'The Young Lenin', 1936, in Irving Howe (ed), *The Basic Writings of Trotsky*, London, 1964, pp325–37.

177. Although during this period he wrote an essay on Engels, and the preface to *The Living Thoughts of Karl Marx* (London, 1940), Trotsky was never able to begin the book. Victor Serge and Natalia Sedova Trotsky (op cit, p252) describe how 'a book he had been dreaming about for a long time was one on the friendship and fruitful life-long collaboration of Karl Marx and Friedrich Engels. The deep understanding that existed between these two great champions of the proletarian cause, their unwavering affection for each other – this is what he wanted to recreate in the written word. But the publishers and the public were more interested in the fearsome tyrant'.

178. Trotsky's *Stalin* was withheld from publication due to pressure from the US State Department during the Second World War, when Russia and the USA were allies, and was only finally issued in 1946. Since it was incomplete, it was heavily edited by Charles Malamuth, who did not share Trotsky's views on many important points. See John G Wright, 'A Biography of Stalin', *Fourth International*, Volume 7, no 7, July 1946, pp210–3.

179. Louis Francis Budenz (1891–1972) had previously been involved with the Trotskyists in the Workers' Party of the United States, but had left in 1935 to join the Communist Party, for whom he edited the *Daily Worker*. He was thus an ideal agent for operations against the Trotskyists. He went over to the Catholic church during the Cold War.

180. Joseph Hansen, 'With Trotsky to the End', in *Leon Trotsky: The Man and His Work*, op cit, pp17–18.

181. Serge and Sedova, op cit, p268. For an earlier account, cf Natalia Trotsky, 'How it Happened', *Fourth International*, Volume 2, no 4, May 1941, pp100–3.

182. This was the Spanish Trotskyist, Manuel Fernández Grandizo (Munis, 1912–1989), who had himself just escaped from a republican prison at the end of the Spanish Civil War.

183. J Gorkin, *L'Assassinat de Trotsky*, Paris, 1970, pp290–316; Leandro A Sanchez Salazar and J Gorkín, *Murder in Mexico*, London, 1950, pp231–5. Julián Gómez García Gorkin (1902–1987) was a writer and a leader of the POUM, himself arrested by GPU intrigues during the Spanish Civil War.

184. Vicente Lombardo Toledano (1893–1969) was the head of the Mexican Workers Federation, and a leading Stalinist.

185. Narciso Bassols (1898–1959), a professor of law, had been minister of the interior before becoming Mexican ambassador in Paris. His position enabled him to infiltrate more GPU agents into Mexico, who mingled with Spaniards fleeing from Franco's triumph in the Spanish Civil War.

186. Ramón Mercader del Rio (1914–1978), Trotsky's assassin, was a Spanish Stalinist trained for the task in Moscow. Since Mexico had no death penalty, he was sentenced to 20 years in jail (Walter O'Rourke, 'The Verdict on the Assassin of Trotsky', *Fourth International*, Volume 4, no 8, August 1943, pp235–9). Upon his release from prison in 1960, he was greeted by prominent government personnel in Cuba on his way back to the Soviet Union. He was decorated upon his arrival in Moscow, but went back to live in Cuba in 1974, where he died of bone cancer (Chris Catlin, 'Trotsky's Killer Reported Alive in Moscow', an interview with his brother, *Washington Post*, 17 January 1977, reprinted in *InterContinental Press*, Volume 14, no 3, 31 January 1977, pp70–1; 'Trotsky's Assassin Dies in Havana', *Guardian*, 20 October 1978; 'Leon Trotsky's Assassin

Dies', *Daily Telegraph*, 20 October 1978; UPI, 'Trotsky Assassin Reported Dead', *The Times*, 20 October 1978; 'Trotsky's Assassin Dies in Havana', *Workers' Vanguard*, 3 November 1978; Joseph Hansen, 'Trotsky's Assassin Reported Dead of Cancer', *InterContinental Press*, 6 November 1978; 'Silence in Havana Over Mercader's Death', *InterContinental Press*, 13 November 1978). He now lies in a Moscow cemetery. His younger brother, Luis, provides some additional details about him in *Ramón Mercader mi hermano*, Editorial Espasa-Calpe, 1991 – see the review by Diego Mocar, 'The Prophet Murdered', *Trotskyist International*, nos 13–14, April–September 1994, pp87–8. A vast literature has since grown up around the murder. The following are the most useful books: Isaac Don Levine, *The Mind of an Assassin*, New York, 1960; Bernard Wolfe, *The Great Prince Died*, London, 1972; Nicholas Mosley, *The Assassination of Trotsky*, London, 1972; Pierre Broué, *L'Assassinat de Trotsky*, Brussels, 1980; Alain Dugrand (ed), *Trotsky in Mexico*, Manchester, 1992; Pavel Sudoplatov, *Special Tasks*, London, 1994, pp65–83. The inside story of the intrigue within the Mexican Communist Party appears in Valentin Campa, *Mi testimonio: memorias de un comunista mexicano*, Mexico, 1968. The relevant parts are translated into English in 'How the Stalinists Planned Trotsky's Murder', *Workers Vanguard*, 3 November 1978, and 'Campa Tells about Plot to Kill Trotsky', *InterContinental Press*, Volume 16, no 48, 18 December 1978, pp1397–9. See Joseph Hansen, 'Campa's "Revelations"', op cit, pp1395–6.

Index

Abd el-Krim 61
Absolutism 176
Action Française 84, 134
Ageloff, Sylvia 225–227
Alma Ata (USSR) 141, 146, 201, 238
Almazan, General Juan 211
Alvahuante, Felipe 229
American Communist Party (CPUSA) 17, 64, 129, 137, 237
Amherst (Canada) 200
Amiens, CGT Congress (France, 1906) 127, 137
Amsterdam International (ICFTU) 127, 137
Anarchism 28, 64
Anarcho-syndicalism 14, 45, 60–61, 195, 212
Anglo-Soviet Trade Union Committee (1925) 137
Anschluss (Austria, 1938) 154–155, 231
Anthemius of Tralles 230
Anti-fascism 160, 164, 195, 210, 214, 220, 223
Antonini 51, 64
Antwerp (Belgium) 166
Anual, Battle of (1921) 62
Aragon, Louis 69, 132
ArcheioMarxists (Greece) 14
Askvig, Carl 180, 235
Athens (Greece) 151
Authoritarianism 29, 36
Auvergne (France) 156
Avanti (Italian Socialist Party Paper) 95
Avenida Viena (Coyoacan, Mexico) 208, 210–211, 224
Balabanoff, Angelica 15
Balkan Wars (1912–13) 203
Barbé-Célor affair (France, 1931) 34
Barbé, Henri 34, 62
Barbizon, France 43, 161–162
Barbusse, Henri 23, 58, 60, 170
Barcelona (Spain) 200, 206, 229
Barnes, Jack 44, 64
Bassols, Narciso 229, 241
Beals, Carleton 195, 197, 237
Belgian Communist Party (PCB) 13–14, 17
Belsen 61
Beneš, Edouard 154, 231
Beria, Lavrenti 238
Berlin 15, 43, 137, 152, 201–202, 237–238
Berthelin, Pierre 91, 135
Besnard, Eugène 86, 134
Béthune (France) 52
Blanqui, Louis 61
Blanquism, Blanquists 23, 61, 92, 125
Bloc Nationale, National Bloc (France) 51
Blum, Léon 136, 178, 235
Bobigny (France) 31
Bolsheviks, Bolshevism 13–14, 35–37, 46, 55–56, 63, 72, 75, 87, 103, 112, 118, 123, 127, 129–130, 134, 136–137, 143, 146, 168, 170, 177–178, 180, 188, 197, 205, 230, 237, 239
Bolshevisation, Bolshevisers 17, 19, 21–22, 24, 26–31, 34, 39, 45, 47, 50, 52–53, 55–56, 58, 65, 67, 70, 90, 116, 118, 121–125, 127–128, 150
Bolshevik-Leninists (Trotskyists) 76, 165, 169
Bonapartism, Bonapartists 37, 63, 163
Bonar Law, Andrew 108, 136
Boulogne (France) 32
Brandler, Heinrich 15, 124, 137
Breton, André 68–70, 77, 132, 211
Bristol Hotel (Copenhagen) 236
British Communist Party (CPGB) 16
Bronstein, Nina 206, 238
Bronstein, Zinaida 206, 238
Broué, Pierre 12
Budenz, Louis 225, 241
Bukharin, Nikolai 13, 17, 56, 98, 102, 105, 135, 146, 148, 203, 230, 234
Bulgarian revolution (1923) 56, 65
Bulletin communiste 23, 27, 30, 40, 50–52, 54, 61, 63–64, 68–71, 86, 132–134
Bulletin of the Opposition (*Biulleten Oppozitsii*) 151, 168, 202
Bureaucracy, bureaucratisation 26, 42, 54, 59
Butov, Georgi 206, 238
Caballero, Francisco Largo 212, 239
Cachin, Marcel 22, 34, 36–37, 58, 60
Cadeau, Paul 84, 86–87, 134
Cahiers du bolchévisme 25–28, 30–31, 54
Cahiers de l'histoire de l'institut Maurice Thorez 37
Caillaux, Joseph 108, 136
Calzan, Claude 86, 134
Cannon, James P 14, 17, 43–44, 64
Cardenas, General Lazaro 190, 211
Cartèl des Gauches (Left Bloc, France) 84, 108
Cells, cell structure, cellulards 45
Célor, Pierre 34, 62
Centrism 41–42
CGT (General Labour Federation, France) 28, 62, 87, 125, 134, 137
CGTU (United General Labour Federation, France) 84, 89, 116, 134

Chambelland, Maurice 33, 51, 62, 89, 136
Chamberlain, John 195, 236
Charbit, Fraim 51, 64, 136
Chauvinism 21, 33
Chavez, Carlos 211
Cheka 73
Class collaboration 158
Clavez, Antoine 14, 17, 35, 62
Clemenceau, Georges 145, 230
Clichy (France) 24, 26, 58, 149
Clique 40, 81, 115
Clynes, Joseph Robert 108, 136
Cogniot, Georges 24, 61
Colonies 22, 32, 58
Comitees syndicalistes révolutionnaires (CSR, France) 86–87, 134
Committee for the Defence of Leon Trotsky 192
Committee for Joining the Third Intenational (France) 21–22, 45, 59–60
Committee for the Resumption of International Relations (France) 21
Communism 17, 20, 23, 25, 32, 73, 169, 177
Communist Syndicalist 113
Communist Youth (Spain) 229
Copenhagen (Denmark) 151–152, 193
Coyoacan (Mexico) 195, 198, 207–208, 212, 216, 222, 226
Crimea (USSR) 73, 136
Critique sociale 68–70
Croce, Benedetto 76, 133
Croix de Feu (France) 232
Daily Mail 112
Daladier, Edouard 153, 155, 159, 162–165, 231
Danton, Georges 188, 235
Daudet, Léon 84, 134
Dawes Plan (1924) 62, 83, 90, 110
Defence of the USSR 217
Delagarde, Victor 15, 35, 50, 54, 59, 62, 65–66, 79, 84, 93, 134, 136
Delegorgue, Judge 193
Democratic centralism 13, 25, 30
Denikin, Anton Ivanovich 105, 136
Desierto de los Leones (Mexico) 224
Desnos, Robert 69
Deutscher, Isaac 11–12, 133
Dewey, John 195–198, 236
Dewey Commission 195–198
Dialectics, dialectical materialism 77
Dictatorship of the proletariat 38
Dies, Martin 210, 239
Dies Committee (USA) 210
Djilas, Milovan 72
Dobbs, Farrell 64
Doriot, Jacques 79, 134
Dostoyevsky, Fyodor 204, 237
Dreyfus, Alfred 193, 197, 236
Drôme (France) 83
Doumergue, Gaston 163, 233
Dual power 158
Duclos, Jacques 26, 33–34, 46, 61
Dunkirk (France) 152
Dunois, Amédée 24, 47, 61, 70
Duranty, Walter 170, 234
Dzerzhinsky, Felix 73, 106, 133
East German Communist Party (Socialist Unity Party SED) 31
Eastman, Max 13–17, 64, 70, 75, 115–119, 133, 137
Electoralism 51
Eluard, Paul 69, 132
Les Embruns 154
Engels, Frederick 32, 178, 225
Entente Cordiale (First World War Allies) 154
Excelsior 222
Fabians, Fabian Society, Fabianism 177, 235
Fabre 135
Fabrol Emile 20, 49, 60, 64
Factions, factional activity, factionalism 32, 85, 87, 100
Factory cells 27, 45, 47, 54, 126
Factory councils 22, 57, 158
Farrell, James T 64, 198, 237
Fascism 28, 50, 84, 91, 126, 135, 155, 157–159, 184, 198, 205
Ferrat, AndrÈ 55, 58, 64–65
Fiori, Giuseppe 77
First World War (1914–18) 12, 33, 51, 141, 209
Fischer, Louis 170, 234
Fischer, Ruth 14, 43, 53, 56, 64, 123–124, 127, 129,
Flandin, Pierre 163, 233
La Follette, Suzanne 195, 236
Foster, William Z 129
Fourth International 15, 43–44, 64, 168–170, 214–216, 218, 220, 226, 228, 233–234, 238
– Founding Conference (1938) 14, 43, 76
Frachon, Benôit 33–34, 62
Freemasonry 35
Freikorps 63
French Communist Party (PCF) 12, 24, 26, 29–33, 36–37, 39, 45, 47, 49–55, 57–58, 60–62, 64–66, 68–69, 85, 87–88, 111, 115, 120–121, 125, 132, 134–135, 141, 150, 155–156
– First Congress (1921) 22
– Second Congress (1922) 22
– Third Congress (1924) 26
– Fourth Congress (1925) 24, 26, 56, 149
– Fifth Congress (1926) 26, 30, 33, 58
– Central Committee 26–27, 37, 95, 99, 115–116, 120, 148
– Politbureau 26–27, 80–81, 83, 92
– Executive Committee 80–81, 85
– Organisational Bureau 27
– Trade Union Commission 23, 50, 82, 90
– Parisian Region 149
– Seine Federation 36, 62, 64, 84, 91,

134
– Centre Faction 22, 36
French Revolution (1789) 167
French Socialist Party (SFIO) 21–22, 28, 47–48, 51, 53, 57, 60–62, 65, 134–136, 232
Frossard, Louis 21–23, 32, 35, 50, 58, 60, 84, 87, 89, 131
Futuro 220, 223, 237
Gallifet, General Gaston 134
German Communist Party (KPD) 31, 56, 124, 157, 168, 215
German October, German Revolution (1923) 36, 55–56
Gestapo 223
Girault, Suzanne 24, 32, 34, 36, 52, 61–62, 87–88, 134
Glazman, Mikhail 206, 238
Godonnèche, Victor 51, 136
Gorkin, Julián 229, 241
GPU, NKVD 69, 76–77, 175, 182, 189, 192, 194, 198, 206, 211, 220–222, 227,
Greece 14
Gruber, Helmut 15
Grumbach, Saloman 95, 135
Guesde, Jules 60
Guillot 91
Guralsky, Auguste (Alfred Lepetit) 25, 28, 54, 61, 63, 137
Hamburg (Germany) 65
Hansen, Joseph 226
Harte, Robert Sheldon 240
Heijenoort, Jean Van 12, 181, 235
Held, Walter 206, 238
Heller, Michel 72
Hernandez, Nestor Sanchez 223
Herring, Hubert 239
Herriot, Edouard 62, 136, 233
Hervé, Gustave 91, 135
Hess, Rudolf 193, 236
Hindenburg, Field Marshal Paul Von 118, 137
Hippe, Oskar 43, 64
Hippodrome (New York) 193
Hirohito (Japanese Emperor) 234
Hitler, Adolf 69, 74, 149, 154–155, 159–161, 165, 168, 192, 205, 207, 209–210, 214–218, 225, 231–232, 238
Hitlerite 159–160, 193
Holland 161, 199
Honefoss (Norway) 166–167
Hostotipaquilla (Mexico) 223
House of Representatives (USA) 210
House Un-American Activities Committee (USA) 239
L'Humanité 33, 38, 51, 53, 86, 89, 91, 103, 115, 117, 120, 124, 126, 141–142, 149, 151, 159–161, 164, 180
Humbert-Droz, Jules 24, 51, 55, 61
Ibsen 13, 17, 183, 235
Ilbert, Léon 87, 134
Imperialism 22–23, 25, 57, 104, 109, 113, 136, 155, 165, 176, 211, 215
Independent Labour Party (ILP) 150, 231
Inprecorr 117, 133
International Brigade 223
Istanbul (Constantinople, Turkey) 141–142, 147, 149, 168
Jacobins 63
Jacobs, Sarah 44, 64
Jacson, Frank (Jacques Mornard see Ramon Mercader)
Jalisco (Mexican state) 223
James, Cyril Lionel Robert 60
Jesuits 77
Joad, Professor Cyril 236
Joffe, Adolf 71, 206, 239
Johns Hopkins (University, USA) 228
Joint Opposition (USSR) 13, 15, 43
Joubert, Jean-Paul 232
Jouhaux, Léon 134, 137
Kaan, Pierre 70, 132
Kahlo, Frida 189–190, 208, 236
Kamenev, Lev 13, 17, 24, 34–35, 46–47, 53, 63, 73, 75–76, 105–106, 118, 135, 146, 187, 188, 230, 235
Kanachikov, SI 104
Kautsky, Karl 72, 133
Kemal, Mustapha (Ataturk) 153, 164, 231
Kerensky, Alexander 42, 236
Kienthal Conference (1916) 76, 121
Kirov, Sergei 189, 192, 236
Klement, Rudolf 206, 238
Knudsen, Konrad 166–167, 178–179, 181, 233
Kolchak, Admiral Alexander 105, 135
Kollontai, Alexandra 152, 231
Korsch, Karl 70, 132
Kostov, Traicho 237
Kremlin 77, 179, 200–201, 216–217, 222
Krestinsky, Nikolai 203, 237
Kristiansand (Norway) 179
Krivitsky, Walter 206, 239
Krog, Helge 187, 235
Kronstadt revolt (1921) 73–74, 77, 133
Krupskaya, Nadezhda 16
Kulaks 74
Kun, Béla 40, 63, 110
Kurella, Alfred (Bernard) 31, 62
Kursk (USSR) 141
Kyeller airport (Norway) 193
Lafayette, Marquis de 137
Landau, Kurt 206, 238
Latin America 61, 223
Laurat, Lucien 70, 132
Lausanne, Switzerland 206
Laval, Pierre 160, 163, 232
League for the Rights of Man 35
Lefebvre, Raymond 22, 59–60
Left Opposition (Trotskyist) 15, 24, 49, 158, 178
Leftism, leftist, ultra-leftism 42, 63–64
Lenin, Vladimir Ilyich 13, 15–16, 20–21, 24, 28–32, 35–36, 38, 40, 42, 46–47, 49, 53–57, 59, 70–76, 78, 82–83, 87, 91–93, 100–118, 122–123, 130, 147, 150, 165, 168, 178, 203, 217,

225
–*April Theses* (1917) 42
– *Testament* (December 1922/January 1923) 15–16, 71, 75, 116, 133
Leninism, Leninist 13–14, 31–34, 45, 47, 53–54, 59, 70, 72, 75, 82–84, 88, 91–92, 95–96 107, 109–110, 123–124
Lenin School (France) 31–32
Leningrad (USSR) 43, 218, 220
Leningrad (Left Centre) Opposition 43
Lepetit, Alfred (see Guralsky)
Lepetit, Jules (Bertho) 22, 25, 27, 59–61
Letter of the 280 15, 24, 61
Leviné-Meyer, Rosa 137
Levi, Paul 15
Le Libertaire 84, 134
Lie, Jonas 187–189, 235
Lie, Trygve 166, 233
Liebknecht, Karl 184, 195, 235
Little Entente (Eastern European Alliance) 154, 231
Litvinov, Maxim 156, 159, 232
Lloyd George, David 108, 136, 145, 230
London 15, 115, 190, 203
Lore, Ludwig 13, 17
Loriot, Fernand 21, 24–25, 47, 60, 91
Louzon, Robert 136
Lozovsky, Solomon 36, 63, 233
La Lutte de Classes 41, 63
Lubyanka prison (Moscow) 21
Luxemburg, Rosa 14, 38, 54, 63, 65, 124, 137, 184, 235
Lyons, France 152
MacDonald, James Ramsay 136, 150, 231
Madrid (Spain) 176, 229
Manuel dihistoire du PCF (1964) 45, 58
Manuilsky, Dmitri 36, 63, 233
Mao Zedong 31
Marinez, Anita 222
Marseilles (France) 151
Il Martello 195
Marty, André 27, 61
Marx, Karl 31–32, 74–75, 77, 132, 150, 156, 162, 165, 225, 237, 241
Marxism, Marxism-Leninism 45–46, 70, 72, 74–75, 132, 168
Maslow, Arkady 14, 64, 124, 137
Matignon Agreement (1936) 233
Le Matin 92, 135
Maurín, Joaquím 70, 132
McCarthy, Senator Eugene 210
Mecca Temple (New York) 197
Mensheviks 118
Mercader, Ramon 226–229, 241–242
Méric, Victor 89, 135
Mesnil, Jacques 70, 132
Mexican Workers Federation 195, 220, 229
Michelet, Jules 133
Mikado (Japanese Emperor) 176, 234
Millerand, Alexandre 84, 134
Molotov, Vyacheslav 238
Monatte, Pierre 13–15, 17, 21, 23–25, 35–36, 39, 42–43, 45, 47–48, 50–51, 54–55, 57–66, 79, 84–85, 89, 93, 129, 131, 134, 136, 138
Monmousseau, Gaston 21, 23, 57–58, 60
Mooney, Tom 196, 237
Morals, morality 77, 134
Morning Post 111
Moscow 13, 15–17, 21, 36, 53, 69, 74, 77, 89, 96–97, 99–101, 110, 121, 141–142, 148–149, 151, 160, 177, 179, 180, 182–184, 190–192, 194, 200–201, 206–208, 211, 218, 220, 229
Moscow Military Academy 229
Moscow Trials 11, 132, 179, 187–198, 203–208, 211, 236–237
Müller, Hermann 151, 231
Munich Agreement (1938) 231
Munis, Grandizo 241
Murmansk (USSR) 60
Mussolini, Benito 60, 108, 131, 133, 161, 206
Muzhik (Russian peasant) 171
Nancy (France) 132
Naples (Italy) 151
The Nation 84, 221, 234, 240
National Union Party (Norwegian fascists) 235
Naville, Pierre 12, 69, 132
Neo-Socialists, Neos (France) 161, 232
New Class Theories (of the USSR) 12, 72
New Deal (USA) 154, 231
New Economic Policy (NEP) 106
New York 15, 146, 151, 190, 193, 195, 197–198, 200, 206, 210, 215–216, 220–221, 225–228
Nikolayev, Leonid 236
Nin, Andreu (Andrés) 206, 212, 238
Nomenklatura (Russian) 72
Norwegian Communist Party 180
Noske, Gustave 184, 235
Not Guilty! 198
Nuremburg War Crimes Tribunal (1946) 236
Offensive, Theory of 40
Old Guard (Bolshevik), Old Bolsheviks 36, 55
Orwell, George 236
Oslo (Norway) 166, 179–182, 193
Ossinsky, Valerian 17, 104, 135
Pablo, Michel 64, 229
Pabloites 45
Palais Bourbon (Paris) 163
Palme Dutt, Rajani 16
Paris 16–17, 22, 24, 38, 61–62, 65, 68, 72, 83, 132–135, 146, 151–155, 161–164, 167, 180, 198, 200–202, 225, 229
Paris Commune (1871) 72
Parliament, parliamentary struggle 33
Parvus, Alexander 134–135
Pascale, Pierre 70
Patri, Aimé 70, 132
Patriciate, patricians 71–72
Peasants, peasantry 42, 51, 74, 84, 96,

102, 112, 115, 126, 159
Pepper (Pogany), John 137–138
Péret, Benjamin 69, 132
Périgny (France) 234
Permanent Revolution, theory of 112, 133
Petit-bourgeois 72, 74, 101, 103, 118, 135
Petrograd (USSR) 105, 135, 200
Petrov 175
Le Peuple 84, 92, 134
Piatakov, Georgi 191–193, 203, 236
Piatnitsky, Osip 39, 63
Pioch, Georges 50, 64, 84
Pivert, Marceau 232
Plekhanov, George 77
Poincaré, Raymond 23, 60, 108
Polish Communist Party 65
Pompeii (Italy) 151
Le Populaire 161, 178, 235
El Popular 220, 223
Popular Front, People's Front 62, 136, 159, 161, 210, 232–233, 235
POUM (Workers Party of Marxist Unity, Spain) 132, 212, 238–239, 241
Poznansky, IM 206, 238
Primitive accumulation 174
Primo de Rivera, Don Miguel 159, 232
Prinkipo (Turkey) 145, 147, 149–150, 153, 156–157, 162, 164, 168, 202, 215
Proletarianisation 39, 54
PSOP (Socialist Workers and Peasants Party, France) 232
Pujol, Antonio 222–223
Purges 47, 61, 63, 208, 231
Putschism, putschists 23, 40, 42, 50
Que Faire? 65
Queneau, Raymond 69, 132
Quiroz, Dr Alfonso 229
Quisling, Vidkun 183, 235
Le Quotidien 84, 92, 134
Radek, Karl 15, 124, 134, 137, 191, 234, 236
Radical Party, Radicals (France) 28, 51, 62, 136, 162–163, 233
Rakovsky, Christian 203, 237
Reade, Arthur 13–14, 17
Red Army 105, 238
Red Day 149
Red International of Labour Unions (RILU) 50, 63–64, 89, 137
Red Referendum (Germany, 1931) 158, 232
Red Saturdays (Russian work details) 200
Reformists, reformism 21, 32, 38, 42, 49, 57, 59, 108–109, 112, 124–126, 128, 137, 235, 237
Reichstag (Germany) 129, 195
Reichswehr (Germany) 65
Reiss, Ignace 206, 238
Renaudel, Pierre 95, 135
Revisionists 226
Révolution prolétarienne 14, 41, 43, 48, 59, 64, 66, 69, 79, 94, 116, 120–121, 130–132, 136
Revolutionary Socialist Party (Dutch RSAP) 168
Ribbentrop, Joachim Von 207
Ridley, Francis Ambrose 14, 233
Rif (Moroccan rebels) 27, 32, 61, 115
Riksdag (Norwegian parliament) 166
Rivera, Diego 189–190, 195, 199, 202, 208, 211, 236, 239
Robespierre, Maximillien 188, 234–235
Rocque, Colonel Casimir de la 232
Rolland, Romain 170, 234
Rome (Italy) 133
Roosevelt, Franklin Delano 154, 195, 228, 231
Rosmer, Alfred (Griot)
– and Communist International 22, 24, 41, 43–44, 51, 53–55, 59, 79–131
– and French Communist Party 11, 21–25, 36, 39–43, 50–51, 54–55, 120–131
– and opposition within Russian Communist Party 15–24, 43–44, 59, 79–131
– and syndicalism 21, 45, 47
– and Trotskyism 13–15, 41, 43–45, 59, 94–113
Rosmer, Marguerite 55, 239
Ross, Edward 195, 236
Rosta (Russian news agency) 89
Royan (France) 154, 156, 161
Royat (France) 156
Rühle, Otto 195, 237
Ruhr (Germany) 23, 27, 56, 58, 60, 65
Russian Civil War (1918–21) 135, 238
Russian Communist Party (CPSU) 32, 37, 53, 94, 106, 116–120, 122–123, 126, 135, 146–147, 159
– Tenth Congress (1921) 74
– Thirteenth Congress (1924) 52, 56, 101, 135
– Politbureau 15, 95, 103
– Central Committee 94, 99–100, 111, 116–118, 120, 146, 149, 159, 180
– Central Control Commission 146
– Left Opposition 24, 49, 60, 63–64, 178
– Right Opposition 175
Russian Revolution (1905) 36, 55
Russian Revolution (1917) 21–22, 29, 31, 35–37, 46, 55, 62, 65, 71, 83, 93, 111, 113, 117–119, 128, 130–131, 133, 137, 143–144, 146, 150–152, 167, 169, 173, 176–178, 195, 198, 220
Rykov, Alexei 101, 104, 146, 203, 230
Saar, Saar plebiscite (Germany, 1935) 161, 232
Sacco, Nicola 237
Sacred Union (*Union Sacrée*, France) 21, 36, 50
St Louis Post Dispatch 209, 239
Saint-Palais (France) 154
Saint-Simon, Comte de 71, 133
Salazar, Leandro 240–241
Santiago de Cuba 229

Sarraut, Albert 164, 233
Sauvage, François 33–34, 39, 62
Scheidemann, Phillip 184, 235
Scheringer, Richard 158, 232
Scissors Crisis (USSR) 96, 100
Second International (Labour and Socialist International) 121
Second World War (1939–45) 12, 61, 132, 134
Sectarians, sectarianism 63
Sedov, Leon (Lev) 145, 151–152, 192–193, 196–199, 202, 206, 230
Sedov, Sergei 206, 238
Sedova, Natalia 12, 231, 233, 236, 240–241
Seine (French department) 36, 40, 62, 64, 84, 91, 134, 161
Seine-et-Oise (French department) 161
Sellier, Louis 28, 36, 62, 89, 135
Sémard, Pierre 21, 28, 30, 32, 50, 60, 62, 86, 89
Senate (France) 210
Serge, Victor 12, 60, 206, 231, 233, 236, 240–241
Sermuks, NM 206, 238
Serrana, Julia Barradas de 222
Serrano, David 223, 240
Serrati, Giacinto 15, 17
Shachtman, Max 135, 230
Shooter, Millicent 14
Sieva (Vsevolod Volkov) 206, 221
Siqueiros, David 221–223, 240
Sklyansky, E 75, 133
Smirnov, Ivan 189, 236
Social Democracy, Social Democrats 21, 25–26, 28, 45, 54, 57, 63, 65, 93, 122, 135, 152, 231–232
Social fascism, Theory of 135
Socialism in One Country, Theory of 25
Socialist Workers Party (German SAP) 168
Socialist Workers Party (USA) 43–45
Sokolnikov, Grigory 110–111, 136
Soudeille, Jean 70, 132
Souvarine, Boris 13–17, 21–22, 24–25, 30, 32, 35–36, 38, 45–47, 52, 55, 60–62, 67–69, 89, 132, 134
Soviet Union, USSR 12–15, 17, 25, 43, 46, 72, 77, 101, 142–143, 146, 151, 167–168, 170, 172, 174–178, 196, 197, 214, 216, 218, 233, 241
- Commissariat of War 95, 103
- Council of Labour and Defence 103, 107
Soviets 41–42, 44, 71, 102, 159
Spanish Civil War (1936–39) 61, 132, 234, 238–241
Stalin, Joseph 17, 24, 31–32, 35, 47, 49, 56, 60–61, 63–65, 69–78, 103, 105–106, 112–113, 133–135, 141–149, 151, 153, 156, 159–160, 177, 180, 182–183, 187–194, 199, 203–207, 210–211, 214, 216–218, 220, 225, 228–234, 236, 238–241
Stalinism, Stalinists 12–13, 20, 26, 28, 34, 42, 60, 62–63, 65, 71 149, 152, 155, 158–159, 161–162, 164–165, 193, 196, 203, 208, 211, 215, 220, 222, 234, 238, 242
Stalin-Hitler Pact (1939) 193, 208, 214, 223
Stambulisky, Alexander 65
State capitalism, state capitalists 173
Stauning, Thorvald 152, 231
Stavisky affair (France, 1934) 232
Stockholm (Sweden) 152
Stolberg, Benjamin 195, 237
Storsand (Norway) 181
Stresemann, Gustav 151, 231
Sundby (Norway) 181–184
Surrealism, surrealists 68–72
Syndicalism, syndicalists 21, 35, 47, 50–51, 59, 89, 92, 127, 129–130, 138, 141
Tampico (Mexico) 189–190, 223
Tartakowsky, Danielle 27–28, 31, 47, 55
Tass (Russian news agency) 142, 179–180, 191, 237
Taxco (Mexico) 207, 209
Teheran (Iran) 229
Le Temps 163
Thalheimer, August 15
Thermidor (France, 1794), Thermidoreans 41, 43, 45, 63, 144, 170, 234
Third International (Communist International, Comintern) 11, 14–15, 17, 20–25, 28–29, 32, 35–36, 38–41, 43, 46–47, 49–66, 70, 73, 81, 89, 91–92, 101, 103–104, 106–107, 109–110, 116–124, 127–132, 135–138, 141, 146–147, 149–150, 164, 166, 168–169, 180, 203, 205, 215, 217, 230–232
- Second Congress (1920) 22, 53, 59, 106
- Third Congress (1921) 28, 30, 40–41, 107–110, 123
- Fourth Congress (1922) 20, 22–24, 29–30, 49, 53, 55, 57–58, 107, 109–110
- Fifth Congress (1924) 20, 24, 38–39, 52, 55, 80–81, 83, 85, 101, 103–104, 122–124
- Executive Committee (ECCI) 15, 24, 53, 120, 124, 128
Third Period, Theory of 40, 62–63, 135, 150, 157, 230
Third Republic (France) 163
Thirion, André 68–70, 132
Thomas, Wendelin 195, 237
Thorez, Maurice 26, 33–34, 37, 52, 60–62, 142, 230
Togliatti, Palmiro 77, 134
Toledano, Vicente Lombardo 222, 229, 241
Tomsky, Mikhail 146, 203, 230
Tories 15, 136
Totalitarianism 20, 194, 217
Trades unions 29, 42, 44, 102, 123–124,

127–128, 137, 158, 230
Tranmael, Martin 166, 233
Treint, Albert 14, 22–24, 26, 28–29, 32, 34, 36, 38, 41–42, 44, 46, 49–53, 60–61, 79, 87–91, 127, 134–135
Tresca, Carlo 195, 206, 237
Triumvirate, Troika 55, 99, 146, 230
Trotsky, Leon Davidovich
– assassination of 220–229
– and Alfred Rosmer 11–12, 15
– and defence of the USSR 214–220
– and French Communist Party 35, 41–43, 46–47, 49, 52–54, 61, 70, 72, 116, 120, 125
– and Frida Kahlo and Diego Rivera 208–211
– and Leon Sedov's death 199–202
– and Moscow Trials 187–188, 190–198, 203–208, 211
– and nature of the USSR 12, 167–178, 217–220
– and Hitler and Nazi Germany 154–161, 208–209, 215
– and opposition in the Soviet Communist Party and Communist International 15, 17, 24, 41–43, 46–47, 49, 55, 57, 59, 64–65, 69, 75, 91, 95–96, 98–100, 102–113, 117–118, 136, 144, 146–148
– and Popular Front 160–162
– and Russian Civil War and Kronstadt 73–74
– and Spanish Civil War 206–207
– and Stalinism 74–78
– and Stalinist slander campaign 141–143, 155–156
– and Third Period 149–151, 155
– exile in France 154–158
– exile in Mexico 187–229
– exile in Norway 166–185
– exile in Turkey 141–153
– *How the Revolution Armed* (1923) 74
– *Terrorism and Communism* (1920) 73, 133, 169, 233–234
– *The New Course* (1923) 77, 99, 142
– *The Lessons of October* (1924) 104
– *Europe and America* (1926) 133
– *Where is Britain Going?* (1926) 133
– *Platform of the Left Opposition* (1927) 200
– *Defence of the Soviet Republic and the Opposition* (1929) 150
– *My Life* (1929) 12, 147
– *The Third Period of the Comintern's Errors* (1930) 150
– *The Stalin School of Falsification* (1932) 146
– *An Open Letter to the Workers of France* (1935) 163–165
– *The Third International after Lenin* (1936) 168
– *The Decisive Stage* (1936) 167
– *The Revolution Betrayed* (1936) 12, 167–178
– *I Stake My Life!* (1937) 195
– *The Case of Leon Trotsky* (1938) 197
– *Their Morals and Ours* (1939) 77
– *In Defence of Marxism* (1940) 12, 214
– *Stalin* (1946) 225
Trotskyism, Trotskyists, Trotskyist Opposition 12–15, 17, 19, 24, 26, 32, 41, 43–44, 46, 49–50, 53, 59, 63–65, 69, 71, 73, 76–78, 83, 92, 94–95, 112–113, 132, 141–142, 148, 160, 175, 191–192, 200, 203–204, 223–224, 236, 238, 241
Tsankov, General 65
Tsarism, 112, 157, 177, 192
Tukhachevsky, Mikhail 204–205, 237
Turatti, Filippo 108, 136
Tzara, Tristan 69, 132
United front 13, 83, 91, 93, 124, 128, 134, 158
El Universal 229
Utopia, utopian 71, 133, 231
Vanzetti, Bartolomeo 237
Velázquez, Fidel 229
Verdier, Guillaume 86, 134
Verdun, Battle (1916) 60
Verfeuil, Raoul 89, 135
Vergeat, Marcel 21–22, 59–60
Versailles, Treaty (1919) 230, 232
La Vie ouvrière 89, 138
Vienna (Austria) 200
Vodka monopoly 112, 136
Vorkuta (USSR) 238
Vorwärts (SPD paper) 95
Vosges (France) 83
Voroshilov, Kliment 204–205, 238
Vyshinsky, Andrei 188, 197, 204, 236
Wall Street, American Stock Exchange 63, 90, 223, 231
Wall Street Crash (1929) 63, 231
Washington 195, 206
Webb, Sidney and Beatrice 177–178, 234
Weber, Jack 64
Weil, Simone 69, 132
Weimar Republic (Germany, 1919–33) 137
Weitling, Wilhelm 150, 231
Weksal (Norway) 166, 178–181
Wells, Herbert George 236
White Guards 155
Wilhelmshaven Revolt (Germany, 1918) 195, 237
Wilson, Woodrow 145, 230
Wolf, Erwin 206, 238
Workers' control 158
Workers Opposition (Russia, 1921) 59, 92, 231
Workers' state, theory of 77, 168, 168, 170, 214, 216–218
Yagoda, Hendrik 188, 203, 236
Yudenich, General Nikolai 105, 135
Zamora, Francisco 195, 237
Zetkin, Clara 53, 65
Zimmerwald Conference (1915) 24, 50, 60–61, 76, 83, 93, 121, 131, 203
Zinoviev, Gregory 13–14, 17, 20, 24, 28,

34–36, 40–43, 46–47, 49, 51–53, 56, 60–64, 73, 75, 95, 100, 105, 118, 135–136, 146, 148, 150, 187–188, 191–193, 230, 235–236
Zinovievism, Zinovievists 13–14, 17, 38, 41–42, 46
Zola Emile 193, 236
Zurich (Switzerland) 200